The Tri-State Terror

The Life and Crimes of Wilber Underhill

By R. D. Morgan

NEW FORUMS PRESS INC.

Stillwater, Okla. U.S.A.

This book may be ordered in bulk quantities at discount from New
Forums Press, Inc., P.O. Box 876, Stillwater, OK 74076 [Federal
I.D. No. 73 1123239]. Printed in the United States of America.

International Standard Book Number: 1-58107-107-8

On the Cover

*Top Left: Mug shot of Wilbur Underhill at Kansas State
Penitentiary.* Courtesy Kansas Department of Corrections.
*Top Right: Several members of the posse, Agent R. H. Colvin, top
left, Clarence Hurt, top right, Jelly Bryce, kneeling right.* Courtesy
Jack Hurt.
Bottom: Wilbur Underhill shortly after the gunfight. Courtesy Rick
Mattix.

Contents

Foreword

Wilbur Underhill—the "Tri-State Terror"—is the Boogeyman of Depression-era outlaws in more ways than one. For nearly a decade in the turbulent period of the 1920s and 30s, he was one of the most infamous and feared criminals in the Southwest. Convicted of one of his murders in Oklahoma he was sentenced to life and escaped, killing a cop and receiving another life term in Kansas, and then escaped again, leading ten others in a mass breakout. In the last months of his life, he rose to national notoriety as a prolific bank robber and suspect in the infamous Kansas City Massacre and became the first criminal ever shot down by agents of that fledgling agency which would soon become the FBI.

True criminal immortality seemed to elude Wilbur after his death, his name eclipsed in the national headlines by the likes of John Dillinger, "Pretty Boy" Floyd, and "Baby Face" Nelson. But scratch the surface and he's still there. From his native Joplin where Underhill began his career modestly as a "lovers lane" bandit, to the Tri-State mining district where he is best remembered as a lone wolf scurrying about the night terrorizing the populace and committing a half-dozen robberies at gunpoint, to Wichita, Kansas where he was known as a vicious cop-killer, to Jeff City, Lansing, and McAlester where he became a legendary figure among the inmate populations and seemingly possessed a talent to break out at will, to the Central Oklahoma oilfields and his hideouts in the wild and wooly Cookson Hills, to the many towns he struck in Kansas, Missouri, Oklahoma, Kentucky, and Arkansas his impact is still felt. The lives he took, touched or made a total travesty of has impacted generations of folks in the Southwest.

His name hasn't been totally obliterated from the history books of course. Most crime buffs are familiar with Wilbur Underhill if not necessarily with the details of his long and deadly career. He's received cursory mention, though usually not long on accuracy in such books as *Ten Thousand Public Enemies* by Courtney Riley Cooper and *The Bad Ones* by Lew Louderback. Cooper, J. Edger Hoover's crony and favorite journalist in the thirties set the tone with a fictional account of how Underhill was kicked out of the Kimes-Terrill Gang (itself a media created fiction) for having a murder complex. Around 1970 Loren D. Estelman based his novel *The Oklahoma Punk* (later reissued in paperback as *Red Highway*) on Underhill. But Estelman's Virgil Ballard really owed more to Cooper's fiction than to any real life events. The 1973 movie *Dillinger* with Warren Oats thoughtfully included Wilbur as a character giving the popular but erroneous version of him being tracked down through his wedding then compounding the fiction by having Underhill personally killed by Melvin Purvis—who wasn't even there. Louderback's paperback was still being sold at the time and probably introduced many crime buffs to the "Tri-State Terror" but his inclusion in the movie might possibly owe something also to the late Clarence Hurt who served as a technical advisor. Hurt, a life long lawman and one of the two G-Men who shot Dillinger, was an Oklahoma City police officer in 1933 and helped bring down Underhill at Shawnee. The Underhill capture may well have gotten him his appointment to the FBI.

Strangely, even the FBI has seemingly forgotten Wilbur. Decades after J.Edger Hoover's death the bureau still promotes it's glorious gangbusting escapades of the thirties, capitalizing on such gangland legends as Dillinger,

Pretty Boy Floyd, and cases in which the bureau's involvement was minimal such as Al Capone and Bonnie and Clyde. But even they seem to be totally unaware today that Wilbur Underhill was the first criminal ever shot by FBI agents, who had no police powers before 1933 and weren't really legally authorized to carry guns until six months after Underhill's demise.

Underhill emerges from the shadows at last in this work, thanks to the tireless research of R.D. Morgan. *The Tri State Terror* is a natural follow-up to Morgan's previous works (especially *Bad Boys of the Cookson Hills)* but easily stands on its own as the definitive biography of a long lost superstar of thirties crime whose position in the criminal constellation is reaffirmed. Previous authors such as Courtney Riley Cooper and Anthony Gish have characterized Underhill as stupid, brutish, moronic thug, a myth carefully maintained in the self-serving recollections of former crime partners such as Harvey Bailey and Jim Clark written many years later when neither Underhill and other witnesses were around to contradict them. Okay, maybe Wilbur was a brute and a thug but he was far from stupid. The prison letters Wilbur wrote to his Mother and sisters, uncovered by Morgan, reveal a somewhat disturbed and anti-social but complex and highly intelligent man, a literate man, a reader of volumes of psychology, and one with a strong sense of irony that is particularly apparent in the closing lines of his last letter before the Lansing crashout. For all his dark brooding persona and cold-bloodedness, Wilbur was also a gentleman in a strange sort of way. One can't help but be a little charmed by his seemingly moral quirk of marrying women before bedding them. And Morgan's painstaking research rounds it all out thoroughly. Book after book, article after article, have repeated *ad nauseum* Harvey Bailey's tale of how he joined the Lansing break only to prevent Underhill from coldly murdering Warden Kirk Prather and how he talked Underhill out of killing the Warden. None of them until now apparently bothered to read Prather's own contradictory account of his abduction printed in local newspapers at the time and left for a first rate objective crime historian like Morgan to uncover. The Boogeyman has emerged from the shadows thanks to R.D.Morgan in this, one of the finest true crime books in years.

Rick Mattix, coauthor of: *Public Enemies: America's Criminal Past, 1919-1940*; and, *Dillinger: The Untold Story* (Revised Edition)

To Naomi and Pug

Acknowledgments

I wish to thank Richard Baine for granting me access to his Great Aunt Dorothy Underhill's large collection of documents, photos, and news clippings having to do with the career of her infamous brother. I also thank Michael Webb and Crimewebb Collectables for use of twenty-seven letters written by Wilbur Underhill (dating from 1924 to 1933) to his mother and sister Dorothy from the Kansas and Missouri State Penitentiaries as well as various other vital documents and photographs. In addition, the author wishes to express his gratitude to Ella DeLisle for information concerning Eva Mae Nichols, as well as John and Dr. Dan Lairmore for providing background on lawman Mark Lairmore and Lester Clark for use of numerous photos, private letters, and documents pertaining to his Uncle Jim Clark. Also, a hearty thanks to old-timers J. E. Jech, Henry Jolliff, Doug Thomason, Henry Peak, Harper Edwards, and Fred Gossett for sharing their remembrances, as well as Rich Green of the Oklahoma Department of Corrections and Bill Miskell along with Brett Peterson of the Kansas Department of Corrections for their assistance. I further wish to convey my appreciation to Jack Hurt, Mike Koch, Stanley Rogers, Robert D. Magness Sr, Fay Halley, Jeffery King, Rick Mattix, Lee Mann, John East, Kitty Mace, Linda Childers, and John Russell Jr. for sharing crucial information. Finally, I tip my hat in memory of the late L. L. Edge, whose book, *Run The Cat Roads*, was the inspiration for this narrative. I walk in his shadow.

About The Author

R. D. Morgan is the author of four non-fiction books concerning Oklahoma Lawmen and outlaws. He has also written numerous articles on the subject for Oklahoma newspapers and historical magazines. He and his wife, Naomi, make their home in Muskogee County, Oklahoma, with their two trusted hounds, Jack and Skeeter.

Preface

The author spent nearly five years researching this book. A host of prison, police, FBI, court, and other official documents along with reams of news articles on microfilm were consulted, dozens of interviews were conducted and a massive amount of never before seen family documents were amassed and studied. Research was conducted throughout a five state area. Extensive tours were made of both the Kansas and Oklahoma State Penitentiaries and the route taken by the 1933 Memorial Day escapees was driven and studied in detail. The physical location of every major event described in this book was visited and photographed by the author and his wife.

It is the writer's hope the reader will come away with a rare insight into the life of one of America's most prolific public enemies. The author has attempted to present an accurate story as can be told given the secretive nature of many of the participants. As for the families of Underhill and his partners in crime, one cannot pick his or her relatives and this book is not meant to be an indictment of them in any way.

For better or worse the story of Wilbur Underhill and the lawmen that tracked him down is a part of our country's history, perhaps not polite schoolbook history, but history all the same.

Chapter One

Early Life

Henry Wilber Underhill was a true product of Middle America. His father, Henry Sr. or "Hank" as he was commonly called, raised near the small southern Illinois farming community of Litchfield located just fifty-odd miles from the metropolitan area of St. Louis, Missouri. It might as well been a thousand. In the days of slow moving horse powered transportation, Litchfield was unaffected by its urban counterpart. A city of only a few thousand souls it featured a classic "Grant Wood" scenario. Stuck smack in the middle of the vast Illinois corn-belt, grain farming was its mainstay. Hank Underhill, born in 1864, was the son of German immigrants and like his own father became one of a million faceless farmers who slaved from sun to sun raising corn, beans, hogs, and children in America's breadbasket. The more offspring the better was the mantra of families in early agrarian society. In the days of animal and people power, a man needed to put as many hands in the field as possible.

Around 1880, while Hank was still in his teens he and his sister Dora left Illinois joining an older sister and her husband in the Southwest Missouri farming and mining community of Newtonia.

While Dora remained with her married sibling as a housekeeper, Hank drifted out into the countryside seeking employment as a hired hand. Obtaining work on a neighboring farm, he was given room and board as well as a few dollars a month for his rigorous labors.

Farming in the 1880s was a backbreaking enterprise. Up before dawn to milk the cows and slop the hogs, then rig up the horses or mules to either plow, plant, cultivate, or harvest the fields depending on the season. Winter work included cutting firewood or rail ties with hand operated crosscut saws and razor sharp axes. In the case of rail ties, they were loaded by hand on wagons and transported to a shipping point. Other cold weather chores included blacksmithing, hog butchering, and fertilizing, which was a nasty business that entailed cleaning out the cow, hog, and horse barns, as well as chicken houses by pitchfork and shovel, loading the smelly substance into an open wagon to be hauled to the fields by horse, mule or oxen and spread onto the soil. Nineteenth century farming methods had little in common with today's modern agricultural operations with its eight to eighteen row planters, air conditioned combines, and oversized tractors. When a inquisitive reporter once asked President Harry S. Truman about his experiences as a turn of the century farmer in Southwest Missouri, he bluntly stated, "Life behind the plow looking up a mule's ass was no dance in the park."

The only recreation a hired man had to look forward to was a rare Saturday afternoon in town, perhaps services at a country church on Sunday or an occasional barn dance. More than likely young Hank first made the acquaintance of his bride to be, sixteen-year-old Nancy Almira Hutchison, who lived with her mother, two brothers, and stepfather on a nearby farm at such an affair.

After a short romance, Hank and "Almira," as she was called, paired off and matrimony was in the works. On taking their vows in early 1887, the newlyweds set up house on a small farm near the Newton County settlement of Seneca. The couple likely began their married life working on shares for someone or farming for kinfolk till they scrimped and saved enough money to make a down payment on their own small piece of ground.

In September 1887, the pair was blessed with the birth of a daughter, Grace, and like clockwork every few years they added to their family unit with the births of sons, Earl in February 1889, and Charles Ernest in September 1894, another daughter, Anna Lea, in 1897 then a third son, Henry Wilber, who was dubbed simply "Wilber" by his folks, on March 16, 1901, followed by a fourth male child, George, born 1903. The final addition to the family was a daughter named Dorothy, born in 1907.

Like most nineteenth century farm families, they were constantly strapped for cash and learned to live without the finer things in life. Earning a living in agriculture was then as now; a risky business, one bad drought or flood could wipe a man out sending him to the poorhouse. After breaking your back for a full year, one could end up with nothing to show but an empty sack, resulting in his scurrying to the bank to borrow future operating funds thus putting the farm at risk of bank foreclosure. Unlike today, where most farm wives drive to town and work an extra job to help make ends meet, in the old days a trip to town was an all day affair making that option impractical.

Around the turn of the century, the Underhills quit farming and moved to a two-story frame rent-house located on the corner of Lincoln and Brook Streets in the nearby county seat community of Neosho where Hank purportedly tried his hand as a door-to-door salesman. Apparently the man of the house had difficulty adjusting to town life, records show he was twice arrested on charges of petty theft and disturbing the peace while in residence.

In 1909 Hank up and moved the family to nearby Joplin which was currently undergoing a construction boom due to the discovery of massive lead and zinc deposits in the area. Soon after the town's conception in 1871, it became the center for the Tri-State (Missouri/Oklahoma/ Kansas) mining district. By the time Hank Underhill and family moved to town four lead smelters were up and running and dozens of mining operations were flourishing in the district employing tens of thousands of miners and even more folks in service industries which catered to them. The city's streets were being paved and multi-story hotels, office, and bank buildings were under construction. Hank quickly found employment as a bricklayer and mason. The family first lived in a small rundown "shotgun" shack located on Pearl Avenue in West Joplin but soon relocated to another undersized rental house located nearby at 1218 Sergeant Avenue. For several years, the Underhills, like the majority of low paid urban dwellers of the time, survived paycheck to paycheck. Tragedy stuck the family on

Downtown Joplin 1910.
Courtesy of the Joplin Chamber of Commerce.

May 22, 1912 when forty-six-year-old Hank's life was cut short by a sudden illness leaving his widow and seven children to fend for themselves.

On the morning of May 25 Almira buried her spouse at Joplin's Fairview Cemetery. Shortly after her husband's untimely death, the widow moved her brood into the home of her son-in-law on Empire Street located in a rough working class section of West Joplin known as "Blendville," which was populated by a host of low paid laborers and their ill-housed, poorly clothed, and undernourished offspring. It proved to be an intolerable existence. Poverty tracked the family like a pack of hungry wolves. With no means of support, the houseguests soon became a heavy burden on her eldest daughter's pocketbook.

Upon the death of the family's chief breadwinner and disciplinarian Almira proved unable to get a handle on the boisterous activities of her three high-spirited boys still living at home. (The eldest, Earl, had married and relocated to Galena, Kansas) Although her and the kids could be seen walking hand in hand every Sunday morning to the Byers Avenue Methodist Church where they attended services and Sunday school, her efforts in regards to religious training just didn't stick.

As for their formal education, the children attended classes at nearby Alcott school. Ernest quit school at the age of sixteen while still in the eighth grade, whereas twelve-year-old Wilber consistently played hooky and ran wild in the streets learning to hustle, drink "rotgut booze," and steal. Before long, both lads evolved into hard-core juvenile delinquents being constantly hauled to the police station on charges of petty theft and fighting. Predictably, the boys soon joined a local youth gang called the

Modern-day view of the Underhill home on Sergeant Street. Photo by Naomi Morgan.

"West-Side Bunch," which hung around Cunningham Park as well as the Brunswick Pool Hall located downtown on Main Street. The gang specialized in small change burglaries and strong-arm robberies, often times jack-rolling drunks on the streets of the central business district. Throughout the Christmas season of 1912 into January 1913 the group committed nearly a dozen robberies before finally one of their victims resisted and tragedy ensued.

According to a confession given by Ernest Underhill, on the evening of January 18, 1913, he and gang members Earl Locke, Sid Devee, and Clyde Howe were stalking through the business district when they spotted a postal employee who was just getting off work named Vawter. On observing him enter a dark alley near the corner of 8th Street and Moffet Avenue, the quartet of thugs confronted their hapless victim with a cocked pistol, forcing him to empty his pockets. The take amounted to a whopping $2.96. Upon completion of the hijacking, the young punks fled the scene on foot. The group of misfits then moved on to 5th Street and Jackson Avenue where they observed several likely targets none of which they figured had a nickel in their britches. Cursing their luck, they let these fortunate individuals pass by.

Around 10 pm, the crew of wannabe badmen broke up after splitting the night's haul, (about 72 cents each). Locke and Ernest wandered the streets until Locke came up with the idea of sticking up an elderly peanut and tamale vender named Phillip Burton. Knowing

Grave of Hank Underhill Fairview Cemetery, Joplin, Missouri. Photo by Naomi Morgan.

the route the vendor used to travel home after his night's labors, the two boys hid in the alley behind the New Joplin Theatre. At just past the midnight hour, Burton, driving his horse and small wagon, entered the alley on his way to his residence. Underhill, armed with a revolver, dashed into the moonlight and demanded his money or his life. Evidently, the old man cared more for his cash than his life cause he refused to cooperate, instead issuing his assailant a firm tongue-lashing. In response Underhill fatally shot the elderly gentleman before completely loosing his nerve and bolting down the alley without bothering to rob his victim. The pair headed for home as fast as their feet could carry them, stopping only long enough to discard the pistol over a fence into a trash pit behind a brewery.

On February 2, one of the gang members, Clyde Howe, was arrested for suspicion of involvement in an unrelated robbery. On being convicted of the crime, Howe, who was a tender sixteen-years-old, was shipped back to the Boonville Boy's Reformatory from where he had only recently been released. Shortly after his arrival, the youth began bragging about his criminal exploits to his fellow inmates, including his knowledge of a recent murder in Joplin. He mentioned several names including that of Ernest Underhill in his loose-lipped colloquy. One of the boys, overhearing Howe's tales snitched to the warden. The next morning, Howe was dragged in front of a group of inquisitive Joplin detectives. The boy clammed up like a seashell but taking their cue from his previous statements, the cops hauled Ernest Underhill into the central police station back in Joplin and began applying the third degree. The youth promptly spilled his guts and he and his partner, Earl Locke, were both charged with the peanut vender's murder. Five other members of the gang were arrested and charged with an assortment of past robberies.

Ernest's little brother, Wilber, was questioned but released due to his tender age and the fact he was considered more or less a hanger-on or "wannabe" as far as his status with the gang at the time.

After the arrest of her wayward son, Almira Underhill, who had become excessively attached to her children after the death of her husband, rushed to the station house sobbing hysterically pleading his innocence and demanding they release him from custody. At his preliminary, Ernest informed the magistrate, "Oh, if I could recall that bullet. I didn't mean to kill the old man. I'm not a murderer for G-d's sake." The following day, a pale, nervous, and shaken Ernest Underhill pled guilty to First Degree Murder. When asked what motivated him to commit such a foul deed, he stated, "One thing led to another. I was running with bad company. I tried getting money without working." When informed he was pleading guilty to a very serious crime, which could result in heavy punishment, Ernest responded, "But I did it, there's nothing else to do." Both he and Locke were sentenced to life at hard labor in the Missouri State Penitentiary in Jefferson City. A broken-hearted Almira Underhill openly swore she would somehow; someday gain his release from the clutches of the law. As she would demonstrate over and over for the next decade and a half, Mother Underhill, who wore heavy blinders when it came to her children, would never admit the guilt of her offspring instead always blaming society and police tactics for their bad behavior.

Although Ernest's crime partner would be paroled in 1920, he would spend the rest of his natural life, minus a few months, confined in the Missouri State Penitentiary. Prison records describe him as five-feet-ten and a quarter inches tall, blue eyes, chestnut hair, and sallow or pale complexion. Asked his religion he stated "None." While incarcerated, Ernest evolved into a degenerate drug addict and general misfit. His prison rap sheet shows him being charged with such infractions as "Shooting dope in the yard," possession of morphine, gambling, stealing, and assaulting other youthful inmates. The parole board time and again refused to consider his release, stating Underhill posed an imminent threat to society due to his immoral behavior.

Back in Joplin, Almira Underhill took in washing and cleaned some of the finer residences in Joplin while her son-in-law worked long shifts as a night watchman in an effort to properly feed and clothe the two families. Sadly, their combined incomes proved insufficient and poverty was again knocking at the door.

Around this time, young Wilber was the victim of a tragic accident. Apparently the lad was rooting through a trash pit located next to the Alcott school on one of the few days he had chose to attend classes when someone inadvertently tossed a case of empty glass bottles out an upstairs window. The load landed directly on Wilber's head, fracturing his skull. According to local and family lore, Wilber was never the same after the accident. He became agitated and temperamental without the slightest motivation and was given to violent outbursts. Shortly after this unfortunate incident the young man quit school and moved in with a relative back in Neosho where he worked odd jobs such as delivering groceries for the local mercantile and sweeping out bars for spending money. Within a few months, he tired of life in the sleepy little berg and relocated back to the big city.

Returning to Joplin, the youth, who had since changed the spelling of his name from Wilber to Wilbur (*Note: Which for the sake of clarity is the spelling that will be used throughout the rest of this narrative) due to his belief it appeared more masculine, made little effort in finding steady employment, making a living by the sweat of his brow obviously held no appeal to the boy. Instead, he chose to follow in the footsteps of his brothers Ernest, who was residing deep in the bowels of the antiquated Missouri State Penitentiary, and Earl who had since involved himself in a Kansas City bootlegging enterprise. Wilbur turned to a life of crime burglarizing the homes his mother was cleaning as well as breaking into the back windows of area "mom and pop" stores after dark, boosting cigarettes, candy, and spare change.

By 1917, Almira and family moved out of her son-in-law's home to a residence located nearby on the corner of 20th and Picher streets then again in 1919 to a two-room shack situated at 1209 West 24th street. According to police reports and descendants, for the next few years the little family moved every time the rent was due.

In February of 1919, Wilbur was caught red-handed burglarizing a swanky Joplin residence. Found in his possession was a gunnysack filled with fine silverware. Lucky for him when the case got to court the Judge slapped his wrist with a three year suspended sentence before instructing him to go and sin no more. Meanwhile, Wilbur's younger brother, George, who was working on a relative's farm near Neosho was so impressed by his older siblings new found wealth he promptly moved back to town and joined the festivities. Within a matter of weeks, he was arrested for

Wilbur Underhill in his early teens. Courtesy Master Detective

burglary and sent to the Newton County Jail under the alias of Leon George. He was later released and placed on probation when it was discovered he was barely sixteen-years-old.

In the summer of 1920, a series of bizarre nighttime robberies occurred on an isolated "Lover's Lane" located in the Tanyard Hollow area just west of Joplin. Apparently, a lone individual would sneak up on young "Neckers" while in the act of pitching woo in their parked "Tin Lizzies" and loudly declare "This is a stick-up," thoroughly scaring the hell out of the bewildered youths. The bandit then robbed the couples of whatever valuables they had in their possession before fleeing the area on foot. Reacting to the hold-ups, which had area residents in a state of near panic, the Joplin Police Department decided to attempt to trap the perpetrator using a decoy.

On the warm foggy evening of June 4, 1920 Detective Ben Butterfield and a young lady became the bait, parking in a car near the scene of several of the past robberies. While the pair made over one another whispering sweet nothings in each other's ears, Joplin Detectives Luther Laster and Ole Maxfield hid in the nearby bushes ready to spring the trap if the "Boogeyman" dared to materialize. An hour or so after the laws had put out the bait a tall roughly dressed individual abruptly appeared menacingly pointing a weapon at the pair while demanding their valuables. Suddenly, Detective Laster leaped out from the thick weeds onto the road ordering the hijacker to surrender. The bandit reacted by firing a round from a pistol, the bullet just missing the officer's head. A general firefight broke out. During the initial exchange of fire, the bandit fell to the ground with an audible "Damn!" before scrambling into the darkness. Although the officers conducted an all night pursuit, nothing was discovered of the suspect but a small blood trail that eventually petered out.

A few days after the aborted ambush, lawmen raided an abandoned shack just inside the Newton County line on an informant's tip capturing Wilbur Underhill who was suffering from a minor flesh wound. The following day Underhill was positively identified by Officer Butterfield as his attacker and was officially charged with Attempted Highway Robbery. On October 13, Wilbur was convicted and sentenced to a two-year term at the Missouri State Penitentiary. Incidentally, during the outlaw's short-lived trial, which took place in nearby Neosho, a spectator in the audience named George Sandsberry suddenly leaped from his seat accusing Wilbur's sixteen-year-old brother, George, who was in attendance, of robbing him at gunpoint several weeks earlier at a local park. George loudly denied the charge before fleeing the courtroom. The following morning he was picked up by Joplin authorities at his mom's residence and transported back to Neosho where he was charged with Highway Robbery and eventually sen-

Inside the Missouri Pen. Courtesy Missouri State Penitentiary

tenced to a term at the Missouri State Boys Reformatory in Boonville.

Arriving at the state penitentiary, nineteen-year-old Wilbur faced a hard and hopeless existence to say the least. The big stone bastille, which sat on a bluff in downtown Jefferson City overlooking the Missouri River, could best be described at the time as a "Hellhole." The massive century old forty-seven acre facility was operated for neither comfort nor rehabilitation. Do as your told or face certain punishment was the name of the game. Brutal guards, poor eats, gang violence, inadequate ventilation in the summer and too much ventilation in the winter along with substandard medical care was the daily fare. Survival of the fittest said it all. Inmates had three options, cowboy up, punk out, or lay low.

For an oversized, raw-boned, ham fisted brute like Wilbur, toughened up by a hundred bloody brawls on the mean streets of Blendville, the first option was the only option. He quickly fell in with his brother Ernest and his pals haunting the cellblocks selling booze, dope, and collecting gambling debts, strong-arm style. Within weeks of his arrival, he was disciplined for both gambling and knife

Missouri Prison. Courtesy Missouri State Penitentiary.

fighting. Punishment for even a small infraction of the rules consisted of whippings with a leather strap along with solitary confinement in a cold dank dungeon subsisting on bread and water.

By the time Wilbur arrived at the prison overcrowding had become a major problem. More than 3000 inmates were lodged six to a cell, which were originally constructed to house three. Youthful first offenders bunked with older hardcore lifers. The only educational opportunities offered at the institution were the well-attended schools of burglary, robbery, and wholesale theft, taught by older seasoned cons that gladly passed on their illicit knowledge. Wilbur graduated near the top of his class, going to the pen a punk thief while coming out a well-schooled criminal.

Chapter Two

Up the River

Upon Wilbur's release from prison on December 13, 1921, he apparently took a few days to visit his mother prior to hitchhiking (He rarely traveled by car due to his poor driving skills) to the nearby Picher, Oklahoma mining district seeking employment. Picher was a good destination for a strapping young buck in need of an opportunity. Since the discovery of lead and zinc deposits in 1904, the Ottawa County, Oklahoma area had mushroomed into an economic powerhouse offering jobs a plenty. A score of small boomtowns like Picher, Douthat, Cardin, Zincville, and Hockerville, had suddenly appeared wherever a mine was sunk. The area was literally awash in employment opportunities in either the mining field or those

Mining Operation, Picher, Oklahoma. Author's Private Collection

catering to the underground toilers. Over time, Picher, which had began as a collection of tents surrounding a company store and a half dozen mine shafts, evolved into a huge conglomeration of ramshackle wooden shacks circling a central business district dotted with stores, theatres, saloons, banks, greasy spoon cafes, and scores of other businesses. Folks used to making a pittance on the farm flooded to the area hoping to get rich. Following in their wake was a crowd of prostitutes, bootleggers, and dope peddlers hoping to fleece the workers from their hard earned wages. Wilbur fit right in.

After working a short spell in the mines at the rate of roughly $8 to $10 a day, which was first-class wages in those days, Underhill again chose the easier life of larceny over labor. Meeting up with several others of his stripe in area pool halls and gaming rooms, he quickly joined ranks with this seedier element of the boomtown society whose chief activity seems to have been peddling illegal liquor to the thirsty miners. Not satisfied with their illicit earnings in the bootlegging business, Underhill and his newfound friends expanded their operations to include the commission of a several nighttime burglaries in the mining towns of Picher, Hockerville, and Cardin. Among their depravations, they were suspected of looting the safe of a lumberyard in nearby Douthat then setting fire to the establishment burning it to the ground. Afterwards, feeling the heat, (literally) the gang split up going their separate ways.

After his foray into the mining settlements, it appears Wilbur drifted back to Joplin moving in with his Ma, sister Dorothy, and brother George, who had recently been released from the state reformatory, in their tiny residence on 24th street.

On the evening of December 14, 1922 about 7 pm,

twenty-one-year old Wilbur, armed with a Colt .38 cal. revolver, strolled into the Wilhoit Oil Filling Station located at the busy intersection of 19th and Main Streets in downtown Joplin. Noticing the intruder burst through the front door, Dean Harvey, the only employee on duty at the time, stood up from his seat behind the counter and inquired if he could be of assistance. Wilbur, who Harvey described as wild-eyed, dirty, and disheveled, ordered him to "Shut up and hold still," while the bandit began rifling the small floor safe and cash till. After retrieving about $25 in mostly silver, Underhill instructed the shaken attendant to turn his back to him and walk into the street. After marching the man a block north to the intersection of 20th and Main, the pair was noticed by an elderly fellow who was also taken hostage. Both men were then forced deep into a nearby-unlit alley and ordered to lie on the ground while the robber explained the health hazards of squealing on him in the future. With that said, the bandit fled onto Main Street and disappeared.

George Underhill
Courtesy Michael Webb

The following morning, Joplin Chief of Detectives William Gibson accompanied by a small army of his trusted minions raided every fleabag hotel, gin joint, and pool hall in the downtown district in an attempt to flush out the robber or at least crowd some hapless small-time hood or street tramp into giving up some information on the hijacker's identity. Naturally, the word was soon put on the street that whoever put the robber "On the spot" would be well taken care of for their cooperation. It appears the forces of law and order was successful in the endeavor. That evening the cops put the pinch on Wilbur while he was peacefully snoozing on his mother's couch at her 24th street residence. Naturally, the young thug denied any involvement in the hijacking but was immediately transported to police head-quarters in order to be more vigorously interrogated by the local goon squad.

After undergoing a night of rubber hose therapy, the close-mouthed Wilbur, who proved to be "Tougher than a cob," and very uncooperative, was forced to stand heel to heel with four other inmates in a line-up. Taking a single glance at the group, Dean Harvey, the victim from the filling station heist, picked out Underhill as the fellow who had robbed him. Confronted with the positive identification, Underhill claimed he had been palling it up at a local speakeasy with a young "Twist" at the time of the robbery. When asked the lady's name he refused to answer in order to protect her sterling reputation. "Balderdash," replied the detectives.

The following morning when Wilbur was being frisked prior to his preliminary hearing, Constable Ezra Hull discovered he was wearing three pair of pants and several shirts. A small hacksaw blade was found sewn into his boxer shorts and another in his shoe. After his hearing, where he loudly decried his innocence to a magistrate, Chief Gibson ordered the prisoner transferred to the Jasper County Jail in nearby Carthage for safekeeping. The authorities described Underhill at the time of his arrest as six-feet-tall, weighing 175 pounds, light brown sandy hair, gray eyes and dark complected with two teeth missing from the upper left frontal side of his mouth. The jailhouse description went on to say he wore a size twelve shoe, and had a series of moles and scars about his face and head.

Others would later describe him as thick bodied, rangy, and snaggle-toothed.

On receiving news of her son's incarceration, Almira Underhill, as was her habit, proclaimed his innocence decrying it was a "set-up" job. For the next two weeks she and Wilbur's younger brother George, religiously visited the inmate bringing him plug chewing tobacco and sugar treats. On the evening of January 8, 1923, jailors discovered three bars on his cell window sawed in half leaving a gaping hole big enough for a man to wiggle through. The alarm went out and all cells were immediately locked down. On a further search of Wilbur's accommodations, two hacksaw blades were found and the youthful gunsel was promptly transferred to an escape proof holding cell. When grilled, Underhill denied the handiwork claiming a past occupant must of accomplished the saw job.

The following morning Sheriff Harry Mead informed the assembled press, Underhill and another inmate, Harvey Karnstrom, a suspected Wobbly, (Radical union man) who was being held for vagrancy along with the notorious Asa "Ace" Pendleton who was currently incarcerated on a fraud charge, were involved in the attempted breakout. He was of the opinion the sharp-eyed jailor had interrupted the break only moments before the trio was set to consummate their plan. Upon completion of his statement, the Sheriff ordered the arrest of Mrs. Almira Underhill and her son George as accomplices to the attempted escape. It appears Almira had visited Wilbur the day before the incident, delivering him a bucket of molasses. Officers suspected the bucket contained more than the syrupy substance.

After holding the fifty-two-year-old woman for several days behind bars, a Judge allowed her to go free on bond but revoked her visiting privileges. The charges against her were later dropped for lack of evidence. Wilbur eventually pled guilty to first-degree robbery and was sentenced to five years hard labor at Jeff City. He re-entered the prison for a second time on Wednesday, February 14, 1923 as inmate #25456. When processed into the facility he listed his occupation as "Mechanic," it could have just as easily read "Habitual criminal."

Around this time, it appears Mother Underhill began to have second thoughts about her loving son and the direction his life was taking. According to a letter written by Wilbur in October 1924 Almira and her daughters had neglected to either visit or correspond with him or Ernest for some time. In response to this act of obvious neglect, Wilbur attempted to bribe her by sending some cash as well as instructions to come and visit him and Ernest, saying, "For you have some money now." Adding, "Everyone seems to be against me."

On the afternoon of September 13, 1925 Wilbur, along with twenty-one other inmates tunneled under a

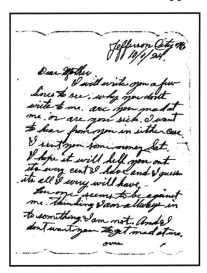

Letter written by Wilbur to his Mother 1924.
Courtesy Michael Webb

Postcard photo depicting Wilbur Underhill, as inmate at MSP, which he sent to his sister. Courtesy Michael Webb.

Wilbur's signature on back of photo. Courtesy Michael Webb.

stage located in the prison's chapel, gaining access to the main sewer line that wound its way to the Missouri River. Unluckily for the escapees, when they arrived at the point where the line ran into the river they discovered the opening blocked with heavy steel bars. Prison officials must of thought the conspirators had suffered sufficient punishment for their actions by spending hours crawling through the smelly sewer line since according to official records only the ring leaders were disciplined for their involvement in the scheme.

Wilbur and Ernest would soon be joined in prison by brothers Earl on June 25, 1925, sentenced to a five-year jolt out of Newton County for burglary, followed by George on March 4, 1926, serving a two year hitch for larceny. For the first time in years, Almira had all four of her boys in one place. Must of felt like old home week.

Chapter Three

Like a Lamb to the Slaughter

On November 9, 1926, Underhill was released from the confines of the Missouri State Penitentiary. On such an occasion society hopes to be greeting a new man, one who has learned his lesson and adjusted his faulty behavior patterns. In Underhill's situation, this proved not to be the case. He came out of the slammer a highly trained criminal, a man filled with bitterness toward society and possessing a great hatred for authority figures.

According to Wilbur, he traveled in his cheap prison issue suit and cardboard shoes back to the hearth of his family in Joplin. He further claimed he sought employment at a shirt factory where he openly informed his employer of his sordid past, adding, he desired a fresh start and intended on going straight for the first time in his adult life. But, as the story goes, his boss and society persecuted him due to his status as an ex-con. Not able to stand the scornful stares of his fellow workers he quit his job and hit the road journeying to the Picher mining district where jobs were plentiful and fewer questions asked.

On his arrival in Picher, he was first hired as a clerk by the Eagle-Picher Lead Mining Company then worked as a miner at Eagle-Pitcher's Crawfish Mine. Underhill maintained that by the end of his first week at the mines, the police attempted to give him the bum's rush due to his criminal record. Wilbur ignored the threat until a pint-sized twenty-three-year-old small-time thief named Ike "Skeet"

Akins, who had recently been fired from his job at the Golden Rod Mining and Smeltering Corporation, informed him of an impending raid on the rooming house where they both were staying. With this knowledge in hand, Underhill and his newfound friend packed up and having no other way of making an honest living he was again forced into a life of crime. At any rate, that's Wilbur's version of events.

Ike Akins
Courtesy Okmulgee Democrat

Underhill went on to assert, the pair fled to nearby Claremore and took up with a local floozy named Sarah Riddle (Often times misidentified as "Sarah Little" in news reports) who would later declare Wilbur married her in a hurried ceremony conducted by a Justice of the Peace. The trio lived quietly until they were forced to move on to Tulsa due to continued police harassment. Of course, the above narrative is based on statements made by both Underhill and his blushing bride who it turns out was as reliable as a broken alarm clock.

The true facts concerning Underhill's movements after his arrival in Oklahoma seem to indicate he had indeed been employed at the mines in Picher for a short spell, but upon meeting up with Akins he plunged back into his familiar role of arch criminal. First, the pair robbed a streetcar conductor named W. H. Hastings on the busy streets of nearby Baxter Springs, Kansas relieving him of several dollars and a .41 caliber Colt revolver as well as his pocket watch. Then they were suspected of pulling off several street muggings on the dark, unlit street corners of the mining settlements before hijacking a sixteen-year-old boy named Fred Smyth on December 12. Apparently, the lad was walking down the Oklahoma Railway tracks near the Piokee Mine (Consolidated #12) heading to a downtown poolroom on a peaceful Sunday morning when suddenly Underhill, Akins, and a third individual accosted him demanding he fork over his wallet. When the boy attempted to flee, Underhill shot him with a .45 caliber pistol, the bullet lodging deep in his right lung. Complicating matters, the teen apparently swallowed his gold tooth during the altercation and nearly choked to death. When the robbers searched his pockets they came up with an empty sack, apparently the boy hadn't a penny to his name. Hearing the shots and the youth's cries for help, neighbors responded by coming to his assistance. His attackers promptly fled the scene. An ambulance was called and Smyth was transported to the newly built forty-bed American Hospital located just a few blocks away where he remained in critical condition for several weeks. Although he had lost a great deal of blood and was suffering from shock and a collapsed lung, he would survive the attack. When the youngster's father, Martin Smyth, was interviewed the day after the assault, he shook his head in disgust over the senseless act of violence saying, "What did those animals think a boy of his age would do when a gun was thrust in his face? He did what any kid would do, he ran."

Young Smyth would later positively identify the man who shot him as Wilbur Underhill. For the next several days, officers swept through the area questioning residents of the town's numerous boarding houses and rousting suspicious persons on the street. Merchant Policeman William Shumulbach thought he was on to something when he spotted an obviously inebriated individual who matched the description of one of the attackers leaning against a lamppost on the corner of Columbus and 4th streets in downtown Picher. On sighting the cop, the man bolted, running up the street. When Shumulbach caught up with him the suspect commenced to throw rocks at the officer who reacted by shooting him in the leg. On questioning the suspect, identified as twenty-seven-year-old Roy Epperson, the cops were disappointed to discover he had nothing to do with the assault on the boy, but had fled from the laws due to his being wanted on an unrelated charge.

The following week, Underhill and Akins hijacked both the J. R. Roberts Grocery Store and the Milo Chew Drug Store in Baxter Springs before knocking off a filling station located on the state line just north of Picher near the Blue Mound Mine as well as an oil company in nearby Galena, Kansas. During this time, the pair was also suspected of jack-rolling a miner named Frank Short on the streets of Picher. When Short resisted, the robbers shot him in the face. Lucky for him the round just grazed his cheek.

For a roof over their heads, the desperate pair stayed in a series of flophouses in the Picher area before moving in with one of Wilbur's honeys named Minnie Gregg in nearby Galena, Kansas. From there, they traveled by rail to Claremore, Oklahoma to stay with Underhill's other gal, Sarah Riddle, before moving on to Tulsa. Underhill described Miss Riddle in a letter to his sister as "Like all my gals, well endowed and plump." Throughout his adult life, Wilbur was attracted to mostly older, hefty sized women.

Alarmed over the recent spat of robberies, some of

which had occurred on their leased lands, the powers that be at the mammoth Eagle-Picher Mining Company, which owned outright or rented from the various Indian tribes nearly 4000 acres of northern Ottawa County Oklahoma, put their crack private investigator Joe Anderson on the case. The forty-three-year-old Illinois born Anderson, who also held a special Deputy Sheriff's commission from Ottawa County, was a force to be reckoned with. He had been a long-time member of the private police force employed by a consortium of

Deputy Joe Anderson
Courtesy Okmulgee Daily Times

Tri-State mining concerns contracted to keep the peace in the vast mining district located on the Kansas-Oklahoma border.

Anderson took down the various descriptions from the victims of the recent robberies and promptly deduced the crimes were the work of the same pair of men, one of them being Wilbur Underhill. The lawman took to the road and was soon hot on the duo's trail tracking them to Kansas then into the booming oil and gas field settlements of central Oklahoma.

On a wind blown, chilly Christmas night, Underhill and his companion arrived by passenger train at Okmulgee, a large oilfield community located in east-central Oklahoma. Apparently, Akins, who had once resided in

Okmulgee, had not been back since he'd been run out of town after serving a short jolt for theft in the county jail. The motivation for this visit was apparently his desire to spend some of the Yuletide season at the home of a married sister, Mrs. D. L. Harrington, who lived on the west side of town. According to statements made the following day by her husband, described as a hard-working local carpenter, Akins and a larger man fitting the description of Underhill arrived unexpectedly at 9 pm on Christmas night. After eating a late dinner, the visitors ventured into the cold on an errand.

At approximately 11:00 pm, the pair was seen loafing in front of the Phillips Drug store by Mrs. M. G. Phillips, the owner's wife. The pharmacy was located approximately fourteen blocks from Ike's sister's residence on West 8th Street. Mrs. Phillips stated, "The pair paced past the store several times peering into the front window before stopping and conferring. They then left walking east." Roughly, forty minutes later the duo strolled into the nearby Purity Drug Store located on East Main (6th) Street near the Frisco Rail Depot. The store's co-owner, Ira Maynard, was standing behind the cash register while his wife was just finishing taking inventory of the day's profits and placing the cash into a bag when they looked up noticing the pair. The bandits, both armed with handguns demanded "The money sack." Meanwhile, Mrs. Maynard discreetly slipped the cash bag between her legs covering it with her skirt while her husband banged open the cash drawer and instructed the thieves to "Take what you want." Grabbing about $26 in mainly silver, the pair finished their business and began to depart when suddenly, eighteen-year-old George Fee and two companions identified as Rex Bell and Carl Kerr, strolled in the front door laughing and filled with Christmas cheer. Little did they realize they were about to bump into the original "Scrooge." Fee refused to raise his hands when ordered figuring the robbery was staged for their benefit as some kind of practical joke. Instead, the unsuspecting youth turned away and sauntered toward the soda fountain. It proved to be the biggest mistake of his life. Akins reacted by firing a single .41 caliber missile, which struck Fee in the arm and passed through the trunk of his body. The lad fell to the floor in a heap and Mrs. Maynard began screaming. The bandits fled out the door bumping into Ira Maynard's partner, George Thornburgh, as he was entering the establishment.

Although an ambulance promptly arrived to transport the gravely wounded Fee to the newly built city hospital the youth died within the hour never fully gaining consciousness. It was reported his mother and wife of eight months were at his side when the end came. Fee's murder was reportedly the 211th homicide in Oklahoma and the 5th in Okmulgee County to occur in the Year of our Lord 1926.

Back at the scene of the crime, Okmulgee police Captain R. W. Stuart along with county detectives, Mark "Lem" Lairmore and Blaine Hill, who had been assigned to the case by Okmulgee County Sheriff John Russell began

Old Okmulgee City Hospital. Photo by Naomi Morgan

questioning the witnesses. After garnering several contradictory descriptions of the perpetrators due to the bad lighting in the store, the officers were able to deduce a short "dwarf-like" man and a large broad shouldered fellow with blondish hair who spoke in a gruff voice committed the crime. Evidently, the shorter man had done the actual shooting. An all points bulletin was issued throughout the state describing the robbers in general terms.

The day after the murder, an individual named Louis Benge of Muskogee was arrested and a big hoopla was made over his capture until lawmen figured out his apprehension was just another red herring. Although Benge was reportedly seen in Okmulgee on Christmas night and physically matched the description of one of the robbers, witnesses declined to identify him as one of the culprits. While investigators didn't like the way the suspect, who they referred to as a "Shady Character," answered their questions and his refusal to offer an alibi for his whereabouts the night of the murder, they were forced to release him from custody.

On December 28, George Fee's funeral was held at Okmulgee's First Baptist Church on 5th street. The event was heavily attended and many businesses including the Oklahoma Tire and Supple Company where Fee was employed closed their doors for the day in memory of the youthful victim. Fee, who lacked two months of turning

Grave of George Fee. Photo by Naomi Morgan

Funeral record of George Fee. Courtesy Kelley Funeral Home

nineteen, had been a popular figure around town. The youth's earthly remains were interred later that afternoon at the Okmulgee Park Cemetery under the direction of the Davis Funeral Home.

Meanwhile, Ottawa County Deputy Joe Anderson had not been sitting on his laurels. Armed with a pair of "John

Doe" warrants, the lawman had taken up the hunt for the two fugitives traveling by automobile from Joplin to Tulsa then to Kansas City apparently staying just one step behind them. After receiving a tip from one of his informants, Anderson again journeyed to Tulsa, Oklahoma where after a bit of snooping discovered Underhill along with Akins and a lady friend had recently been spotted hanging out in the downtown district. Enlisting the aide of a pair of Tulsa cops named B. P. Grace and L. O. Gibson, the lawman set up surveillance on the corner of 4th and Main streets. He didn't have a long wait, within the hour Underhill came lumbering up to the intersection looking like he didn't have a care in the world. On spotting the outlaw, Anderson and his fellow officers moved quickly surrounding the badman with weapons at the ready ordering him to "Get 'em up!" Knowing he was bested, Wilbur raised his hands in submission offering no resistance. When searched the fugitive was found in possession of a pair of Colt revolvers, one a .41 caliber (The same type used in the slaying of George Fee) and the other a .45, along with a pair of hacksaw blades sewn into the lining of his britches.

An hour later, with Wilbur safely tucked in the Tulsa County Jail the officers captured Ike Akins and Sarah Riddle exiting a flophouse located on East 2nd Street. Akins was unarmed at the time of his arrest but a search of his person turned up two .41 caliber bullets.

The following day all three were transported to the Ottawa County jail where the wounded boy, Fred Smyth again positively identified Underhill as his assailant as did several other of his recent victims. Anderson, aware of the reward offered for the capture of the two individuals involved in the Okmulgee murder case, who in his opinion closely matched the description of Underhill and Akins, also contacted Sheriff Russell suggesting the witnesses in that affair come take a gander at his pair of prisoners, just in case.

When C. B. Kerr, one of George Fee's companions at the time of his murder, arrived in Miami he was immediately taken to a lineup of prisoners featuring Underhill and Akins as the headline act. It was a great disappointment to the assembled officers when he stated the pair was not the men he had observed in the Purity Drug Store the night of the crime. Anderson, who was not convinced of their innocence in the affair, requested Okmulgee officials to keep at it.

The following day, Okmulgee Captain Riley W. Stuart along with Detective Bob Shackelford motored into town with witnesses Rex Bell and Ira Maynard in tow. The lawmen were overjoyed when the pair of eyewitnesses identified Underhill and his companion as Fee's slayer. A few days later Okmulgee County Deputy Sheriffs Blaine Hill and Mark Lairmore arrived in Miami by rail with a pair of warrants charging the duo with first-degree murder. The prisoners were rapidly escorted back to Okmulgee to face the music.

On the pair's arrival at the receiving room of the Okmulgee County Jail, a local news reporter in attendance described the duo as a couple of "hard eggs," adding, "While Akins, who was the smaller of the two, bit his nails, fidgeted, and chain smoked, Underhill strolled about nonchalantly joking with the deputies as they photographed and fingerprinted him." The reporter went on to describe Wilbur as a typical "tough mug," with a prizefighters face, small gray eyes, brown hair, and a pleasing smile. As for Akins, the journalist depicted him as small in build with long dark slicked-back hair and high cheekbones.

On January 26, 1927, the fugitives were given their preliminary hearings before Justice of the Peace George

Bob Shackelford
Courtesy Okmulgee Daily News

Captain R. W. Stuart
Courtesy Okmulgee Daily News

Gibson. Attorney E. M. Carter, who appeared unconcerned throughout the affair, represented the suspects. Mrs. and Mrs. Ira Maynard as well as Rex Bell stood up in court and identified the pair as Fee's assailants. "Skeet" Akins's sister testified of the pair's arrival at her home on Christmas night although she refused to identify Wilbur as her brother's companion at the time saying, "He looks familiar but taller than the man I saw." The Justice ordered the pair be held without bond and closed the hearing.

Naturally, the day after Wilbur's preliminary his long-suffering mother showed up at the county jail protesting his innocence. Her youngest daughter, Dorothy, who reportedly worshiped her brother, accompanied her, as did

Wilbur's ever-faithful moll, Sarah Riddle, who Ottawa County authorities had recently released from a charge of harboring fugitives from justice. Speaking with Sheriff John Russell, Almira tearfully pleaded with him to allow her to visit her "baby" who she swore was as harmless as a lamb. Russell, sideswiped by the woman's hysterical outburst, relented allowing Mrs. Underhill and her crew permission to visit the prisoner.

In the early morning hours of January 31st Underhill, Akins, and two other inmates identified as "Red" Gann and Duff Kennedy, sawed through the bars of their individual cages making their way into the jail's main corridor. From there the quartet sawed a single steel bar of an exterior window squirming through the small opening climbing onto a narrow concrete ledge which encircled the fourth floor jail before lowering themselves down a makeshift rope made of blankets and sheets to the frozen earth and freedom. Once the prisoners hit the ground, they split up into pairs, Underhill and Akins in one group with Kennedy and Gann in the other.

At approximately 7 am, a woman living in a hotel located on the 7th street side of the jail looked out her window and spotted the long jury-

Almira and daughter Dorothy Underhill
Courtesy Michael Webb

rigged rope protruding out a window of the fourth floor jail falling onto the sidewalk. She immediately telephoned Sheriff Russell at his home stating, "I think you have a problem." After contacting his Undersheriff, Russell sped to the jail. At approximately the same time as Russell had received his call, a city cop named Dick Wells spotted the free hanging rope and hotfooted it to the jailhouse. On the lawmen's arrival, Jailors Claude Goin and W. W. Mayor, who were both just coming on duty, joined them. The pair, who had secured the cellblock at midnight, was shocked to find the quartet of prisoners missing. When the remaining prisoners were questioned, they all denied any knowledge of the escape claiming they were sound asleep at the time.

In a statement issued by Sheriff Russell he stated, "I believe they broke out between midnight, when the jailors made their last round, and 6 am." This position was fur-

Inside the old Okmulgee County Jail. (Not in current use). Photo by Naomi Morgan

Okmulgee County Jail today (no longer in use). Photo by Naomi Morgan

ther re-enforced when officers questioned moviegoers who had been attending the late show at the nearby Orpheum Theatre. The movie house which was and still is located a block from the jail, was currently showing a popular silent western named *The Nervous Wreck* starring the original Harrison Ford and Chester Conklin which lasted until 11:45 pm. Of the several hundred persons in attendance, many who had parked their vehicles adjacent to the courthouse and jail, not one had noticed anything out of the ordinary.

Above: Ledge encircling fourth floor jail. Photo by Naomi Morgan.

Left: Okmulgee County Jail-window the escapees sawed through to gain access to ledge. Photo by Naomi Morgan.

A huge posse was immediately organized and the manhunt was on. The county's noted tracking hound, "Midnight Sun," a large German police dog belonging to W. H. Gragg, was drafted into the chase but soon lost the escapees' scent. A car had been reported stolen during the night and the auto shop belonging to Hugh Hancock located on the Beggs Road was reportedly broken into and the cash box rifled for 300 pennies. Lawmen thought they were onto something until city officers informed the posse the man who had stolen the vehicle and robbed the garage had been identified and captured several hours earlier.

In the meantime, officers in nearby Okfuskee County began conducting a series of raids of the known whereabouts of several acquaintances of both Kennedy and Gann. The pair was incarcerated for sus-

Advertisement from time of escape from Orpheum Theatre. Courtesy Okmulgee Democrat

picion of committing a dozen robberies of an assortment of filling stations, garages, and country stores in Okfuskee County, which all occurred on the night of November 19, 1926. Their short-lived crime wave culminated in the murder of an elderly Creek Indian who resisted their efforts. The duo was captured several weeks after the conclusion of their crime spree when two Okfuskee lawmen ambushed them at an isolated farmhouse outside of Louisiana, Missouri after being tipped-off to their whereabouts by one of their ex-crime partners. Ironically, Kennedy and Gann had been transferred to the Okmulgee County Jail from Okemah for safekeeping just a few days before their escape. Okemah officers figured the Okmulgee jail was more secure than their own facility.

Back at the jail, officers were convinced inmates Mike Murphy, a hot check artist and Aaron Davis, a convicted forger, had taken part in the jail delivery since blankets and sheets from their cells had been used to construct part of the improvised rope. A search of the Underhill's now empty cell turned up several letters written by Almira Underhill which suggested she had previous knowledge of the impending escape. Officers questioned her but drew a blank when she vigorously denied any involvement in the affair, saying, "I never wrote a thing in a letter that I didn't want the laws to read, for I knew they would." Had the authorities been aware at the time of her association with Wilbur's 1923 Carthage jail escape attempt they would have surely questioned her more forcefully. Sarah Riddle, who was staying at the Paul Hotel, was also questioned. When she tried to dummy up and stonewall the officers, Russell, who suspected she knew more than she was telling, ordered her arrested for vagrancy, claiming she was an "Idle person having no visible means of support." Since word around town suggested she had been pulling tricks at a local roadhouse as of late, the charge was probably not out of line. When Wilbur's attorney, E. M. Carter, was quizzed, he also pled ignorance. Since Riddle, Carter, and Mother Underhill were Wilbur and Ike's only visitors, and Deputy Blaine Hill had sat in on all of Riddle's visits observing her every move, County Prosecutor A. N. "Jack" Boatman publicly concluded that Wilbur's ma was probably the culprit who smuggled in the hacksaw blades. Not possessing enough evidence to make a case that would stick, the prosecutor stated he was unfortunately unable at that time to officially charge her with the crime of jail breaking.

In response to the escape, county officers mailed some 1500 circulars with mug shots of the four fugitives to various police departments across the nation. In a statement to the press, Sheriff Russell stated all four escapees should be considered dangerous, especially Underhill and Akins who would likely resist if cornered. He further informed his deputies to take no chances with these men, instructing them to shoot to kill if the occasion demands.

Wanted Poster for Wilbur Underhill and Skeet Akins originating from Okmulgee County. Courtesy Michael Webb.

Chapter Four

The Tri-State Terror

No sign of the fugitives was reported until the evening of February 5 when a Pittsburg, Kansas taxicab driver reported he had been kidnapped by two men matching the descriptions of Underhill and Akins and forced to drive them to Fort Scott, Kansas. Reacting to the report officers throughout Kansas and Missouri set up numerous roadblocks at bridges and crossroads across the area but the fugitives somehow slipped the net.

On the afternoon of February 9, a rural Missouri constable named Floyd Selby, was flagged down on a road just outside of the community of Lamar by what he described as a short man in raggedy clothes standing next to a 1926 Ford Touring car, which was mired in the mud. When the constable inquired if he could be of assistance, the lone man replied he could use a ride into town. Noticing the automobile (which had been stolen off the streets of Wichita earlier that week) had no license plates; Selby began questioning the individual. Getting no straight answers, the lawman promptly gave the man a lift directly to the county jail, later explaining, he felt the fellow was probably wanted somewhere. Taken into the presence of Barton County Sheriff J. L. Garrett, the officer thought the man looked familiar. When quizzed about his identity, the stranger responded his name was Bill Jones of Tulsa, Oklahoma. Garrett filed a charge of not carrying a legal auto tag against the little man and had him held in the county jail overnight for good measure. On reviewing a stack of wanted posters the following morning, Garrett came across one originating from Okmulgee County, Oklahoma containing a description and mug shot of Skeet Akins, which perfectly matched his newly acquired prisoner.

After being informed of Skeet's possible capture, Sheriff Russell wired a full set of fingerprints to the Missouri officers in order to complete the identification. Later the same evening, Okmulgee authorities received word of conformation from the "Show Me" state. Russell wired back saying he was on his way, adding an admonition to the Missouri authorities suggesting they hire an extra guard to watch over the elusive outlaw until his arrival. The following morning, Russell, and his Undersheriff, Mark Lairmore, loaded up and began traveling towards Missouri driving in the Sheriff's late model Chevy Coup.

Okmulgee County Sheriff John Russell. Courtesy Okmulgee Public Library and John Russell Jr.

Deputy Sheriff Mark Lairmore. Courtesy Okmulgee Public Library and John Lairmore.

On their arrival in Lamar, Russell discovered he'd been double-crossed. Evidently, Sheriff Garrett, upset over the recent extradition and subsequent escape of the notorious outlaw Ray Terrill while being transported to McAlester from nearby Jasper County, Missouri, declined to release the prisoner to the pair of cowboy lawmen. Garrett had instead given the prisoner up earlier that morning to officers from Columbus, Kansas, where he was wanted on a grand theft charge.

Apparently, Akins had readily agreed to extradition to Kansas in order to avoid his being delivered to Oklahoma where he would be facing a murder rap. The pair of frustrated "Okie" lawmen reacted by motoring to the "Sunflower" state and began bargaining with the authorities there for the right to extradite the bandit. After dickering back and forth for most of a day, the Cherokee County prosecutor finally agreed to turn over the suspect with the provision he would be released back to them once the Oklahoma boys were done with him. Russell agreed, saying, "I doubt he'll be much use to you by then." His prediction would prove to be on the money.

Finally, about 10:30 pm Friday, February 11, the prisoner, handcuffed and flanked by officers Russell and Lairmore, departed the Cherokee County Jail. Exactly how Akins legally came into the clutches of the Oklahoma lawmen when it is known the fugitive had repeatedly refused extradition to the "Sooner" state is unknown. Most likely, it was a case of pure skullduggery on the lawmen's part. When questioned as to the whereabouts of his crime partner, Akins claimed he and Underhill parted company several weeks ago, adding, "I've been spending time with my wife ever since." He followed that pearl of information by stating he had nothing else to say.

Unfortunately for the officers, coinciding with their departure from Columbus was the advent of a major winter storm in the form of a blizzard. When visibility dropped to near zero, the lawmen were forced to stop and seek shelter from the storm in Miami, Oklahoma located just across the border. Upon lodging the prisoner in the Ottawa County jail for safekeeping, Russell and his pal flopped on a pair of cots in the jail's waiting room and got some shut-eye. Incidentally, Russell reportedly paid the jailor an extra $5 to keep a close eye on the prisoner. The jailor in turn informed the Sheriff that for five bucks he'd look in on him every five minutes. According to reports later made public, Akins had informed his fellow inmates at the jail he dreaded going back to Okmulgee and would "Take the first chance I get to escape from custody."

Come morning, the officers ate a hearty breakfast of bacon and eggs while their prisoner dined on a tasteless bowl of grits and soggy toast before beginning the last leg of their journey. At midday, the trio stopped and ate dinner

Modern day view of spot where Sheriff Russell killed Ike Akins.
Photo by Naomi Morgan.

at Claremore before checking in at the Rogers County Jail where they had been informed a prisoner who matched the description of Wilbur Underhill, was being lodged. Turned out the inmate in question didn't look a bit like the elusive outlaw. The frustrated manhunters continued their trip heading down Route 66 until they hit Sapulpa and turned south on Highway 75. While motoring through the small Creek County community of Mounds the prisoner became agitated telling Detective Lairmore he feared he was about to become the featured guest at a necktie party. When the big shamus told him he was probably right, the fugitive began to fidget in his seat and softly moan and weep. Larimore's only reaction was to snort and turn away. Russell, who wasn't the tenderhearted type to begin with, didn't pay a lick of attention to the prisoner's apparent misery. He had his hands full fighting the freezing rain and accumulating snowflakes gathering on his windshield due to his windshield wiper motor going on the blink.

As darkness set in, Russell was forced to pull off the road at both Beggs and Preston to wipe the windshield. He stopped a third time at a location a half-mile north of the Okmulgee city limits near the county garage. According to a statement made by Lairmore later that evening; "When John dismounted the car, Akins suddenly leaped out the side door and I grabbed at him but just caught his coat tail. I yelled 'Watch out'. He broke my grasp just as John fired the first time. Akins screamed 'ouch' or something, then as he regained his balance he began running into an open field, John shot him twice more, both times in the head."

Lairmore rushed to the wounded man's side while Russell calmly strolled to the county garage to call an ambulance. When the meat wagon arrived, Akins was reportedly breathing, but just barely. After loading the wounded

Ike Akins funeral record. Courtesy Shurden Funeral Home.

prisoner, the ambulance began speeding toward City Hospital with red lights flashing and siren wailing. (Ironically, young George Fee had perished six weeks earlier at the same hospital).

According to the ambulance physician, a Dr. Lowe, the outlaw attempted to speak to him on the drive but couldn't get the words out. "He just made a gurgling sound." Akins was dead on arrival at the emergency room.

Unmarked grave of Ike Akins, Okmulgee, Oklahoma. Photo by Naomi Morgan.

Over the next twenty-four hours, Russell would grant several interviews to the local press. The Sheriff told reporters "I certainly hated to shoot him. It looks like I'll be the fall guy in this case. I'm sorry I killed him, but I had no choice." Turns out, Akins was the third prisoner Russell had slain in the performance of his duties in less than a year.

In early 1926, a pair of men identified as Ben Rosekrans and a Creek Indian named "Snakeye" was arrested in Pecos, Texas for trespassing. When the two were searched, they were found in possession of certain items, which had been stolen from a store in Okmulgee. After Texas authorities informed Russell's office back in Oklahoma of the fugitives capture the lawmen announced he would personally travel to Texas to bring the pair to justice. It was later learned Russell had been raised near Pecos and hankered to visit his kin there, thus the journey would kill two birds with one stone or bullets as it turned out in this case.

On arrival in the desert community, the local laws informed the Sheriff or "Big John" as he was otherwise known, that the prisoners had been boasting they would never arrive back in Oklahoma for trial. Russell just smiled and went about visiting his relatives for a few days before arriving back at the jail with extradition papers in hand. The following morning, the trio left for Oklahoma in "Big John's" spanking new Chevy Coup (The same Chevy Akins would later escape from). At a location about 30 miles east of town, Rosekrans suddenly grabbed the coup's steering wheel. According to Russell, the car, which was traveling approximately 40 miles per hour, spun uncontrollably into the ditch rolling over, throwing the passengers clear of the wreck. As soon as the lawman hit the ground, he righted himself and pulled his .45 caliber six-shooter. Russell stated, "When Rosekrans started toward me I shot him between the eyes then turned and shot 'Snakeye' who was crawling some distance away in the back of the head. Both men were dead where they fell."

Within minutes of the conclusion of the shooting, a passing Mexican cattle buyer drove up in a stock truck and helped Russell load the bodies in the back of his rig, transporting them and the lawman back to town. A few months down the trail, a Texas grand jury exonerated "Big John" of all guilt in the matter.

****

Back in Okmulgee, County Attorney A. N. Boatman refused to charge John Russell with any wrongdoing in the killing of Akins, stating the Sheriff acted in the finest tradition of the Oklahoma peace officer. Referring to the recent successful escape of the infamous Ray Terrill, who had jumped out of a running carload of lawmen just outside the prison gates in McAlester, the prosecutor concluded "There will be no Terrill fiascos in Okmulgee

County." The following day, in response to mounting public criticism of Russell's deadly tactics, the Okmulgee Lions Club, which Russell was a member, unanimously passed a "Declaration of support" endorsing the Sheriff's actions. Club President W. C. Vernon announced, "We fully stand behind our Sheriff in his killing of 'bad men' who threaten our town's peace and dignity."

Meanwhile the hunt for Underhill had hit a brick wall. Although there were rumors of his being spotted near his mother's home in Joplin, Missouri, as well as a drug store in Baxter Springs, Kansas, and a café in nearby Cardin, Oklahoma, none of these sightings could be confirmed.

On the evening of February 13, J. D. Wineland, owner of the Mystic theatre located at 111 East 2nd Street in the mining community of Picher, Oklahoma had just gathered up the week's receipts, approximately $800, and was placing the cash in his strongbox in his upstairs office which overlooked the ticket window, when he looked up noticing a rough looking individual enter the theatre's foyer with his right hand stuffed deep in his coat pocket. The fellow approached cashier Mrs. E. E. Burkholder at the cashier's window demanding she fork over the money in the till. The terrified woman handed over the cash, which amounted to roughly five dollars in change (Some reports claim the take was $52.00). Wineland withdrew his pistol from his desk drawer and contemplated shooting the bandit on the spot before coming to the conclusion he didn't want the man's death on his conscience for a measly few bucks. After completion of the robbery, the bandit rushed out of the theater into the street where according to the cashier, a pair of scraggly dressed individuals joined him. Wineland immediately summoned Constable George Fuller by phone giving him the details of the hijacking and the description of the suspects.

At approximately 9:30 pm, Fuller, accompanied by a twenty-one-year-old miner from nearby Douthat named Earl Robert O'Neal spotted a man who fit the description of the robber standing at the counter of the Owl Drug Store located a block from the theatre at 305 South Main. Fuller and his unarmed companion approached the man as he exited the pharmacy with a milkshake in one hand and a detective magazine in the other. When the Constable reached within touching distance of the suspect, he drew his revolver and ordered him to raise his hands and turn around placing them on the drug store's front plate glass window. When the suspect did as he had been instructed, Fuller tossed a pair of handcuffs to his young friend and told him to cuff the fellow. Just as O'Neal stepped between the constable and his quarry, the man abruptly whirled about smashing the youth in the face with his elbow while simultaneously snatching a pistol from his belt. Suddenly, several loud explosions rocked the store's windowpanes and echoed down the street as O'Neal slumped to the sidewalk, blood flowing in rivulets onto the curb and into the street. The fugitive bolted into a nearby alleyway while Fuller and Night Policeman George Norton, who had witnessed the shooting from across the street, began firing in the direction of the fleeing robber who dashed into a parking lot keeping his head down scurrying from one car to another using their steel bodies as cover. Although lawmen fired over a dozen shots in the melee, one shattering a plate glass window of a furniture store while another tore a gaping hole in the front door of a second hand shop, none hit their intended target. Even though nearly one hundred armed miners eventually joined the manhunt, which lasted well into the night, nothing further was seen of the gunman. O'Neal was promptly taken by ambulance to the American Hospital but expired on the operating table from internal bleeding due to a massive wound to his abdomen.

After questioning the witnesses on the scene, Picher Chief of Police Lon Bone, surmised the missing gunman was Wilbur Underhill who was well known in the area. He further concluded Underhill had acted alone in the theatre robbery and subsequent shooting. Carl Wallace, the proprietor of the Owl Drug Store informed lawmen the shooter had entered his store exchanging five dollars worth of quarters for a five-dollar bill before buying a milkshake and a magazine, he then began inspecting an automatic pistol displayed in a showcase. "The man appeared much interested in the gun."

Later the same night, two hundred miles to the southwest of Picher, the body of Ike Akins was put on display at the Davis Funeral home in Okmulgee. Ironically, he was laid out in the same viewing room as was his victim George Fee back in January. According to news reports, several thousand morbidly curious citizens filed past the open casket. The following day, the coffin was transported by hearse to the potter's field section of the Okmulgee Park Cemetery. With only the undertaker and a minister as witnesses, the body was lowered into the grave. (*Note: Oddly, official cemetery records incorrectly list his name as "Wilbur Aiken," burial plot #996, while Davis Funeral Home records notes "Ike Akins, plot #995."). Not a single relative or friend showed up for the graveside service. Glaringly absent was his sister who lived in town and his widow and two small children who resided in Kansas. News reports stated, "Not a tear was shed." A solitary spray of flowers with the inscription "Friends" decorated the grave.

The following night at 8:30 pm, a lone individual strolled into the Blue Mound Grocery Store located on the Oklahoma-Kansas state line just north of Picher and robbed the proprietor of roughly $50 at gunpoint. The description given of the bandit perfectly matched that of Wilbur Underhill. At the very moment lawmen were arriving at the grocery store in response to the robbery call, the same gunman entered the State Line filling station, located only a short distance from the store, producing a heavy caliber revolver, ordering the owner, A.W. Bradney, to step aside and raise his hands to the ceiling. After rifling the till of fourteen dollars, the gunman forced Bradney to walk a hundred feet down the road into the dark night before going through his britches stealing an additional eleven dollars. The bandit then informed Bradney he was, "Broke and needed some cash to get to Dallas, Texas." The filling station operator recognized the robber as Wilbur Underhill who had hijacked his station several weeks ago. Within minutes of the dual robberies, lawmen, joined by armed vigilantes began scouring the area on foot. Picher Mayor J. H. Klimefelter took up a collection from area miners

Picher, Oklahoma today. Photo by Naomi Morgan

and the proceeds, some $400, was offered as a reward for the capture of the outlaw "Dead or Alive."

The following morning, Deputy Sheriff Blaine Hill arrived from Okmulgee with the high-powered tracking dog "Midnight Sun" to join the chase. The posse began a new hunt starting from the scene of the previous night's robberies near the state line. By midday, it was reported a large group of angry miners from nearby Baxter Springs, Kansas armed with shotguns and clubs joined their Oklahoma cohorts in the search for the badman. A Joplin newspaperman stated, "These fellows had blood in their eyes and several ropes were produced. It seemed a necktie party was in the works." He may have been right, young Earl O'Neal had been a popular man in the Picher-Douthat mining area.

The district was soon engulfed in a climate of fear. Squads of law officers from neighboring Missouri and Kansas joined the hunt. Area boarding houses, pool halls, and mining shacks were searched. Sheriff E. E. Simpson posted armed guards at isolated cafes and filling stations as well as on interurban rail cars. The mining camps evolved overnight into an armed camp. Even farm folks began locking their doors with the coming of darkness.

A clever newspaper reporter dubbed the elusive Underhill "The Tri-State Terror" due to repeated assaults on businesses in the Tri-State mining district. Another journalist noted, "This Underhill, is a real 'Mad Dog'." The home of Minnie Gregg, one of Wilbur's girlfriends, was again put under round the clock surveillance, as was the residence of his mother in Joplin. A rumor began to circulate which purported Constable Fuller had accidentally shot his partner during the scuffle at the Picher drug store instead of Wilbur. Other wild rumors swept through the area like a windstorm. Over the next twenty-four hours, citizens reported sighting the fugitive at a café in Picher, exiting a privy located behind a residence in Cardin, and on the streets of Baxter Springs. In an act of frustration, the Ottawa County Sheriff's office issued a statement promising the next newsman publishing any false and misleading rumors in regards to the manhunt would be arrested and charged with obstruction of justice.

J. D. Wineland, the theatre operator, publicly stated he wished he would of "Shot the son of a bitch when I had him in my gun sights." Ottawa County Prosecutor A. L. Commons went before Justice of the Peace J. C. Baker and officially filed a murder complaint against Underhill.

On February 16, the funeral of Earl O'Neal was held at the home of his father-in-law William Turner near the tiny community of Century located a mile south of Picher. Burial was at the G.A.R. Cemetery in nearby Miami, Okla-

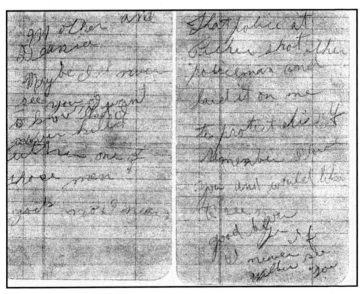

Handwritten note left by Underhill to his mother shortly after the O'Neil murder. Courtesy Michael Webb.

homa. The victim's young widow stood in silence at the graveside numbed by the senseless act of evil that had befallen her family. Back in Picher, there was still no sign of the perpetrator of that evil. The authorities were of a mind Underhill had fled to the Joplin area.

They were indeed correct in their assumption, according to a statement later made by the outlaw and confirmed by witnesses, in the wake of the shooting, Underhill had found sanctuary at a boarding house located only a block from the scene, where he had been rooming under a false name. Apparently, he locked himself in his room, staying put till the midnight hour when he scurried out of town making use of the dark alleyways and back roads. He evidently walked or rode a freight train into nearby Baxter Springs, Kansas where he stayed a day with a pair of acquaintances who were in the bootlegging business. From there, he managed to get to his old haunts in Joplin. After his arrival in his hometown, he walked to his mother's house and under the cover of darkness slipped a hastily written note under her door, which stated he had not killed O'Neal and informing her she would not likely see him alive again. It went on to claim Constable Fuller had accidentally slain the youth during the confusion and in turn blamed it on him.

The note read in full… "Mother and Deanie, Maybe I'll never see you. I want you to know I never killed either one of those men. Gods no I never. That police at Picher shot other policeman and laid it on me to protect his self. Remember I love you and would like to see you. Goodbye if I never see you…Love, Wilbur"

In the early morning hours of February 17, the manager of a rooming house in the small Ottawa County mining community of Hockerville, Oklahoma located on the border just east of Picher, phoned the town constable breathlessly informing him he had just spotted Wilbur Underhill entering the back door of his establishment. The constable reacted by calling Ottawa County Sheriff E. E. Simpson before rounding up a group of armed vigilantes. The armed posse surrounded the boarding house positioning a guard at every exit. News of the sighting raced through the community like a brushfire. Businesses closed up and residents armed themselves behind locked doors. Folks raced between houses warning friends and kin that "Mad Dog" Underhill was in the area.

After standing around over an hour in bone chilling subzero temps the vigilantes were joined by Sheriff Simpson and a pair of deputies. The jittery lawmen entered and searched the rooming house for over an hour but obtained no results. Sheriff Simpson commented, "If Underhill was in there, he slipped out the back door before they surrounded the place."

Chapter Five
Trial And Punishment

On the afternoon of March 28, Heavener, Oklahoma Night Constable Jimmie Johnson was informed by a local merchant of a stranger who had recently arrived in town and was indiscreetly flashing a wad of cash around, spending money like a drunken sailor in port. According to the shopkeeper, the man was often times accompanied by Lucille McDowell the daughter of a local hotel proprietor. Since new residents in the small mountain community, located roughly forty miles southeast of Sallisaw, was a rare occurrence, Johnson decided to investigate. Curious of the man's identity, Johnson began to observe the couple whenever they were in town. No one in the area seemed to know the man's business. After reading a description off a recent wanted poster issued from Okmulgee County, the lawman thought it possible the individual was the notorious Wilbur Underhill. Being a practical man, Johnson wired both Okmulgee and Joplin, Missouri inquiring if there was a reward offered for the fugitive. Okmulgee Police Captain Riley Stuart wired back informing the constable of a $1000 standing reward from the authorities in Picher (actually $400) and another $100 from Okmulgee. When Johnson asked for further "dope" on the fugitive, Stuart mailed a packet containing a photo as well as a full set of fingerprints to the officer. At the time, Captain Stuart thought nothing of the communication between him and the officer since there was no apparent sense of urgency in the request. Over the past few months, many departments across the southwest had contacted him seeking information pertaining to the elusive fugitive.

Constable Johnson stayed a respectful distance from the high spending couple until he received the photo from Okmulgee. One glance at the forwarded picture and he rushed to the home of his friend and fellow officer Laflore County Deputy Sheriff Charles Crawford who had accompanied Johnson on a surveillance of the man the previous evening. Crawford agreed the picture was the spitting image of the bad man. Further motivating the officers was the fact Stuart had stated in his letter the terms of the reward for the outlaw's capture was listed as "Dead or Alive." An attempt to capture the bad man under those stark terms simplified things greatly. Smacking their lips over the fat cash reward, the two officers immediately began making plans to entrap the fugitive.

For the next few days, the lawmen shadowed the pair while they formed a plan of action. It made no difference to them if they had to kill the bandit outright in order to affect a capture since the reward would be paid either way. Matter of fact they were counting on "Giving the works" to the violent desperado. No sense in taking undue risks with a gunsel of Underhill's caliber.

On the night of April 19, a fellow officer in Heavener phoned Johnson instructing him Underhill (who was using the name Ralph Caraway at the time) and his female companion had hopped into a Ford Coup and began driving north on the newly graveled highway. Somehow, Johnson also received word the pair's ultimate destination was Muskogee, Oklahoma, but first the couple purposed to spend the night at a hotel in the community of Panama, Oklahoma located about twenty miles north of Heavener. A little bird also whispered in his ear the fact Wilbur intended on catching the Kansas City Southern passenger train bound for Muskogee the following evening. Although the information was never made public, it's obvious someone in Wilbur's entourage (possibly a relative of Lucille's) was acting as a stool pigeon for the police.

Just south of Panama, Underhill and his girlfriend ran into a flooded roadway. (Due to recent heavy rains, the nearby Poteau River had overflowed its banks) The couple parked their car and walked the several miles into the village.

****

In the meantime, Officer Johnson connected with Deputy Crawford at Heavener's new city hall and the duo set out for Panama in Crawford's automobile. Like their quarry, the officers had to park a few miles out of town and hike in with their pants rolled up through the flooded backwaters. On arrival in town, the officers spotted the couple smoozing it up in the café and began a surveillance of the pair patiently waiting for their chance to strike.

After eating, the lovebirds sat around shooting the breeze with the restaurant's owner and his wife for an hour before leaving. On exiting the eatery, the pair was observed checking into the nearby England Hotel taking a room on the second floor. The lawmen, hot on their heels, took their positions on the bottom of the stairwell hoping to pounce on the badman come morning.

At approximately 6:45 am, the sleepy eyed officers heard the couple moving about in their room. They drew their weapons readying themselves for action. A few moments later, the lady came strolling down the stairs with Underhill lagging a step behind carrying a grip in one hand and a hatbox in the other. When ordered to "Throw up your hands" Underhill dropped the grip while flinging the hatbox at Deputy Crawford before gallantly placing his body between the officers and the woman, shielding her while simultaneously reaching into his back pocket. While his partner was busy dodging the hatbox, Johnson nailed the big thug with a single .38 slug. The round grazed the fugitive's left forearm and penetrated his thigh. The outlaw stiffened and stood motionless while shouting his surrender. Johnson approached the now demure fugitive frisking him before placing handcuffs on his wrists. No weapon was found in the desperado's pockets although a .45 automatic pistol was recovered from his suitcase.

Instead of transporting the wounded fugitive to a hospital, the lawmen took him back upstairs to his hotel room and placed him in his bed. According to the officers, Underhill immediately began letting out a fearful groan accompanied by a crescendo of cries demanding he be taken to a hospital while informing the cops he was surely on the brink of death. In lieu of seeking medical care for their wounded captive the cops first made a telephone call to Okmulgee County informing Captain Stuart they believed they had Underhill in

Wilbur's current wife, Lucille.
Courtesy Wichita Eagle

their possession and demanded the reward money.

When interviewed by Johnson, Wilbur's lady friend announced she was his legal wife. She further claimed she knew nothing of his illegal activities insisting her betrothed had told her he was a traveling salesman who was being pursued by the authorities over a bad debt, which he was unjustly accused of owing. After several hours of intense questioning, the young "Chippy" was released from custody and sent back to the bosom of her family.

Meanwhile, back in Okmulgee, Sheriff Russell and Prosecutor Boatman was overjoyed with the news of Wilbur's capture. Russell and Deputy Ernest Hulsey hopped into the Sheriff's trusty Chevy and began burning rubber to Panama. On their arrival, Russell was forced to fork over the $100 reward for the prisoner and pledged his word he would assist the officers in gaining the $1000 bounty offered by Ottawa County before he was allowed access to the fugitive. (Eventually Officers Johnson and Crawford would each receive $200 from Ottawa County) They also informed the Sheriff he almost missed gaining hold of the prisoner due to their plans to transport him to the hospital in Fort Smith, Arkansas for treatment. Russell demurred, informing his brother officers he would assume full responsibility for the health and welfare of the prisoner who had been loudly complaining of his wounds. His protests fell on deaf ears. The Okmulgee officers loaded him up and began speeding towards Okmulgee County. When the fugitive again screwed up his face and began to moan and groan telling his captors he needed medical attention, Russell informed him he'd best layback and shut his doughnut hole. The big lawmen also instructed the prisoner not to try to escape because his treatment for that disease was "Two rounds to the head." It was reported Underhill was a model prisoner for the remainder of the trip. According to Russell, the fugitive told them he was innocent of the Fee killing stating he was in Picher, Oklahoma at the time of the murder. He also claimed he did not shoot the Picher miner; instead the constable had accidentally shot him. Saying, "I'll get clear of these charges you watch and see."

When Russell asked the fugitive of his whereabouts over the past months, Underhill informed him that after the Okmulgee jail break he and Akins had hitchhiked and hopped freights to Kansas then traveled to Joplin to visit Wilbur's mother. Deciding to journey to Mexico, the pair walked to the Joplin rail depot where Akins somehow got hold of a pint of whiskey, " He got so drunk, I left without him, riding the rails to Laredo, Texas."

Soon after his arrival in Laredo, he entered Mexico. After a few days of drifting through the streets he re-entered the US commenting, " I had no money and couldn't speak the language."

Discouraged by his futile expedition south of the border, he hopped a freight to Kansas City and on his arrival walked to the passenger depot where he was spotted by a couple of railroad dicks who seemed to recognize him. The fugitive fled into the lady's restroom hiding in a mop closet several hours until he figured the coast was clear. He then rode the interurban to Picher where he bunked with a pair of bootlegger acquaintances. After the O'Neal shooting, he fled back to Joplin before riding the rails to Oklahoma. Hopping off an empty boxcar at Heavener, he spent the night at a boarding house where he met and began romancing a young lady whose folks ran the place. With the few dollars she had saved, the couple traveled by passenger train to Winfield, Kansas where on the morning of March 14, 1927, a Justice of the Peace married them. From Winfield the newlyweds went to Parsons, Kansas where they intended to honeymoon. (Parsons being the Niagara Falls of Kansas, I presume). Their efforts at consummating their marriage were interrupted when a beat cop spotted the pair walking into the hotel and began questioning them. As soon as the patrolman left the scene, a nervous Wilbur and his newly acquired bride scurried back to Oklahoma.

****

When the officers arrived with their catch back at the Okmulgee jail, a doctor was allowed to visit the prisoner to treat his wounds, which were described as "slight." The outlaw reportedly kept jailor Claude Goin jumping all night long running errands fetching water, towels, aspirins, blankets, and extra pillows.

The following day, Wilbur's momma and baby sister came steaming into town on the afternoon train. The pair took rooms at a boarding house located at 216 East Main Street. When she requested visitation rights from Sheriff Russell, he flatly refused, telling her lawyer, E. M. Carter, he suspected the woman of assisting in her son's January 31, 1927 escape. In due time Wilbur's ex-shack up job, Sarah Riddle, who loudly claimed she was Wilbur's legal spouse, showed up in Okmulgee from Tulsa. She was refused visiting rights as well and was duly informed she would be residing in the unfriendly confines of the Okmulgee County Jail where she had spent several weeks after Underhill's escape the previous winter on a charge of vagrancy, if she didn't watch her step. As the reader will notice as the story progresses Wilbur practiced the art of bigamy throughout his adult life. One of his few redeeming qualities was the fact he evidently rarely bedded down a woman unless he first put a ring on her finger. Of course, he may of have been married to two or three ladies at the same time. In his case, chivalry was not dead, just a little twisted.

Not to be denied a chance to toot her horn, Almira Underhill promptly paid a call on the local newspaper and began her well-worn public relations campaign to seek her son's release, telling reporters her boy was a victim of circumstance and although she was old and poor, she would stick by his side if it meant her being "Reduced to rags and begging in the streets." The gray haired matriarch also informed the press; Wilbur's case was one of mistaken identity, pure and simple. That same night, Wilbur's brother-in-law, Otto McDowell, (Lucille's brother) showed up at the jail demanding a visit with the prisoner. Jailors refused his request and sent him packing. An hour later, a call came into the Okmulgee Police station from the nearby Oklahoma Hotel stating an inebriated individual had entered an unlocked room and passed out on a bed without registering as a guest. When the cops arrived on the scene, the brother-in-law, who was described as "Well pickled" was promptly escorted to the town limits and given the bum's rush.

Back at the county jail, Sheriff Russell was taking no chances with his famous prisoner, ordering him chained and shackled head to foot. A heavy steel trace chain was wrapped around his waist and padlocked to the bars. His hands were handcuffed and heavy manacles bound his ankles together. Extra guards were hired to observe Underhill's every move around the clock. They were instructed to shoot to kill if the prisoner made even the slightest effort to escape.

Underhill's trial was scheduled to begin May 25, but was delayed a few days in order to allow for the completion of the trial of Mae Hamilton, an obviously deranged woman who was accused of murdering her fourteen-year-old son by means of a strychnine laced watermelon in an attempt to collect the proceeds of a large life insurance policy she had recently put in effect. When the Hamilton trial ended, several days were spent in jury selection. A panel was finally agreed on and Underhill' s court date set.

On June 1, the case against Underhill began in earnest. The defendant was escorted into court surrounded by three armed officers and leaving a trail of blood on the floor in his wake. He was wearing handcuffs and iron leggings which when removed showed deep lacerations and abrasions around his ankles and wrists. Wilbur's court appointed attorney, E. M. Carter, protested the harsh treatment of his client and when Judge John L. Norman asked the defendant about his treatment at hands of the officers, Underhill scrunched up his face and looking about as pitiful as one man could, squeaking it was "Pretty bad." The Jurist then firmly chastised the Sheriff's department for

Okmulgee County Courthouse around the time of Wilbur's trial.
Courtesy Okmulgee Public Library

their apparent cruelty. The jailors in turn protested the wounds were self-inflicted in an obvious attempt to gain sympathy with the jury and his honor. As this debate was raging, Wilbur's female kinfolk and his supposed "wife" Sarah Riddle, now joined by another of the desperado's sisters, Mrs. Anna Lewis, sat in the front section of the courtroom awash in tears, loudly sobbing and moaning, while the family of murder victim George Fee sat nearby in stony silence.

When the chief prosecutor, A. N. Boatman, announced he would seek the death penalty, Lawyer Carter responded by demanding a change of venue. He also protested the biased stories being written by the press about his client, claiming Wilbur was the victim of a lynching by print. Judge Norman ignored the remark; instead, he informed the spectators who had packed the courtroom, he would charge anyone who caused a disturbance with contempt of court. The defendant, who was described as ashen white, sat staring at the floor throughout the Judge's instructions.

First to take the stand, were the witnesses from the scene of the crime, each described the robbery as well as the murder of Mr.

A dapper Wilbur.
Courtesy Tulsa World

Fee in detail. At the end of their testimonies, they all pointed to Underhill as one of the guilty parties. Wilbur's ever-faithful paramour, Sarah Riddle, testified she was with both Underhill and Ike Akins at a rooming house in Tulsa on the night of the murder. The owners of the establishment, a Mr. and Mrs. Ballinger, informed the jury the trio were indeed registered at the inn on December 23 through 25, but added they did not see the subjects on the night in question. Deputy Ernest Hulsey, a tough World War veteran who had been with the department for two years, testified the defendant had informed him and Russell on the trip back from Panama he was in Picher at the time of the Fee killing, thus contradicting Riddle's testimony. Deputy Joe Anderson, who had captured Underhill off the streets of Tulsa on January 7, testified the defendant had informed him he was visiting in Okmulgee at the time of Fee's murder. It appears Wilbur and his girlfriend was having a hard time keeping their stories straight.

The state then called Ira Maynard to the stand. The druggist positively identified Underhill as one of the raiders of his business. Ike Akins's brother-in-law, D. L. Harrington, testified he had entertained the pair shortly before the robbery, claiming the duo left his home on West 8th Street about 10 pm. A Fred Thompson swore he saw the pair walking on 6th Street at roughly 10:15 on the night of the murder, and Mrs. M.G. Phillips, the wife of the owner of the Phillips drug store, located at 105 East 6th Street, spotted the same two men loitering in front of her husband's business a half hour later.

In testimony given later that afternoon Dr. Fred S. Watson described George Fee's fatal wounds, saying the single bullet caused two wounds, plowing through the victim's arm prior to plunging into his side and continuing through his trunk before finally making it's exit. The cause of death was massive internal bleeding due to gunshot wound.

The following morning, Wilbur took the stand, and after swearing to tell the whole truth on the bible, he launched into a pack of lies and half-truths that would have shamed the devil himself. The defendant began his testimony complaining of the brutality he had suffered at the hands of the law over the past few weeks beginning with his capture in Panama where he stated the lawmen had shot him down unmercifully without giving him a chance to surrender peaceably, adding, "I was living the life of an honest citizen when out of the blue these two laws ambushed me on the hotel stairwell." He further declared, "The cop shot at me five times but only hit me twice." He then spoke of his devotion to G-d and motherhood before telling the jury a highly fictionalized account of his life. First, he spoke of his childhood, claiming he and his brothers had constantly been victims of police persecution while growing up. He then addressed his two terms in the Missouri State Pen where according to him; he had endured a tormented existence due to the cruelty of the guards. He dubbed himself a lifelong victim of society, blaming the law for his present predicament.

When grilled by Prosecutor Boatman, he denied he had made any statement to the officers on the trip from Panama to Okmulgee. He also denied he was in Okmulgee on the night of the killing, insisting he had spent Christmas night in the Tulsa boarding house laid up in bed with Sarah Riddle deep in the grip of romance. Furthermore, the defendant instructed the jury he was in Panama with his newly acquired bride (Lucille) on the night Earl O'Neal was slain in Picher. Both statements were in direct contradiction to numerous statements he had made in the past. When asked why he escaped from the Okmulgee jail, he insisted he fled due to his having no money to hire a decent attorney to effectively combat the false charge he was being held for, adding, "They wouldn't even allow me to communicate with my ma." He went on to describe his travels over the past months ending his testimony with a curse for cops in general, calling them corrupt, brutal, and dishonest.

Next up to bat was Wilbur's attorney who in his closing statement informed the jury his client was merely the victim of a poor choice of companions, inferring Akins had pulled the trigger instead of the defendant. The prosecutor retorted under Oklahoma law when several persons planned and perpetrated a crime that resulted in a homicide all those involved were equally guilty of murder in the first degree. On the completion of closing arguments, the trial concluded. The jury received the case at 9 pm. After taking a quick ballot, which was 10-2 in favor of conviction, the panel retired to their rooms for the night. The following morning, deliberations began in earnest. At roughly 9 am, the jury foreman informed the bailiff the jury had reached a unanimous decision. After gathering back in the packed courtroom, Miss Helen Hale, the deputy court clerk, read the verdict. "Guilty as charged with a recommendation of life at hard labor."

Within seconds of the announcement, Wilbur's white haired mother swooned and hit the floor passed out cold. His sisters burst into tears and a distraught Wilbur leaped from his chair to come to the aid of his ma. A crowd of guards quickly surrounded the badman as he ripped his shirt off and began fanning the prostrate old lady with it while cursing the cops. Judge Norman suggested the court recess and Mrs. Underhill who seemed to be coming to, be taken to a couch in his office. Wilbur was allowed to accompany the officers as they carried the elderly lady to the Judge's chambers. Within minutes, she seemed to be reviving from the shock. Wilbur, in an attempt to console her, began tenderly stroking her hair while whispering, "Poor mother, I know I've broken your heart. I've caused you a lot of trouble, but I'll never make you sorry again."

Later that same day, the Judge followed the jury's recommendation and sentenced Wilbur to life at the Oklahoma State Penitentiary. Underhill's mother again flopped off her chair and an ambulance was summoned to take her to her boarding house. A crowd of several hundred citizens who had gathered on the courthouse lawn, watched as the attendants carried the prostrate woman to the waiting ambulance on a stretcher. Back in the courtroom, Attorney Carter filed for a new trial in the case. It was denied. An Ottawa county official asked the Judge to turn over the defendant for trial in Miami for the murder of Earl O'Neal. Prosecutor Boatman stated they could have him after he reached the penitentiary.

The next day, the Ottawa county prosecutor filed papers with Oklahoma Governor Henry S. Johnson seeking permission to try Underhill in Miami for the murder of O'Neal. They also asked the Okmulgee Prosecutor to turn over the .45 automatic pistol found in Underhill's possession at the time of his capture in order to conduct ballistics testing (O'Neal was slain by a bullet from a .45 automatic). District Attorney Commons stated he intended on placing Underhill's ass in "Old Sparky," the nickname for Oklahoma's electric chair, "Come hell or high water."

The following Monday morning, Sheriff Russell and Deputy Lairmore transported the prisoner to the state pen in McAlester. On the way, Wilbur managed to slip a hand out of one of his handcuffs. When Underhill inquired if Russell would shoot him if he escaped and fled into a crowd, the double tough lawmen retorted, " You make a break and see." The rest of the trip went smooth as silk.

Back in Okmulgee, Underhill's devoted mother gave a lengthy interview to the local newspaper while resting on a feather bed in her boarding house room, saying, "I have a mother's heart and in my heart I believe him still. I don't understand how those officers could say such ugly things about my boy. They stood before the judge and lied. I have all the world of respect for law and order but how could they have kept him chained like a dog. I love my boy, believe in him, and have always tried to teach him right and wrong. Perhaps I erred when I defended him and his brothers so staunchly when they were accused of pranks when they were children. I know I have said things in defense of my boys over the years that gained the enmity of the police.... I'll not blame G-d for this, everything happens for a purpose. I have faith." Over the next few years, her baby boy would put the old lady's faith to the test time and again. To her, her son could do no wrong, no matter what pain and suffering he caused the rest of the world. She would remain Wilbur's staunchest defender to his dying day. Later that same day, Sarah Riddle drove the grief stricken woman and her daughters back to their Joplin home.

On the morning of June 5[th,] a young woman named Peggy Austin appeared at the office of County Prosecutor Jack Boatman declaring she was Wilbur's lawful wife. Boatman, who had "Heard the wind blow" before by several other "ladies" in the past, looked at her with a cautious eye and asked her what her story was. Austin, who was a resident of Maud, Oklahoma had read about the trial in the newspapers. She claimed Miss Riddle's story stating she was with Wilbur on December 23 to 25 was false and she was willing to testify she was honeymooning with Wilbur on December 24. The woman went on to declare she had married the desperado in Joplin, Missouri on December 18. She stated her motivation for exchanging vows with the badman was due to his promise to buy her a fur coat. Boatman shook his head in disgust and had her firmly escorted out of his office.

Chapter Six

Big Mac

On June 7, 1927, the gates of the Oklahoma State Penitentiary slammed shut on Wilbur Underhill. Prison officials were aware they were not getting a rookie with the notorious outlaw. After two terms in the Missouri pen and a number of stays in county and city lockups throughout the tri-state area, Wilbur knew the ropes. When processed he claimed his downfall was caused by "Bad Company" and listed his religion as "Methodist," his trade as "Plumber," and stated he had received ten years of formal education. According to several sources, the big man immediately started throwing his weight around. His aggressive nature was a plus on the cellblocks of the violence ridden correctional facility where survival often depended on raw muscle as well as street smarts

Built by inmate labor shortly after statehood in 1907-09 the prison was noted as a tough place to do time. In

Wilbur's mug shot OSP. Courtesy Michael Webb

OSP login sheet. Courtesy Oklahoma Department of Corrections-
Rich Green

1927, the prison population totaled 2364 inmates doing time behind the walls and on the surrounding "P" farms. Three hundred and thirty-seven inmates were confined for the crime of murder, 201 for manslaughter, 251-burglary, 189 for grand larceny, 132-auto theft, 113 for possession of narcotics, 46 for violation of liquor laws, and 1095 for various other indiscretions.

The majority of prisoners listed their occupation as "Farmer" and only 119 stated they don't drink, smoke, or chew. There were 366 lifers and nine inmates were awaiting execution on death row. Seminole County held the proud distinction of most inmates per capita due to its explosion of squalid oil boom communities.

The chief disciplinary problem inside the walls was drunkenness followed by fighting. Convicts, bored by life inside the joint, dreamed up a hundred ways to make intoxicating spirits. Those working on the farms and in the kitchens had access to sugar, yeast, and vegetables, which they turned into hooch. Tough guys like Wilbur sold the

Oklahoma State Penitentiary. Courtesy OSP

stuff or forcefully collected monies due. During the 1920s, there were several recorded incidents of inmates dying of poisoned "rot gut" whiskey made of wood alcohol or spiked with dangerous chemicals added to give the product some "kick." In 1927, four inmates died in a single incident in which they all drank from the same batch of homemade booze, which had been fermented and mixed in a discarded fifty-gallon drum that once held a poisonous insecticide. Other victims were more fortunate and only became sick for a day or two or were afflicted with a temporary condition called "Jake leg" a syndrome caused by the consumption of "Bad likker" that caused the victim to walk clumsily with a stiff leg and sometimes twitch and shake violently as though stricken with an epileptic attack.

Within days of Underhill's arrival at McAlester he connected with a vicious thug named Chester (Alton) Purdy who along with thirty-six-year-old Missouri born, Ace Pendleton (who had accompanied Wilbur in his unsuccessful jailbreak from the Jasper County Jail back in 1923), Jake Cook, Ralph King, and Wesley (Grandpa) Harrison had been involved in a lengthy crime spree which occurred mostly in Okmulgee, Creek, and Okfuskee Counties. The Purdy Gang had began its rein of terror in 1924 with a series of home burglaries which culminated with the murder of an Okmulgee merchant policeman named Robert Tyree in April, 1925. Apparently, Tyree spotted Purdy crawling out a window of the residence owned by a C. E. Campbell located at 1621 East 8th Street in Okmulgee. When the officer ordered the thief to freeze, Purdy began to run. Tyree took a potshot at the fleeing suspect who responded by drilling the lawman with a .38 slug to the heart, killing him instantly. A few months later, Detective Mark Lairmore captured both Purdy and Ace Pendleton after a brief gun battle in which no one was injured. While transporting the handcuffed fugitives to the county jail, they both jumped out of the lawman's car when it halted at a stop sign. To Lairmore's chagrin, the pair of suspects fled into a nearby wooded area and quickly disappeared.

Over the next two years, Purdy's band of cutthroats steered away from residential break-ins, switching to commercial burglaries committing over a dozen jobs in both Creek and Okmulgee County. The gang was partially splintered in June 1926, when Pendleton was arrested in Shawnee, Oklahoma, and charged with attempted burglary. The wayward thief was subsequently convicted of the charge and sentenced to a year in state prison. Meanwhile, Purdy along with "Grandpa" Harrison and Bob King plundered the Hummell Department store in Beggs, Oklahoma for an estimated $5000 in merchandise in early December. Pendleton was released from "Big Mac" on January 31st and quickly rejoined his cohorts in crime. On February 26, 1927, the gang struck a wholesale grocery business in nearby Okemah killing a local police officer named Claude Ryan during the heist. Soon afterwards, "Grandpa" Harrison was arrested in Kansas on a burglary charge.

On the afternoon of March 21, 1927, Creek County Deputy Sheriff John Willard spotted Purdy riding alone in a touring car just south of

Ace Pendleton. Courtesy Joplin Globe

Mounds, Oklahoma. He immediately phoned Sheriff John Russell who after being joined by Deputy Lairmore began driving north on the Beggs highway. In an effort to box in the fugitive, Deputy Willard, now joined by Mounds Chief of Police Paul Harmon, began motoring south towards Okmulgee. At 2 pm, the Okmulgee officers sighted the outlaw at a point four miles north of town. After the officers shot out the fugitive's two back tires Purdy pulled over raising his hands in surrender. He was cuffed and lodged in the county jail where he fessed up to numerous robberies but denied involvement in either of the cop killings.

Purdy, described by reporters as "dapper" and a "real dandy," was lodged in the Okmulgee County Jail just two weeks prior to Underhill's arrival at the bastille. The following week, Purdy along with Bob King, who had recently voluntarily surrendered to custody, were transferred to the Okalahoma Penitentiary for safekeeping while awaiting trial. Harrison joined them upon his extradition back from Kansas.

According to prison sources, within days of their commitment Purdy and several of his henchmen partnered-up with George Kimes, the brother of the infamous Matt Kimes, who was doing time for murdering Sequoyah County Deputy Sheriff Perry Chuculate. Kimes, described by officers as mean as a snake, had apparently ran a bootlegging and strong-arm operation at the prison since his arrival. When Underhill arrived at "Big Mac," as the prisoners referred to the correctional facility, he quickly joined up with Kimes-Purdy bunch in their sordid activities.

In early August, Underhill and his newfound partners in crime attempted an escape from their top tier of cells by gaining access to the building's roof by sawing through a barred door with hacksaw blades provided by Kimes who didn't make the trip. Once on the roof they were quickly spotted and gave up in mass when a pair of tower guards fired several warning rounds over their heads. When searched the escapees were found in possession of a sixty foot of coiled rope, civilian clothing, several shivs, (home-made knives) and a quantity of foodstuffs. As punishment, Wilbur was sentenced to nearly a year in solitary confine-ment while Purdy, Harrison, and King were promptly trans-ferred back to Okfuskee County where they were tried and convicted of murdering Officer Claude Ryan.

George Kimes was also tossed in the hole due to his being suspected of engineering the aborted breakout. In a statement given the day after the break, the prison's assis-tant warden stated, "Although Kimes is a rough customer, Underhill is the meanest man we have ever had at this insti-tution, he refuses to work, sits about cursing the guards all day, and is involved in most of the skullduggery going on within these walls."

A week after the attempted bustout, five other pris-oners staged another break. On the evening of August 21, an inmate named Clarence Eno, who was one of five Mis-souri born brothers who were all career criminals, claiming he was deathly ill, made a request to be transferred to the prison infirmary. When an escort showed up, Eno jumped him placing a copper wire around his neck forcing him to open an adjoining cell occupied by four other inmates. The group was made up of Charles Dotson, a one-time crime partner of the infamous Ed Lockhart who was imprisoned on a hijacking and attempted murder charge out of Craig County, as well as Leonard Bagby and Tommy Mason both imprisoned on robbery charges along with J.C. Andrews, a convicted forger out of Greer County who had been in-volved in two previous unsuccessful escape attempts in the past year. Dotson and Andrews were armed with pistols that had somehow been smuggled into the prison. The five men and their hostage made their way to the hospital where they were met by Night Sergeant Sam Fields who had gone in search of his missing guard. When the group of prisoners encountered Fields, they shot him before beating him unmercifully about the head with their pistol butts and a steel table leg. Afterwards, the escapees broke into the main yard where they were met by the gunfire of three tower guards. After the group's leader, Clarence Eno, took a slug to the leg, his cohorts, seeing the futility of their actions threw up their hands and surrendered. Officer Fields would eventually recover from his injuries.

Warden Newell immediately called for an investigation and had the five men thrown into the overcrowded segregation unit. Due to a lack of space, Dotson was housed in the same cell as Wilbur. Both were shackled to heavy trace chains to the wall. Over the next few months, the two naturally became fast friends. Incidentally, in the not too distant future, Dotson, along with Clarence Eno would reconnect with Underhill in the free world and there would be hell to pay.

Underhill would one day boast of spending nearly half of the next four years at "Mac" in solitaire, chained and beaten almost daily by the "hacks." In his condensed autobiography written shortly after his release from OSP in 1936, the legendary Ray Terrill wrote of Wilbur, " Underhill occupied a cell not far from mine. They once kept him in chains for months. I have seen his ankles and wrists swollen and bloody where the shackles rubbed him cruelly. He was a particularly dangerous fellow, but I do not agree with many who described him was a born killer, I believed society made him that way." After Underhill's final release from segregation, he was assigned to the prison brickyard as a mason and immediately began to plot his next escape attempt. This time he would go solo.

On the morning of July 14, 1931 as Wilbur and a group of 150 inmates were marching in a long line four abreast to the brickyards, located just outside the prison gates, the crafty outlaw jumped off a footbridge which spanned a small creek and lay silently in a foot of water while the column trudged past him. When the sounds of the column grew faint, he scrambled to the opposite shore and hid in a tall growth of cane growing on the stream's edge. He quickly stripped off his prison issue garb and wearing civilian clothes underneath, calmly walked into town in plain sight of the guards. According to most reports, the fugitive was not missed until the mid-day roll call several hours later. After swimming several sizable streams, he fled into the fastness of the heavily forested Ouachita Mountain Range heading east. The outlaw later stated that on one occasion a group of his pursuers mounted on horseback accompanied by a pack of tracking dogs led by the famous bloodhound, "Old Boston," came within a few feet of where he was hiding in a small cave. The outlaw further claimed he traversed the rugged mountain range walking nearly 60 miles on foot with no food or

George Kimes on left, with friend.
Courtesy Tami Babione

water until he arrived in the small community of Wister where he retrieved a bag of money he had hidden shortly before his capture in nearby Panama, Oklahoma in 1927. Whether he visited his ex-wife Lucille, who resided just a few miles distant in Heavener but had reportedly divorced him and remarried by this time, is unknown. After grabbing his loot, the fugitive apparently hopped a train bound for Missouri. Wilbur declared that on his arrival in Joplin, he marched a handful of hobos he had befriended on the train to a café and stood them all grub before visiting his sister, Mrs. Anna Lewis.

Although Wilbur had entered the Oklahoma pen during the fabulous "Roaring twenties" a period of great eco-

Inside the central rotunda of "Big Mac." Photo by Naomi Morgan

nomic prosperity, at the time of his escape he entered a new world, the American economy had taken a nosedive of historic proportions. After the stock market crash of 1929, financial institutions began to fold up and economic chaos spread across the land. A worldwide depression soon enveloped the globe. Millions were thrown out of work, unemployment hit as high as 40% in parts of the nation. Jobs and hard cash became a scarce commodity. Even crime didn't pay; there was nothing of any value left to steal. Over the next decade, the average take in an armed robbery (nearly 500 in 1931 nationwide) resulted in only a few hundred dollars, compared to several thousand in the 1920s. Slim pickings indeed.

Tens of thousands of down and out families had taken to the road-traveling west seeking work in the orange groves and cotton fields of California while multitudes of mostly single men and teenagers hopped freights, sleeping in hobo jungles, working odd jobs and panhandling for their daily bread.

Cellblock roof Underhill and pals attempted to escape from. Photo by Naomi Morgan

Despite the ongoing depression, life went on, 1931 saw the construction of engineering marvels such as the Empire State Building and the mammoth George Washington Bridge, cultural achievements in literature and entertainment abounded. *The Good Earth* by Pearl Buck was published. Films like *Frankenstein, The Champ,* and *The Public Enemy* were released." Classic radio programs such as *Little Orphan Annie* and the *Bing Crosby Hour* debuted.

In sports, Max Schmelling was crowned heavy weight boxing champion, Alabama won the Rose Bowl, and Babe Ruth and Lou Gehrig both smacked 46 home runs. The current craze in the Sunday morning funny papers was "The Katzenjammer Kids" and "Gasoline Alley." The newest edition to the world of candy was the "Tootsie Pop" and "Scarface" Al Capone was sentenced to eleven years for income tax evasion. A new Model "A" Roadster went for $430 and a first class stamp cost two cents.

Old Boston. Courtesy Muskogee Times-Democrat

P. O. BOX 393   Oklahoma State Penitentiary   No. 2422

S. E. BROWN, Warden.

RULES FOR WRITING AND RECEIVING MAIL

All incoming and outgoing mail must pass through the office of the mail clerk where it will be opened, examined and placed on record before it is mailed or delivered to prisoner. All officers are strictly forbidden to pass out or deliver prisoner's mail. Write plainly and confine yourself to business or family matters. No objections will be made to the receipt of mail in accordance with these rules, but none other will be permitted. All letters must be addressed in care of Box 398, McAlester, Oklahoma.

If you desire to send money send Post Office Money Order. Currency sent in letters is at the risk of sender and personal checks will be returned. All funds for prisoners are deposited to prisoners credit with the Warden.

These article only are admissible thru the mail. General and local newspapers direct from the publisher and books of proper character will be permitted to enter the prison. Ample provision is made by the State for all articles of clothing and shoes for the prisoners and no package of any kind or description will be permitted to enter the prison. Any received will be returned at the expense of the prisoner addressed, or destroyed.

All prisoners will be permitted to write one letter per week, but will be permitted to write only to his or her wife or husband, father, mother, brother, sister, sons and daughters. All letters sent prisoners must have name and address of sender written plainly on upper left hand corner of envelope.

Visiting Rules:—Father, mother, sister, brother, wife, husband, son or daughter will be permitted to visit the prisoner once every 30 days. These visits will be allowed any day in the week, including Sunday and the hours are from 9 A. M. to 4 P. M. No exception to these rules will be allowed except with the special permission of the Warden or Deputy Warden. The Warden will at all times arrange to allow prisoners to see their attorney.

LETTERS MUST BE SIGNED WITH FULL NAME

McALESTER, OKLAHOMA, Oct 1 193___

Rules and regulations concerning correspondence and visiting privileges for inmates-circa 1934. Author's private collection

Chapter Seven

Wichita

On the evening of July 21, Underhill checked into a Cherryvale, Kansas hotel registering under his familiar alias of Ralph Caraway. According to Wilbur, he also bought an interest in the hotel from a man named Nichols and soon made the establishment his base of operations. Sometime around this period he took time from his busy schedule to marry a woman named Ethel from nearby Independence, Kansas, while simultaneously carrying on an affair with a thirty-six-year-old waitress named Margaret Smith who also boarded at the hotel.

On the evening of July 28, Deputy Sheriff Blaine Wilburn looked up from his desk located in the front hallway of the Sedgwick County Jail in nearby Wichita observing two men, one wearing a light covered cap pulled over his eyes and another wearing white britches and walking with a limp, enter the main door. According to the Deputy, the lame individual approached him inquiring if he and his pal could visit with an inmate named R. Elam while his companion stayed back in the shadows. Wilburn directed the pair to the office of County Sheriff Charles E. Grove stating "You'll have to get permission from the boss." The young man then walked into the Sheriff's office where he inquired if he could "Visit with prisoner Elam for a spell?" Grove declined stating it wasn't visiting hours. The pair then hastily withdrew from the building passing Deputy Bill Johnson in the hallway as they exited. Although the officers thought nothing of the visit at the time, they would all three later positively identify the pair as Wilbur Underhill and his nephew, Frank Vance Underhill. It was later learned Elam was being held on a federal liquor violation and was an old acquaintance of Underhill's. It was never discovered what the pair had in mind, but it was assumed they intended on breaking the prisoner out by force of arms but changed their minds when faced with the sight of the trio of heavily armed lawmen. The following night a solitary bandit matching Wilbur's description knocked off the Skaggs Drug store in Wichita for a few hundred dollars. The cops failed to make the connection at the time.

A few days later on a warm Sunday night, a lone man sashayed up to the ticket window of the Midland Theater in Coffeyville, Kansas relieving the cashier, twenty-year-old Rhea Payne, of the night's proceeds, amounting to roughly $220. According to Miss Payne, the hijacker, who she would later identify as Wilbur Underhill, was armed with a handgun and stuffed the loot into a white canvas money-bag before fleeing on foot. Ironically it was "Bank Nite" at the theatre, a weekly promotional feature commonly held at movie houses throughout the nation during the depression, which entailed bringing a child from the audience to draw a numbered ticket from a large jar during intermission. If

Sedgwick County Sheriff Charles Grove. Courtesy Sedgwick County Sheriff's Department

the drawn ticket matched that of an audience member, they won the jackpot, usually $5.00 or a gift certificate from the local hardware store.

Reportedly, it took several minutes for theater goers to notice the cashier's screams due to the crowd being riveted in their seats watching the bloodcurdling performance of Bela Lugosi in "Dracula." Apparently, while the heist was taking place, the "Count" was in the process of obtaining his evening meal by plunging his evil fangs into the juicy neck of some breathless starlet who reacted by screaming her fool head off and was in turn joined by a host of hysterical females sitting in the audience, thus making it difficult to hear the commotion taking place in the lobby.

The following day, Sunday, August 2, around dusk Mrs. Sam Wilson and her husband were driving home from a family reunion being held at a small park located approximately eight miles east of Wichita near the Travel Air Field, when suddenly a tan Ford touring car came flying down Central Avenue Highway at a high rate of speed nearly sideswiping their vehicle. Reacting to the near disaster, Mrs. Wilson screamed at the driver who she could plainly see, "Watch out, Buster." The driver responded with a vulgar gesture and drove on. After arriving home she received a call from her daughter, Mrs. Guy Bright, who lived in nearby Towanda, complaining of a wild-eyed motorist who had ran them into a ditch just moments after the reunion broke up. After comparing notes, the pair agreed they were victims of the same reckless driver. The next day, Mrs. Wilson received news of a robbery-homicide, which had occurred the previous evening at the Neely Cities Service Station located less than a mile from her home. According to eyewitnesses, the getaway car used in the robbery was similar in appearance to the one being driven by the careless driver Wilson and her daughter had encountered earlier that same evening. Strangely, the ladies kept their own council and failed to report their observations for nearly two weeks.

The fifty-six-year-old operator of the filling station, William E. Neely, had been held-up twice before. The first time he had beaten the bandit to a pulp with his fists and on the second instance he knocked the robber out cold with an old car spring. The best witness to the homicide was a W. L. Davis who lived just south of the station. According to his statement to the police, he observed two "youths," one taller than the other drive up in a tan Ford Model "A" about 8 pm and park about 100 feet south of the station. One of the men, described as six-feet tall and 180 pounds, walked to the garage but returned to the car when a customer (Mrs. Myrtle Ringwald) drove up, stopping to add air to a tire. After the customer left, the big fellow returned to the station. Moments later Davis heard three shots. Seeing the car depart carrying the two individuals, he dashed to the road in an attempt to take note of the license plate but was thwarted in his efforts due to the darkness and the automobile's headlights being off. He was also unable to get a good description of the suspects' faces. Also hearing the shots was a neighbor, Lee Pray, and Neely's brother-in-law, C. E. Boren, who lived nearby. Upon noticing the "commotion," Prey and his wife rushed to the station and discovered Neely lying in front of the cash

Slain filling station operator William Neely. Courtesy Wichita Eagle

register on his right side, one bullet having pierced his breast while another entered his right arm. A third round had missed its target, lodging in a wall. The coroner soon showed up pronouncing Neely dead on the spot. Lawmen discovered size eleven footprints imprinted in the mud behind the station where one of the suspects had been standing.

In a statement to the press Sedgwick County Sheriff Ed Grove told newsmen, "It looks like the Neely job may have been pulled by the same pair of fellows who hijacked John Bain's filling station in Wichita a couple of weeks ago. In that case the robbers also used a Ford as a getaway car and one of the men was a big man, maybe 180 pounds and armed with a small caliber handgun." Over the next week, dozens of individuals were questioned and roadblocks set up in an effort to locate the murderers. Shotgun toting officers manned surveillance posts at several rural gas stations hoping to ambush the pair.

Scene of the Neely killing. Courtesy Wichita Beacon

On August 7, Wilbur, once again posing as Ralph Carraway, purchased a nearly new Ford Roadster, license plate Kansas S-11674. In a statement later made to investigators Wilbur claimed shortly after acquiring his new wheels, he motored to Kansas City, Missouri in order to visit his mother and youngest sister who were currently living in an apartment complex under the names of Almira and Dorothy Dean. After a tearful reunion, Wilbur slipped out of town driving to his sister Anna's residence in Joplin with his nineteen-year-old nephew Frank Vance Underhill in tow. Apparently, Wilbur had promised the teen, who was Earl's son, he could have the use of his new car for an entire week if he would act as his driver on a short journey. (Wilbur had a well-known aversion to driving automobiles, preferring to hop freights, hitchhike, or hire a chauffer). It would turn out to be the worst decision of the young man's life.

Frank, who walked with a decided limp due to a bout of infantile paralysis that left two of his toes permanently curled, was an odd choice for a companion for an arch-criminal like Wilbur. According to family members, Almira had taken in the lad in 1915 when he was only three years old due to the death of his mother and incarceration of his father. Although the boy got into a few minor jams while growing up in Joplin he apparently kept his nose clean after the family relocated to Kansas City, regularly attending services at the Oakley Methodist Church and joining a Christian youth group. He had a good job at the Pittsburg Plate Glass Company where he had been employed since he had dropped out of Kansas City's Northeast High School while in his junior year. In an effort to avoid the stigma of the Underhill name, the young man had apparently dropped the Underhill from his name shortly after moving to Kansas City and was known to his friends, teachers, and employer as simply Frank Vance.

****

At roughly 9:45 pm on the night of August 13, twenty-year-old Cecil Honick was sitting behind the counter of the Texaco filling station located at the intersection of Ida and Kellogg Streets just east of Wichita's central business district when he noticed a tall, dark complected man walk into the business and politely inquire if he had a pay phone. Before the youth was able to answer, the big man, who he would later identify as Wilbur Underhill, whipped out a large automatic pistol demanding, "The dough, or I'll kill ya." Faced with the ominous looking barrel of a big bore handgun pointing right between his eyes, Honick, knees knocking and teeth chattering, immediately complied with the robber's demand forking over the cash in the register which amounted to $18.24. The individual then ordered the lad to walk in front of him down a nearby alley for about fifty feet before forcing him to lie on the pavement telling him, "I ought to blow out your guts so you can't squawk." The big man then hopped into a Ford Roadster which was idling with its lights off, parked roughly 200 feet down the alley. Honick could vaguely make out a figure sitting in the driver's seat, but due to the darkness, he could not distinguish the individual's features. The car traveled over a block with the headlights off before the driver turned on his lights and punched the accelerator squealing rubber heading west. According to police reports, several bystanders sitting in a nearby yard witnessed the fleeing automobile and gave excellent descriptions of the car and driver.

An hour later Wilbur and his young companion were motoring down South Lawrence Road with Frank at the wheel when a car driven by J.A. Walker of Fairview, Kansas sped through a stop sign broad-siding them. Both cars were badly damaged and were towed by wrecker to a garage on South Water Street operated by R. C. and Floyd Lucas. Accepting full responsibility for the accident, (Apparently Walker had been drinking at the time of the collision) Walker requested the pair meet him at a certain location in downtown Wichita the following morning in order to settle with them. Underhill quickly agreed. A helpful citi-

Wilbur and his nephew Frank Vance. Courtesy Michael Webb

zen named Harold Siegel then drove Wilbur and his side-kick to the Wichita Hospital, where a Dr. Chow treated Frank for various cuts and bruises.

Afterwards, the duo caught a lift to the Lucas Garage in order to check on Wilbur's wrecked vehicle. Around 2 am the pair walked to the nearby Iris Hotel situated at Douglas and Water Streets where they checked into room #15 located on the third floor of the establishment. Wilbur registered as Ralph Caraway and Frank as Frank Vance.

At approximately 8:15 am the following morning forty-eight-year-old Wichita Police Officer Merle R. Colver, who had been on duty for roughly an hour, began his morning rounds checking out recent arrivals at downtown hotels and boarding houses, as was his habit. Entering the Iris Hotel, he strolled to the front desk where Innkeeper Cora Brotherton greeted him. When she informed him a pair of suspicious looking fellows, one with a bandage on his face, had registered earlier that morning, Colver decided to roust the pair just to be on the safe side. On reaching the third floor, he strolled to room #15 and banged on their door with his nightstick ordering the occupants to open up.

Just moments after Officer Colver had entered the room; a series of loud explosions rocked the hotel bringing a curious Mrs. Brotherton and two female housekeepers out into the hallway of the second floor. The trio soon spotted the new lodgers sprinting down the stairs leaping two and three at a time. According to the landlady, the older of the pair who was shirtless but carrying a suit coat, stopped just long enough to toss a blood-soaked shirt into a vacant room before turning toward her saying "There's been an accident upstairs, you had better call the cops." Brotherton reportedly dashed up to room #15 and peeked in. Seeing the officer sprawled on the floor in a pool of blood, she sent a maid, Mrs. Jennie Quigley to call the cops.

Due to a misunderstanding, officers were incorrectly directed by the police dispatcher to the Allis Hotel. Quickly discovering their mistake, they switched gears and rushed to the Iris. When officers finally arrived on the scene, the suspects were long gone. Directed to the room in question by the landlady, they discovered Officer Colver lying motionless on the floor with a bullet wound to the trunk of his body as well as another to the neck and head area. The room was reportedly in shambles and detectives discovered a stack of pictures lying underneath the officer's body and a moneybag (later identified as the one used in the theatre holdup in Coffeyville) on the floor nearby. Colver's .45 caliber service revolver was missing. After getting a description of the room's former occupants from the landlady, an all points bulletin was issued and dozens of hastily armed citizens (Mostly members of the local American Legion and VFW) joined up with a large contingent of law enforcement officers and began scouring the downtown area. All major roads leading out of town were guarded by shotgun toting lawmen. Several plainclothes officers were posted at the rail passenger depot as well.

Back at the Iris Hotel, Acting Coroner L. S. Markel assisted by Deputy City Marshal Tex Thompson began a crime scene investigation. Officer Colver's body was lying just inside the

Officer Merle Colver. Courtesy Wichita Eagle

room's door. One of the bullets had struck him in the left side of his neck near his ear, exiting out his shoulder blade on the right side of the back. Another round had hit him in the left side under his back shoulder blade passing through his body coming out his right groin. The bullet paths through the victim's body signified he was in a stooped position when shot. Deep powder burns, indicating he was shot at point-blank range, characterized both entrance wounds. Powder burns also marked the thumb and forefinger of his right hand. On a closer examination of the premises, Deputy Thompson discovered four spent steel-jacketed .45 caliber bullets, one in the mattress, a second imbedded in the dresser, a third on the floor and the fourth fell from Colver's clothing when the coroner rolled him over onto his back.

Glancing at the photos discovered under Colver's body Thompson noticed the name "Wilbur Underhill, Joplin, Missouri" scratched on the backs. When the pictures were shown to the hotel's manager she identified the individual

Officer Colver being loaded into ambulance. Courtesy of Sterling Detective, May 1934.

as one of the men she had rented the room to earlier that morning. When investigators contacted the authorities in Joplin inquiring if they knew anything of a Wilbur Underhill, they were quickly informed he was an escapee from the Oklahoma Prison system and a convicted murderer. Also found at the crime scene was the title to a 1930 Ford Roadster made out to a Ralph Caraway of Cherryvale, Kansas. A further search of the hotel turned up a discarded blood-soaked shirt with a set of car keys stuffed in the pockets lying on the floor of a vacant room. (Room #18) An inspection of area garages was promptly instituted and fortunately for officers, the suspect's wrecked automobile was discovered at the first garage the officers explored. The vehicle had 1180 miles on the odometer.

Meanwhile, a huge crowd of curious citizens had gathered in front of the Iris Hotel. Hopping off a nearby streetcar Officer Colver's sixteen-year-old daughter walked into the crowd asking what had happened. On being informed, she burst into tears and collapsed in grief. A kindly bystander drove her back to her home.

After nearly ten hours of beating the bushes the pair of fugitives were spotted lying exhausted under a tree next to a baseball diamond in Linwood Park about a mile and a half southeast of the scene of Colver's murder by Officer Ray Mitchell (a rookie) and ex-Wichita cop Jack Myler. When the officers ordered the men to "Get em high." Frank immediately complied but Wilbur who was shirtless and carrying a coat in the crook of his arm, attempted to pull out Officer Colver's revolver from the coat pocket but dropped it when the hammer snagged on a piece of fabric. Myler responded by firing several wildly aimed shots in his direction, one which randomly struck a year-old toddler named John George Colliate (the round passed through the child's right hand nicking his abdomen) that was sitting on his mother's lap in a nearby swing, the infant's three-year-old sister was standing only a few feet away. Underhill then attempted to yank out his automatic from the other pocket but was beat to the draw by Myler who sent a well-

Top Left: Jack Myler. Courtesy Wichita Eagle. *Lower Left: Patrolman Ray Mitchell.* Courtesy Wichita Eagle. Right: *Wilbur under arrest.* Courtesy Wichita Eagle

placed slug into the left side of the outlaw's neck, temporarily paralyzing his arm causing him to drop the second gun. Wilbur then began sprinting across the park. Myler took up the chase while Mitchell cuffed Frank. After pursuing the fugitive nearly five blocks and firing several more rounds that whizzed past the outlaw's head, Myler temporarily lost sight of him in an alley located between Kansas and Hydraulic on the south end of the park. Hearing a noise emitting from a nearby shed the officer fired a slug into the structure just to observe a pair of squalling cats come hightailing from the building. He then noticed Wilbur lying in a nearby patch of tall weeds curled up in a ball. When Myler confronted the fugitive, he gave up peaceably. While being handcuffed, Underhill began moaning and stated he was "Bound to die from his wound." Ironically, the date of Wilbur's capture coincided with the one-month anniversary of his escape from the Oklahoma State Penitentiary.

When the two suspects were hauled to the station they again gave their familiar aliases and Underhill continued to

St. Francis Hospital, Wichita. Author's private collection

cry and shriek in pain stating he was near death and feared blood poisoning from the his injury which turned out to be a minor flesh wound. He was transported to St. Francis Hospital where Dr. Herman J. Kloecker treated his wound with Mercurochrome and a sterile bandage. When officers attempted to question him, Underhill suddenly laid back on a stretcher and appeared to faint. Figuring he was faking unconsciousness, the city physician, Dr. R. E. Hobbs, was called in to examine him. Hobbs stuck him in the foot and arm several times with a needle but got no response but when a Wichita Eagle photographer named Harold Lyle photographed the badman, Underhill leaped off the gurney wide-eyed and full of fight when the flash bulb popped. Seeing their prisoner was not going to take a "dirt dive" on 'em, lawmen transported the now snarling and snapping Wilbur in leg irons to the city jail where he was lodged in a cell as far from his nephew as possible. Fingerprints and mug shots were taken and Detective Joe Maness who was placed in charge of the investigation began interrogating the prisoner. When asked his name, the stoic Wilbur responded, "I ain't telling you nothing. I'm no squealer" He didn't. Finally giving up on his uncooperative suspect, Maness stormed out of the room and the older Underhill was placed back in his cell where he reportedly slept like a log.

Unable to get the "straight dope" out of Wilbur, Detectives Maness and Captain W. O. Lyle hauled young Frank down to the interrogation room, where he was sat on a hard wooden chair in a bare room under a glaring light bulb surrounded by the pair of grim looking cops. The lads in blue then commenced to put the fear of G-d into the boy who according to them appeared about to soil his drawers. It didn't take much prodding on the gumshoe's parts, the youth quickly caved in, "Singing like a yellow-winged songbird." The gist of his lengthy confession amounted to "I didn't do it, Uncle Wilbur did. I was just along for the ride." You get the picture, right?

Meanwhile back at the St. Frances Hospital the wounded child was listed in critical condition. Thankfully, the toddler would fully recover.

On the morning of the 15th, the chickens began to come home to roost. The witnesses from the Iris Hotel, (the landlady and two maids) came to the jail and positively identified both Wilbur and his nephew as the individuals who had been staying in room #15 on the morning of the murder. They also stated they had seen the pair running down the stairs only moments after hearing the shots coming from

Mug shot taken Wichita Police headquarters. Courtesy Wichita Beacon

upstairs. A few hours later, Mrs. Sam Wilson and her daughter showed up claiming they had recognized Frank's picture in the Wichita Beacon (both Wichita papers, the Beacon and the Eagle, had given the story wide spread coverage) as the individual driving the car that nearly ran them off the Central Avenue Highway near the Travel Air crossroads just hours before the William Neely murder on August 2. That evening, Cecil Honick, the operator of the Texaco station, also identified Wilbur as the lone gunman who had held him up on the evening of August 13, saying, "It's either him or his twin brother."

That afternoon, Montgomery County Sheriff Bob Lewis and a deputy came calling at the jail with the cashier from the Coffeyville Theatre robbery in tow. The witness took one look at Wilbur and stated, "That's him." Meanwhile J. A. Walker of Fairview, Kansas had come forward identifying the Underhills as the occupants of a car, which he had slammed into on the night before the murders. Upon discovering the suspect's wrecked automobile parked at the Lucas garage, both Frank and Wilbur Underhill's fingerprints were pulled off of it. Later that day, several eyewitnesses who had been standing down the street from the Texaco station when it was robbed, came forward and ID'd young Frank as the driver of the getaway car. As the evidence and number of hostile witnesses began to mount, Maness decided to again confront Wilbur with some pointed questions.

Sitting in the sparsely furnished interrogation room at roughly 11:40 am on the morning of the 16th, Wilbur was informed by Detective Maness both he and his young nephew were about to be charged with first-degree murder and highway robbery. Not knowing Frank had already dropped a dime on the pair confessing to only "Being there" when his Uncle "Popped the cop," but denying involvement in any robberies, Wilbur decided to take the rap for his nephew. This occasion marked one of the few times in his otherwise wasted life that Wilbur ever demonstrated a sense of decency. The following day the Wichita Eagle printed the badman's confession word for word. After answering a few general questions about his early life and criminal history, Wilbur was asked....

Q: Where did you go after your July 14 escape from the Oklahoma State pen?

A: I went to Cherryvale, Kansas

Q: How long did you stay at Cherryvale until you made a trip to Kansas City, Missouri?

A: I stayed there about three weeks.

Q: After you arrived in Kansas City, did you visit any relatives?

A: My Mother.

Q: And what is your mother's address?

A: 3735 Garner

Q: Did you visit anyone else?

A: Mother, sister, and nephew.

Q: What is your nephew's name?

A: Frank Vance Underhill

Q: Did you later leave K.C. in company of Frank?

A: That same evening, August 11

Q: Where did you go?

A: Joplin, Missouri to my sister's house.

Q: How long did you stay?

A: About an hour

Q: And then where did you go?

A: Back to Cherryvale. I had to get my car worked on.

Q: How long did you stay in Cherryvale?

A: We stayed all day the 12th.

Q: Then where did you go?

A: Tulsa

Q: How long did you stay there?

A. Overnight

Q. Then where?

A: Wichita

Q. Do you recall the date you arrived in Wichita?

A: The night of the 13th.

Q: Where did you and Frank go after arriving in town?

A: We went to this garage about a block from here where we had our car pulled from outside town. We'd had a wreck. We stayed there trying to get this car straightened out until early morning, when we checked into the hotel.

Q: What time was it when you checked in?

A: About two or three O'clock in the morning.

Q. Do you know where this hotel is located?

A: No, it's about a block from that garage, wherever it is.

Q. Did you then go to bed?

A: Yes.

Q: Did you and Frank leave word to be awakened the next morning?

A: Yes, I did.

Q: Did someone awaken you the next morning?

A: Yes, I suppose it was the landlady.

Q: Did anyone else come to your room?

A: A police officer.

Q: Did you know him by name?

A: No

Q: You did know he was a police officer.

A: Oh yes

Q: Now Underhill I'm going to ask you to state in your own words just what took place in the room you and your nephew were in. Which is located in the Iris Hotel at the corner of Water and Douglas in Wichita, Kansas on the morning of August 14, 1931.

A: The officer came to the door, knocked, and said "This is the police," and before I could go to the door he came on in. He said it was his duty to check these hotels every morning. He sat down on the foot of the bed and was talking to us about our business and what it was in Wichita and where we lived and asked us when we were going to leave and I told him my business was a hotel in Cherryvale and I showed him my papers on the car, proving my identity, and he seemed convinced. Then he asked Frank who he was and where from and where his business was, and he didn't have any papers to prove his identity and the officer said 'I don't want you to feel hard towards me for inquiring into your business for it is a matter of duty.' He was smoking a cigarette and I asked Frank for a butt and Frank got the package and gave me one and took one his self. We asked the officer for a match and the officer said 'Buddy I haven't any but I will give you a light.' We lit up and in the meantime, I was about half dressed, standing by the side of the bed. Frank was in front of the mirror putting on his tie. The officer got up and looked through some packages sitting on the dresser and then looked under a coat on the bed and then looked under a pillow, started over to a window to look behind a window shade and then he started over to the other bed and I seen that he would find the pistol I had hidden under the pillow, my being wanted for being an escaped convict I couldn't stand the arrest, so I walked over and got the pistol from under the pillow as he reached for it. He stepped back a couple of steps and I told him to put his hands up. Instead, he started striking at me with his club, hitting me on the head and neck. In the meantime, I had fired one shot. He kept grabbing at me and in the scuffle. I shot three more times. He began to let loose of me. He fell and in the meantime Frank was standing at the foot of the bed wringing his hands and hollering, 'Don't.' When the officer fell, I told Frank 'Lets get out of here.' Frank picked up a couple of parcels and ran out the door. I started to run out and happened to think about my money being in the pillowcase and my cap. I returned and got the dough and my cap, in coming out, I had to step over the officer, and he was moving his arms. I reached down and got his pistol and went on out. We ran down the steps and three ladies was asking 'What was the trouble' and I told them an accident happened up there, to call the officers. We went on down to the alley back of the hotel and got out to the edge of town. Frank was cursing about the trouble that I had caused him and wanted to know why I had done it. I told him that I was an escaped convict, that I had life and I couldn't stand the arrest. Knowing I would be taken back. I didn't know at that time that I had killed this officer, but I did know I had emptied my gun in him. I told Frank that I would get him out of town and that I wanted him to go home and that I didn't want him with me. Later in the evening two officers stopped us and I started to walk away. I was carrying a coat on my arm with both pistols in the inside coat pocket. They hollered 'Halt' and instead I kept walking trying to get my pistol out of my coat pocket. It hung in my pocket and this officer seen I was going for a gun and he shot. The bullet hit me in the neck and it caused my arm to go numb and I dropped my coat with both guns in it. I didn't have time to pick it up. The officer fired approximately four or five more shots and I started running across the park. We ran three or four blocks after we got out of the park. I fell down and was laying in some weeds when he ran up on me. They took me to the hospital and got my wound dressed and then to the county jail and from there to the city jail.

Q: How many guns did you and Frank have at the time the policeman came into the room?

A: I only had one and Frank didn't have any. I had a .45 automatic.

Q: How long had you had this .45?

A: A week or so.

Q: Do you recall where you got this gun?

A: Yes, I stole it out of a car in Tulsa, Oklahoma

Q: Did you have the automatic at the time you left Cherryvale going to KC, MO.?

A: Yes.

Q: In other words, you packed a .45 automatic all the time.

A: Yes.

Q: You stated at the time you went back to get your money and cap the officer was moving his arm.

A: Yes, as if he was trying to lower his arms to his hips.

Q: Did you speak to the officer at the time you reached down and took the pistol from his holster?

A: Yes

Q: What did you say to him?

A: I told him 'Don't move, buddy.'

Q: Did the officer answer you?

A: Yes, he said 'I won't.'

Q: Where was Frank at the time you and the officer were struggling?

A: Standing at the feet of the right hand bed going into the room and I was in between the officer and Frank.

Q: Did Frank at any time get mixed up in the shuffle?

A: No.

Q: Did he at any time touch the officer?

A: No

Q: You said a while ago you dropped two guns, just which two guns did you have reference to?

A: My .45 auto and the gun I had taken from the officer.

Q: Was the gun that you took from the officer loaded at the time you dropped it in the park?

A: Yes, a full six shells.

Q: Was your automatic loaded at that time?

A: No, it was empty

Q: At the time you were shooting this officer did you empty your gun?

A: Yes, three or four shells was all I had.

Q: But at any rate, you shot as long as you had ammunition?

A: I emptied the gun, yes.

Q: At the time the officer jumped you up in the park did you shoot at either of them?

A: No, I didn't. I tried to but my gun hung and I

couldn't get it out of my pocket and then he shot me and I dropped the coat.

Q: At the time you were trying to get the gun out of your coat pocket you intended fully to shoot.

A: Yes

Q: In other words, you did not intend to be taken alive?

A: No

Q: What was Frank doing at the time you were trying to get your gun out at the time you were apprehended in the park?

A. He was standing about twenty feet from them just standing there close to the police officer's car. When I seen the car coming I starting walking off, thinking it was the law, that's how come us to be separated.

Q: Did Frank make any attempt to get away?

A: No, not while I was there with him.

Q: How long had it been since you had seen Frank since you visited him in KC?

A: Well, It had been close to five years.

Q: At the time that you were in the room in Wichita and at the same time as the officer came in the room, did you have some Kodak pictures in your pocket?

A: Yes

Q: Did you loose them in the scuffle with the officer?

A: I think so.

Q: Did you at the time you ran out of the room throw your shirt in an adjoining room?

A: Yes

Q: Did you realize at the time you threw your shirt in the room it had your keys to your car in it?

A: No.

Q: You claimed in your statement you were in a wreck coming into Wichita.

A: Yes

Q: Do you know what caused the wreck?

A: Yes sir, a drunken driver run me into the wrong side of the road.

Q: Whose car was you and Frank riding in?

A: Mine, I bought it last Saturday new.

Q: Where did you buy it?

A: Cherryvale.

Q: Where did you get the license for the car?

A: Independence, Kansas.

Q: Under what name?

A: Ralph Caraway.

Q: Which is not your correct name?

A: No.

Q: Would you state the officer died fighting?

A: He didn't die while I was there.

Q: Would you say this officer was fighting all the time you were shooting?

A: Ya, he was holding on and fighting.

When quizzed about the Neely killing, he declared he was in Cherryvale on the night of the murder. Asked about the robberies of the Coffeeville Theatre and the Texaco station, he sat mum. At the end of the session, he willingly signed the confession although there is some question whether he did so due to his belief the authorities intended dropping the charges against Frank in return for his full cooperation. Detective Maness would later emphatically declare no such deal ever existed outside of Wilbur's imagination.

Chapter Eight

Guilty as Hell

Confronted with a vast array of eyewitnesses to his dastardly deeds, Wilbur caved in on the afternoon of the 16th admitting his participation in both the Coffeyville Theater and the Wichita Texaco station robberies. He then asked the Sheriff if he could write a letter to a lady in Cherryvale, Kansas. While Underhill claimed the woman was his partner in a hotel he co-owned there, turns out the lady in question was his current girlfriend who just happened to live and work at the hostelry. He also requested he be allowed to contact his so-called wife, Ethel, at her residence in Independence, Kansas. One wonders what would have happened if all Underhill's wives and girlfriends had ever gotten together. Sheriff Grove begrudgingly allowed his request although he assumed the suspect was either attempting to set up an alibi for the night of the Neely killing or planning a "bustout" from the jail.

Later that day, Deputy Warden Ed Nolen of the Oklahoma State Penitentiary breezed into town attempting to claim Underhill stating the outlaw was wanted in Oklahoma for escape while serving a life sentence. He further claimed Underhill would be tried for the O'Neil killing, which had occurred in 1927 on the streets of Picher, Oklahoma. District Attorney Adams sent the official packing, saying, "We will not release Underhill to anyone until he has been tried for Merle Colver's murder."

The following day, Perry Porter, the Ottawa County, Oklahoma Prosecuting Attorney, publicly denied he had any intention of trying Underhill for O'Neil's murder in the

---

near future, claiming the state's case had too many holes in it. He added; "Warden Nolan had his spurs tangled when he made his statement."

Shortly after the conclusion of Wilbur's latest confession, the outlaw was given a perp walk for a gathering of reporters and allowed to talk with the newsies for a couple of minutes. When asked if he knew Porter Meeks, an Oklahoma outlaw who had been slain by Officer Colver in a shootout in 1927, he stated, "Ya, but I didn't know he had bought the farm." Meeks' luck ran out when the automobile he, Herman Barker, (Ma Barker's eldest son) and Charles Stalcup were riding in was stopped by motorcycle officers J. E. Marshal and Frank Bush at the 1100 block of North Lawrence Avenue (now Broadway) in the early morning hours of August 29, 1927, only a few hours after the trio had robbed an ice plant in nearby Newton, Kansas. When Marshal stuck his head into the car's window and began visually searching the rig with his flashlight, Barker, sitting in the driver's seat, grabbed him around the neck and shot him point blank in the head several times with a 9mm Lugar pistol. Officer Bush in turn opened fire wounding all three suspects, but the severely injured Herman Barker was somehow able to drive the car away from the scene leaving Meeks, who fled on foot into the darkness between two nearby houses, to fend for his self. After traveling about six blocks south, Barker lost control of the vehicle at the intersection of St. Francis and Pine smashing into a tree. He then fled on foot into a patch of weeds where minutes later, the outlaw, who was suffering from a severe head wound, which had caused him to go temporarily blind, turned his own gun on himself and blew his brains out. Stalcup, who was wounded in both legs and the right arm, was discovered at dawn hiding in a patch of tall weeds located only a short distance from the crash site. A couple of days after the shootout, Colver, who was a detective at the time, was tipped off Meeks had been seen in the vicinity of 23rd and Market on the city's north side. Rushing to the scene, Colver quickly spotted the fugitive ordering him to halt. Meeks turned and called the officer a vile name before whipping out a pistol and firing four shots, several smashing into the officer's car. After a furious exchange of gunfire, Colver came out the winner when two of his rounds found paydirt, one striking the outlaw square in the pump while another accidentally struck a teenage bystander named Harold Burkholder in the leg. While the lad recovered from his wound, the outlaw did not. Several weeks after the shootout, Colver's mates in the department presented him with a long-barreled .45 cal. revolver in honor of his bravery. He carried the gun until the day he died when Wilbur Underhill stole it off his dying body.

****

Asked by the reporters if he had freely confessed to Colver's murder, Wilbur responded, "I guess I'll take the rap alright," but added he was innocent of the Picher, Oklahoma murder charge as well as the Neely slaying. Sometime that same day, Wilbur's gray-haired mother, and two of his sisters, Dorothy Underhill and Mrs. Anna Lewis, arrived from Missouri in hopes of seeing the defendants. Sheriff Grove refused to allow the three visitation privileges. Mrs. Underhill collapsed on hearing the bad news and was reported to be in grave condition. Dorothy told an assemblage of newsmen "Frank is a good boy and has not missed church in years." On hearing this piece of information, the plainspoken Sheriff quickly retorted, "Ya he's a real pip, the little angel was caught playing poker and cussing like a sailor last night with a couple of drunks in the bullpen." According to jail guards, Wilbur, who had spent several hours grooming himself in preparation for his mom's visit, was deeply disappointed on receiving the news, saying, "Well, maybe she can come see me in Lansing." (Location of the Kansas State Prison)

On the morning of August 17, Underhill and his nephew were led manacled from their cells in the city jail to a courtroom in the county courthouse for a hearing in front of Judge Leigh Clark. Nearly a hundred spectators stood on the front lawn of city hall hoping to catch a glace of the prisoners. Meanwhile, a lawyer from Kansas City named B. B. Anderson arrived to represent young Frank. The attorney cloistered himself with Chief of Police O. W. Wilson and Deputy County Attorney J R. Mayall in a room off to the side of the courtroom in an effort to cut a deal. He offered Wilbur on a platter if the charges were dropped against Frank. The Prosecutor cut him short stating, "We intend on trying the boy for murder and will make no deals. We have an open and shut case and that's on the level." Wilbur's confession was read aloud in open court and his preliminary hearing was set for August 21. Frank's lawyer requested a delay in the proceedings against him, which the Judge consented to.

Later that same day, services were held for the fallen officer at the Presbyterian church in nearby Clearwater, Kansas

Wilbur sitting in the can with a sore shoulder. Courtesy Kansas City Star

with most of the Wichita Police Department in attendance standing at attention dressed in their summer blues and donning white gloves. Colver, who had a sterling reputation and was a very popular officer, had joined the force in 1924 and been cited several times for bravery in his career. He had twice ran for Sedgwick County Sheriff, both times being narrowly defeated. His wife and two teenage children survived him. He was the ninth Wichita officer to die in the line of duty in the past decade. As for his attitude toward his dangerous job, he was often quoted as saying, "I will die when my time comes and not a second sooner or later," adding, "Providence will clock me out, not a cowardly killer." He was half right anyway.

On August 18, Clarence B. Sowers, a well-known Kansas City shyster breezed into town. After conferring with Lawyer Anderson and Ma Underhill, he immediately

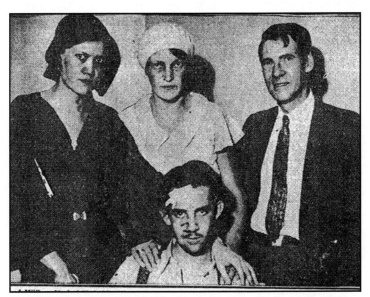

Frank Underhill surrounded by his Aunts Dorothy, top left, and Anne Lewis, top center, as well as his co-council, B. B. Anderson. Courtesy Wichita Beacon

made tracks to the courthouse where he protested the Sheriff's refusal to allow Mrs. Underhill a visit with her son and grandson. Judge I. N. Williams, moved by his argument, eventually issued a permit to the family providing for visitation rights, stating, "The defendant is innocent until proven guilty."

On the morning of the 21st, Wilbur was led into the courthouse to attend his preliminary in front of Judge Fred K. Hammers. Over 500 citizens were present either in the courtroom or on the courthouse lawn. Wilbur, who was handcuffed to Marvin Cox, the Court Marshal, was clean-shaven and neatly dressed in a blue shirt and matching tie.

Crowd taking a look-see at Wilbur and Frank. Courtesy Wichita Beacon

The desperado sat wide-eyed and stared intently at all the proceedings going on around him. When asked where he got the fancy shirt, he exclaimed "Someone gave it to me since mine was lost in the scuffle and is now part of the evidence." He was also overheard whispering to Marshal Cox "There are a lot of witnesses here, but not one of 'em for me."

When asked how he pleads, Underhill pointedly declared, "Not Guilty." When Attorney Sowers went on to suggest to the Judge that Wilbur should be turned over to Oklahoma since he was listed as an escapee doing life for murder in that state, Hammers dismissed his request out of hand.

The prosecution's star witness was Cora Brotherton, the manager of the Iris Hotel who testified she had observed Officer Colver walk upstairs to the third floor, then heard an explosion followed by the sounds of a struggle then three more thunderous bangs in succession before

Before the bar of Justice. Courtesy Wichita Beacon

hearing a loud thump. She continued her statement saying she then saw Wilbur and his nephew race down the stairs

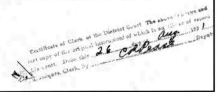

STATE OF KANSAS

vs.

WILBUR UNDERHILL, alias RALPH CARAWAY and
FRANK VANCE UNDERHILL   DEFENDANTS.

O R D E R.

Now on this 26th day of August, A.D. 1931, the same being a regular judicial day of the April A.D. 1931 term of this Court, this matter comes on to be heard upon the application of Mrs. Amelia Underhill, the mother of Wilbur Underhill and Grandmother of Frank Vance Underhill, to see and visit with each of the above-named defendants, Mrs. Amelia Underhill being represented by her attorney Clarence R. Sowers, and the Court having examined into the facts finds:

That the application should be sustained.

IT IS THEREFORE CONSIDERED, ORDERED and DECREED that C. E. Grove, the Sheriff of Sedgwick County, Kansas, be and he is hereby ordered to permit Mrs. Amelia Underhill to see and visit with Wilbur Underhill and Frank Vance Underhill for a period of time of thirty minutes each.

J U D G E.

Approved

ATTORNEY FOR WILBUR UNDERHILL AND AMELIA UNDERHILL.

Legal document allowing Almira to visit Frank and Wilbur.
Courtesy Michael Webb

pausing just long enough to tell her there had been an accident upstairs. Her testimony was followed by that of twenty-year-old Cecil Honick, the operator of the Texaco station, who identified Wilbur as the robber that stuck him up the night before Colver's death. Two citizens, Miss Fern Clark and Mrs. F. B. Macy, who were standing less than a block from the filling station at the time of the heist, identified Underhill's vehicle as the one involved in the robbery. Following the testimonies of several other damning witnesses and the re-introduction of Wilbur's confession, the Judge set his bond at $45,000. When asked if he could make bail, the defendant sneered. The Judge declared him in default ordering him lodged in the county jail until the October term of the district court.

That afternoon, Frank's "mouth-piece" waived his client's preliminary hearing and Judge Hammers set his bond

Wilbur and Frank holding court document. Courtesy Wichita Eagle

at $25,000 on a charge of murder and $10,000 for high-way robbery. His honor then set the youth's trial date for October 19 on the robbery charge and late-November for the Colver murder. Once again, reporters from the local newspapers were allowed to interview the suspects. When the pair was asked to strike a pose for the cameras, Frank grabbed a copy of the indictment papers and took a pose, which appeared as though he was reading the document. When a reporter informed him he was holding the paper upside down, the youth remarked, "Who cares?" When Wilbur was asked to comment on a recent editorial written by an area minister that implied he should be executed, the bandit responded, "Aw, all they want to do is kill me. Them preachers are all hypocrites. The bible says 'Judge not', don't it?"

Adding to the circus-like atmosphere, the *Wichita Beacon* hired the noted psychologist and character analyst, Professor John Jenson, to study photographs of the suspects and make a conclusion as to their strengths and weaknesses. The result of this "scientific" study appeared in a large spread of the Sunday edition of the paper, which showed both defendants faces with

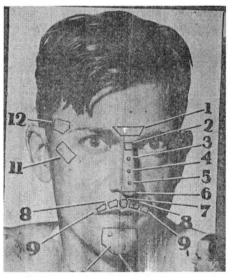

Psychoanalysis of Wilbur's face by Professor Jenson. Courtesy Wichita Beacon

arrows drawn to their pertinent features. The Professor, who took his job very seriously, noted in his conclusions that Wilbur was the aggressive sort (no joke) but given the proper environment could of been a leader of men and an individual of great importance and standing in the community. He went on to state the killer's face showed he had little faith in his fellow man and was anti-social to the extreme. The good doctor also noted Frank was a passive weakling of a man, definitely lacking in leadership. Not to be outdone, the Wichita Eagle hired there own expert a Dr. W. H. Mikesell of Wichita State University to do a similar character study.

Meanwhile, with Wilbur and his nephew safely tucked into separate cells in the Sedgwick County Jail awaiting trial, investigators were busy backtracking Wilbur's movements since his July 14 escape from the Oklahoma pen as well as laboring to make a connection between the suspects and the murder of William Neely. Kansas authorities also suspected the pair of involvement in the August 1 murder of a Wyandotte County Deputy Sheriff named Frank Rohrback. It appears the deputy was slain shortly after he was observed questioning a pair of men (One which according to

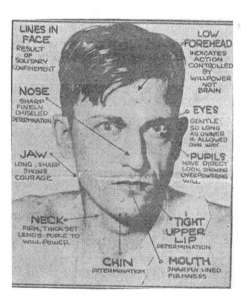

Dr. Mikesell's competing analysis.
Courtesy Wichita Eagle

eyewitnesses resembled Wilbur) seated in a car, which he had pulled over just outside of Kansas City, Kansas.

While on a visit to Cherryvale, Kansas checking out Wilbur's alibi for the night of the Neely murder, Detective Joe Maness hit a stonewall. The couple operating the hotel where Wilbur was staying swore they did not remember if he was in his room the night of the murder or not. A waitress at the hotel's restaurant (Wilbur's newest love interest, Maggie Smith) stated that although her memory was kinda foggy as to specific dates, she believed she and Wilbur had spent the evening in question locked in the grip of romance in her room. The lawmen's luck improved on his arrival back in Wichita; when he was greeted with a telephone message from a Kansas City resident named Mrs. William Reed who claimed to possess important information about the Neely case. When Maness returned her call, Mrs. Reed, who stated she had known Wilbur since childhood, swore to the officer she had seen the outlaw accompanied by a young companion in Wichita on August 2, the day of the Neely murder. Apparently, she was in town that day visiting relatives. The various conflicting testimonies given in the Neely case would evolve into a Mexican standoff with neither the defense nor the prosecutors gaining ground.

Another troubling aspect of the case was the fact Sedgwick County Sheriff Charles E. Grove along with a pair of deputies had all sworn they encountered Wilbur and his nephew at the Sedgwick County jail when the pair attempted to visit an inmate named Elam prior to the Neely murder. When questioned about the visit, which occurred on July 28, Wilbur denied it and Frank stated he had not joined up with his uncle until the night of August 8.

Meanwhile, on September 1 the newspapers reported extra activity at the jail when news was received of Wilbur's brother George having escaped from a Montgomery County Jail work gang near Independence, Kansas where he had been doing a 90-day jolt for larceny. Lawmen were convinced George and Earl Underhill were now actively conspiring to spring their infamous brother. A dozen extra guards were posted at the jail entrances and other added security measures were instituted by Sheriff Grove. In reality, it was a simple case of paranoia on the lawmen's part; Earl was presently residing six hundred miles away in Roswell, New Mexico where he was working as a mechanic at a truck stop. As for George, since his 1927 release from the Missouri State Pen where he was doing a five-year sentence for burglary, he had evolved into a classic drifter aimlessly wandering across the Midwest hitchhiking and hopping freights, moving from town to town. He had been incarcerated on numerous occasions, sentenced to a night or perhaps thirty days or six months for such crimes as burglary, petty larceny, trespassing, and illegal drug possession. In 1930, he spent six months in the Jasper County Jail forced to work the Zinc mines by day and locked down at night. Shortly after his discharge from the Jasper County slammer, George, who had developed into a hardcore morphine addict, was arrested for shoplifting in Coffeyville, Kansas. Since his escape from the Montgomery County work farm he was suspected of perpetrating a series of small town drug store burglaries in Kansas and Missouri. The authorities needn't of wasted their time and resources on George, he was more worried about George and where he would get his next fix than whatever was happening to his big brother.

On the morning of September 2, Wilbur's attorney informed Prosecutor Adams, his client was now prepared to change his plea from "Not guilty" to "Guilty" of the murder of Merle Colver.

In the District Court of Sedgwick County, Kansas

THE STATE OF KANSAS,
Plaintiff.
vs.

Wilbur Underhill

Defendant.

A Regular Day

April Term, A. D., 1931

Cause No. 77526

JOURNAL ENTRY

Now on this 4 day of September 1931, a regular day of said term of this court, this cause comes on for arraignment and assignment, as to defendant, Wilbur Underhill George L. Adams, County Attorney, appearing for and on behalf of the State of Kansas and said defendant appearing in person and by Attorney Clarence Sowers

Thereupon the information herein was read to said defendant Wilbur Underhill charging him with Murder in the first degree

Whereupon said defendant entered a plea of guilty and did then and there plead guilty to Murder in the first degree

And afterwards, to-wit: On the 4 day of September 193 of said term, this cause came on to be heard upon the motion of the County Attorney for judgment of sentence herein the parties hereto appearing as aforesaid, which motion was sustained.

The Court then informed said defendant, that he had been charged, by an information filed against him herein by the County Attorney, with Murder in the first degree

and that he had pleaded guilty to said charge.

The Court then inquired of said defendant Wilbur Underhill if he had any legal cause to show why judgment of sentence should not be pronounced against him and said defendant, failing to show any such cause and none appearing, the Court proceeded to pronounce judgment of sentence against defendant as follows:

It is the sentence of this Court and it is hereby ordered and adjudged by said Court that said defendant be taken to the jail of said County, and thence be taken by the Sheriff of said County to the State Penitentiary at Lansing, Kansas, there to be confined at hard labor, subject to provisions of law, for a term of the rest of the defendant, Wilbur Underhill's natural life time.

It is further ordered and adjudged by the Court that the defendant, pay the costs of prosecution, taxed at $ and that execution issue at the close of said term of said Court for said costs.

To all of which ruling, orders, and sentence said defendant duly objected and excepted.

O. K. Geo. L. Adams

J. E. Alexander
Judge.

Certificate of Clerk of the District Court. The above is a true and correct copy of ... original Instrument of which is on file ... in this court. ... this 5th day of Sept. 193 1
A. E. Jacques, Clerk, by ...

Wilbur's Guilty plea for first-degree murder. Courtesy Kansas Historical Society

INFORMATION

THE STATE OF KANSAS, ⎫
                     ⎬ ss.
COUNTY OF SEDGWICK. ⎭

In the District Court of Sedgwick County, State of Kansas

THE STATE OF KANSAS, Plaintiff,
Against

Wilbur Underhill and
Frank Vance Underhill

INFORMATION.

Defendant.

IN THE NAME and by the authority of the State of Kansas, I, George L. Adams, County Attorney in and for the County of Sedgwick, in the State of Kansas, who prosecute for and on behalf of said State, in the District Court of Sedgwick County, sitting in and for the County of Sedgwick, and duly empowered to inform of offenses committed within said County of Sedgwick, come now here and give the Court to understand and

be informed that Wilbur Underhill and Frank Vance Underhill

late of said County of Sedgwick, at and within the County of Sedgwick, in the State of Kansas aforesaid, and

within the jurisdiction of this Court on the 14 day of August A. D., 1931,

did then and there unlawfully, feloniously, wilfully, intentionally, purposely, designedly, deliberately, maliciously, premeditately, with felonious intent and malice aforethought, being then and there armed with a certain deadly weapon, to-wit: a pistol, commonly called a revolver, loaded with gun powder, leaden or steel balls and percussion caps, a more definite and certain description of which the affiant at this time is unable to give for the reason that he does not know the same, then and there held in the hands of them the said Wilbur Underhill and Frank Vance Underhill, being armed with said deadly weapon as aforesaid, did then and there unlawfully, feloniously, wilfully, intentionally, purposely, designedly, deliberately, maliciously, premeditately with felonious intent and malice aforethought, make an assault upon one Merle Colver; and that the said Wilbur Underhill and Frank Vance Underhill in making said assault upon the said Merle Colver, did then and there shoot off and discharge from said revolver into the body of him the said Merle Colver a certain leaden or steel ball, then and there held in the hands of them the said Wilbur Underhill and Frank Vance Underhill; a more definite and certain description of which affiant is now unable to give for the reason he does not know the same, and a more definite and certain description of which wound affiant is now unable to give for the reason that he does not know the same, then and thereby inflicting upon him the said Merle Colver with said deadly weapon, one certain mortal wound and from the effects of the said mortal wound so received at the hands of them the said Wilbur Underhill and Frank Vance Underhill and in the manner and by the means aforesaid, he the said Merle Colver did then and there die, and that the said Wilbur Underhill and Frank Vance Underhill in the manner and by the means aforesaid at and within the County of Sedgwick and State of Kansas as aforesaid, did then and there unlawfully, feloniously, wilfully, intentionally, purposely, designedly, deliberately, maliciously, with felonious intent and malice aforethought, shoot, kill and murder him the said Merle Colver.

contrary to the form of the statute in such cases made and provided, and against the peace and dignity of the State of Kansas.

Geo. L. Adams .... County Attorney

Charges in Sedgwick County against Wilbur Underhill. Courtesy Kansas Historical Society

After spending several fruitless weeks trying to tie the Underhills in with the Neely slaying, Detective Maness requested County Attorney George Lee Adams put that investigation on the back burner and go ahead and accept Wilbur's guilty plea in regards to the Colver murder case figuring it made little difference if they convicted the thug of one murder or ten since Kansas did not have the death penalty.

On September 4, 1931, a heavily manacled Wilbur Underhill was led into the courtroom of Judge J. E. Alexander where he pled guilty to first-degree murder. Attorney Sowers informed the Judge, "Wilbur is obviously making a guilty plea in hopes that his young nephew does

COMMITMENT   77526

STATE OF KANSAS, SEDGWICK COUNTY, SS:

The State of Kansas to the Sheriff of Sedgwick County, Kansas:

WHEREAS, on the ....4th.... day of ....September.... 19 31 in a cause then pending in the District Court of Sedgwick County, Kansas, Division No. ....1...., wherein the State of Kansas was plaintiff and ....Wilbur Underhill.... was the defendant, judgment was rendered that

Wilbur Underhill serve a sentence in the Kansas State Penitentiary for the rest of his natural life. Said defendant having plead guilty and being guilty of murder in the 1st degree.

You are therefore commanded to take and commit said defendant to the jail of Sedgwick County, Kansas, there to remain until said judgment is complied with.

Given under my hand this ..5th.. day of ....September.... , 19 .31.

A. E. Jacques
Clerk of the District Court

By C. H. Rau
Deputy

O. K. Geo. L. Adams
County Attorney

Wilbur's commitment paper. Courtesy Kansas Department of Corrections

not have to atone for the same offense." County Attorney George Lee Adams replied, "Hopes are all he has." Judge Alexander then sentenced Wilbur to serve the rest of his natural life at the Kansas State Penitentiary in Lansing at hard labor. The outlaw was immediately flown by plane (the cops were still convinced a jailbreak would be staged by the Underhill Gang) to the prison where he was checked in as prisoner # 2337.

A few weeks later, jury selection in the case of the State of Kansas verses Frank Vance Underhill for highway robbery got under way. The state publicly announced Underhill, who had been dubbed "The Kid" by the local press, would be tried for the murder of Merle Colver as soon as the robbery case was completed.

With the trial soon to begin, Almira Underhill and her attractive daughter, Dorothy, who the newspapers pegged a "Greta Garbo-Marlene Dietrich type, tall, slender, and good-looking," again swept into town. Almira began holding mini-news conferences in which she asserted her grandson's innocence, saying, "I pray G-d in his infinite wisdom will have mercy on Wilbur and Frank."

Once Frank's robbery trial got under way in the court of District Judge J.E. Alexander, it moved rapidly. On the

Wilbur's login sheet-KSP. Courtesy Kansas Department of Corrections

morning of October 19, the state presented it's case calling the Texaco filling station attendant to the stand, who although he had not seen Frank, did identify the getaway car and gave the details of the heist. Several citizens who had witnessed the aftermath of the robbery positively identified young Underhill as the car's driver. Defense Attorney Sowers claimed the lad had no idea his uncle was going to rob the station when he had him stop the car. Wilbur, in his confession, had stated he only told the boy to park and "Keep the motor running, I'm going to see a friend." Co-Council B. B. Anderson introduced a letter written recently from the Kansas state prison from Wilbur to his mother in which he stated he was sorry for the predicament his nephew was in since he was solely to blame, adding, "Frank committed no crime." The prosecutor in his closing statement presented Frank as a desperate criminal. The jury didn't buy it and promptly acquitted the lad. The entire robbery trial lasted but three days.

Undeterred, the prosecution in a statement to the press claimed they would easily convict the boy in the upcoming murder trial, which was due to start the following month, stating it would be a "Cakewalk."

On the morning of November 6, news was received that George Underhill was found dead on the floor of the Gilbert Boarding House in Garnett, Kansas. According to the local coroner, George was a victim of a sodium barbital overdose. The powers that be suspected he had stolen the drugs in question from a locked cabinet of an area drug store, which had been broken into the previous night. He was identified by a jailhouse tattoo on his right arm, which read "Kid Underhill Joplin Mo." Although Wilbur pleaded with Kansas prison officials for permission to attend his brother's funeral, which was held at the Blendville Christian church in Joplin, they wouldn't hear of it. The body of the twenty-eight-year-old miscreant was laid to rest at the Ozark Memorial Park.

****

The day before Frank's murder trial was slated to begin, a particularly nasty piece of old business came up. Attorney Sowers, reviewing the Coroner's report, noticed the slain officer's exact cause of death was not noted. Actually, according to Sowers, the document was replete with errors and was a sloppy a piece of work as was ever beheld. When County Attorney George Lee Adams was informed of the glaring omission he immediately got an exhumation order and had Colver's body disinterred and a Coroner's inquest held in Clearwater, which was the site of his burial. Coroner D.G. Heckman and Wichita City Physician R. E. Hobbs conducted the second autopsy. As was assumed, the postmortem examination confirmed the cause of death as "Death by Gunfire."

The trial of Frank Vance Underhill for the murder of

Grave of George Underhill. Photo by Naomi Morgan

Patrolman Colver finally got underway on November 25th. A bevy of witnesses from the murder scene (the Iris Hotel) as well as Officers Jack Myler and Ray Mitchell, who had captured the Underhill's at Linwood Park, were called and testified for the prosecution. Incidentally, Myler had since been overheard commenting to fellow officers he wished he had shot a few inches to the right at the time of Wilbur's apprehension. Deputy Coroner Leonard S. Markel presented a convoluted theory involving ballistics, blood spatter, and bullet trajectory suggesting Frank had initially shot Colver in the back while Wilbur was grappling with the officer. Sowers promptly tore the theory asunder on cross-examination.

Late that night, Frank's Great Aunt Dora Barnes, accompanied by a twenty-year-old family friend named Dorothy Ruppert, were on their way from Kansas City to Wichita to testify in Frank's behalf when they hit a patch of loose gravel and spun into a ditch near Rosalia, Kansas. Mrs. Barnes had her chin laid open while Dorothy was cut about the nose and chin The pair sought medical attention at the nearby El Dorado, Kansas Hospital before catching a bus toward their final destination. When the pair arrived at the courtroom the next day they both limped to the witness stand where they testified, bandages, bruises, stitches and all, that Frank was a fine young man and good Christian. The attractive Miss Ruppert, who was employed as a telephone operator back in Kansas City, was a big hit in the morning edition of the Wichita papers with her eye-catching mug splashed across the front page along with an account of her adventures of the past twenty-four hours.

The following day, Frank, pulling a long face, took the stand in his own defense testifying to a packed courtroom. He gave his life's history beginning with how he came about landing on his Grandmother's doorstep at a tender age, his mother dead and father imprisoned. He piled it on thick about his being a churchgoer and a good student, as well as being fully employed for the past three years. When prodded by Attorney Clarence Sowers, the youth gave his version of the details of the crime. He basically told the same story he and his uncle had told the police in their previous confessions, although he added, that while the two antagonists were engaged in mortal combat, he froze with fear and begged the officer not to resist. He claimed Colver struck the first blow with his nightstick before Wilbur "Gave him the works." He added, "I have no personal knowledge of any robberies. I was just along for the ride, Wilbur had promised me the use of his new car for a week if I drove him to Cherryvale and back. I'm on the square, honest Injun." Although Prosecutor Adams tore into the youth attempting to shake his goofy story, Frank held firm to every detail.

While Sowers was wrapping up his closing augments, Officer Colver's widow fainted and had to be carried from the courtroom. The lawyer continued his colloquy claiming the youthful defendant was a victim of circumstances, a fine, virtuous lad unwittingly led astray by his hardened criminal-minded Uncle.

In his final remarks, the prosecutor asserted the youth was no "Jesus carrying the cross. No Sunday school boy" as his defense attorney made him out to be, but a "Desperate killer trying to make a sap out of the jury." The jury received the case at 4 pm on the afternoon of December 1. After a couple of hours of debate, they broke for supper then returned to the jury room. Unable to agree on a verdict they were sent home for the night. The following day, the jury debated the case throughout the day and into the evening. At 7 pm, after a third ballot was taken, they buzzed the bailiff stating they had come to a decision. Not guilty.

A joyous Frank was taken back to the jail to get his personal belongings and be discharged. He stopped by the office of Sheriff Grove who like the slain Colver was a native of Clearwater, Kansas. Evidentially when the "Kid" tried to shake his hand and say no hard feelings. Grove threw him out of his office instructing him to "Get your things and get out." When he returned to his cell, the inmates cheered him but when the lad approached his captor, now jailor, Jack Myler, on the way out of the building, Myler instructed him to, "Beat it kid before I loose my head and smash you with these keys." Frank then left the scene with no further ado, staying the night with a friend before journeying back to Kansas City.

The following day the Wichita papers were flush with editorials condemning the jury for their verdict. A contemptuous city detective was quoted as saying "It just goes to show ya, it's no crime to kill a cop in Wichita."

Frank Vance Underhill.
Courtesy Michael Webb

Chapter Nine

Greetings From the Big House

Wilbur Underhill was officially received and logged in at the Kansas State Penitentiary in Lansing on September 5, 1931. Records show Sedgwick County Sheriff C. E. Grove escorted him to the prison gates. On his medical examination, Underhill's physical characteristics were noted as 5'11", 170 pounds, medium-large build, dark complected, gray eyes, light brown hair, thirty years of age, gunshot scars on forearm, side, thigh, and shoulder with noticeable moles on face and neck. He listed his birthplace as Missouri and nationality as German. For occupation he stated: Electrician: Crime: First Degree Murder, and sentence: "Natural Life."

For purposes of visitation and correspondence, the badman listed his mother, three brothers, and sisters Grace, Dorothy, and

Mug shot Kansas State Penitentiary. Courtesy Kansas Department of Corrections

---

Anna Lewis along with Margerette Smith of Cherryvale, Kansas. The latter name was a "ringer." Miss Smith was not his sister but a girlfriend. He was obviously attempting to keep in touch with his sweetie through subterfuge. At the time, only close relatives of an inmate were allowed visitation rights. Wilbur stated his current wife was Ethel Underhill of Independence, Kansas. Asked how long he had been a resident of Kansas he stated, "Not, I'm a transient." Quizzed about the crime he was currently incarcerated for, he answered, "I don't care to make any kind of statement in regards to this charge. I entered my plea and have nothing else to say." When the prison chaplain quizzed him as to what caused his downfall he responded "My past record." He was placed in a crowded two-man 6'x 10' cell in "C" Block and assigned to the twine plant.

By the time Underhill arrived at the Kansas State Penitentiary the institution was already nearly three quarters of a century old. Construction of the prison began in 1864 and was an ongoing affair. The eleven acre main prison contained the newly refurbished A and B cellblocks as well

Main entrance, KSP, Lansing, Kansas. Courtesy Kansas Department of Corrections

as C and D blocks along with a hospital, laundry, dining hall, punishment unit (#2 Cell house), recreation yard, baseball field, and various other facilities surrounded by a high stone wall topped by towers occupied by armed guards located on each corner. Adjacent to the central compound was a coal-fired power plant and the prison industries, which included a brickyard that produced an average of 2,000,000 bricks per year, a twine plant, as well as tailor, harness, machine, furniture, plumbing, and tinker shops. In 1881, the powers that be ordered a coal shaft be sunk which eventually worked its way under the nearby Missouri River. Over the years, the mines produced an average of 250 tons of coal a day, employing roughly 455 convicts. By 1931, the prison population had swelled to over 1800 inmates. Prisoners who worked earned up to two dollars a month and those who slaved in the coalmines received two days credit for every day served. A well-stocked commissary dubbed the "Chouteau Store" carried just about every legal article a prisoner had need of offered at competitive prices. The store, which was created by a $100 donation from a previous inmate named Jerry Chouteau, was a nonprofit institution, which gave away its meager profits to destitute families of the inmates (Wilbur's mother Almira would receive a small check every month for over a year from the fund). The store also operated a gift shop that sold handmade crafts, which the inmates in the tinker's shop constructed out of refuse, pieces of string, wire, and tin to the public.

Due to the current economic crisis (the depression) and invariable financial cutbacks, the prison strived to be as self sufficient as was possible through prison industries (bricks, coal, etc.) and the production of food on the institution's 2000-acre Stigers Island farm in the form of beef, pork, and vegetables. There was also a modern milking operation stocked by a herd of seventy cows. The current Warden of the correctional facility was the recently appointed fifty-year-old John "Kirk" Prather, an ex-real estate agent turned "political hack" who had been rewarded the job in June 1931 by Kansas Governor Woodring for past services rendered to the state's Democratic party.

The key words in describing life at KSP (now the Lansing Correctional Facility) were monotony, uniformity, and discipline. Although the prison's undersized, antiquated (built in 1872) dining hall had long been known for serving a bland tasteless diet of red beans, rice, and potatoes along with stale bread and molasses, by the time Wilbur arrived, meat, dairy products, and fresh vegetables had been added to the daily fare. Discipline was strict and punishment for an infraction of the rules, swift. According to the prison's biennial reports, there were 443 breaches of discipline in the year 1932 alone. Prisoners were allowed to purchase

---

————VISITORS————

Close relatives are allowed to visit men of this institution any day except Saturday afternoon and holidays once every thirty days.

Sunday visits are limited to one hour. Visiting hours on all days are from 8:30 until 3:30. As previously stated, this does not apply to Sunday visits, which are one hour.

Any other persons except close relatives are prohibited from visiting, except they bring a letter of permission from the family of the man they wish to visit, or in case of an outstanding emergency of some sort, at which time visitors must satisfy the management of their identification and the urgent need of a visit.

Do not ask for visits on Saturday afternoons and holidays; nor after 3:30 P.M.; or for more than one hour on Sunday.

Respectfully,

KIRK PRATHER, Warden.

Notice regarding visitors to the prison, circa 1932. Courtesy Michael Webb

NOTICE

☞ Inmates may receive packages containing eatables on CHRISTMAS ONLY, consisting of the following

1. Cakes, Cookies, Crackers, Candies [not wrapped in paper], Cooked Meats, Fried Chicken, Butter, Loose Pickles, Cube Sugar, Apples and Oranges, Shelled Nuts. Nothing in glass or tin will be permitted. Perishable eatables generally arrive in a spoiled condition, causing a loss to the enire box.

2. Underwear, Safety Razors, Hose, Garters, Shoes, Suspenders, Handkerchiefs, may be sent any time. Hose must be plain solid dark color, nothing fancy. Sweaters must be black.

3. No Books, Magazines or Papers will be admitted to inmates of this institution unless sent direct from the publisher.

Articles sent here—Not Included In Paragraphs 1 and 2—Will Not Be Returned To Sender.

It is the desire of the management of this Institution to give the Inmates all reasonable accommodations. In order that your relatives may have Fresh Fruits, Candies, Nuts and Tobacco, these are kept at the Chouteau Store, and can be bought any day of the year. Most any article received from the outside, can be purchased here at the same price as outside. You can save yourself and the Management a lot of trouble by placing money to the credit of Inmates in the Chief Clerk's Office.

☞ In making remittances to Inmates, send Drafts or Money Orders, BUT NOT CASH.

KIRK PRATHER, WARDEN.

Prison notice regarding gifts and Christmas packages, circa 1932.
Courtesy Michael Webb

Bull Durham tobacco and Browns Mule plug chewing tobacco in the commissary but tailor made (factory rolled) cigarettes were considered contraband. Unlike other prisons of the era, inmates were allowed to talk to each other. Due to overcrowding and understaffing, (130 full-time employees) the convicts were not as closely supervised as at some facilities. Morphine was readably available for a dollar a packet and homemade or even bonded booze could be purchased on the black market. Marijuana, grown on the prison farms, was commonly available. Homosexual queens openly offered their wares for two dollars a shot in the exercise yard and fights which sometimes involved shanks (homemade knives) were a frequent occurrence. Prisoners entering the institution were designated third class inmates with very few privileges and worked their way to first class and assignment to the honor farm if they behaved. Most didn't.

For recreation, the prison had its own semi-pro baseball team dubbed the Red Sox who for obvious reasons played mostly home games. A basketball team was fielded in the fall and winter. The prison band played concerts every Sunday evening during good weather and a movie followed by a comedy short and current newsreel was shown every Saturday afternoon. According to prison officials, no films that glorified banditry or depicted the slaying of a law enforcement officer were screened. For those who wished to attend, religious services were held every Sunday afternoon. Inmates could also check out books from the prison library, which contained some 7789 volumes.

As for medical care, the institution's forty-three-bed hospital was equipped with an x-ray machine and modern operating room. According to prison reports, the inmate's chief physical complaint was gastrointestinal upsets (so much for the food) followed by heat exhaustion in the mines.

Surgeries performed ranged from gunshot and knife wounds to hemorrhoid removal. Although the spread of TB was much less prevalent at the prison compared to other institutions located throughout the country, VD was widespread; some 30% of inmates tested flunked the Wasserman test. In 1932 and '33, serious outbreaks of influenza swept the prison. The standard treatment for most complaints was listed on official medical reports as bismuth, aspirin, and or Mercurochrome.

The inmate population was made up of 100 armed robbers, 45 bank robbers, 61 murderers, 26 rapists, and 500 thieves of one sort or another followed by a host of other categories including five convicted of possession of illegal drugs (Harrison Drug Act). According to inmates, the chief cause of their downfall was need of money followed by circumstantial evidence, bad associates, liquor, and unemployment. Only ten percent of the prison population was high school graduates (roughly 2% were collage graduates) and 80% used alcohol and tobacco. The majority of prisoners were married and first offenders. The average age upon incarceration was twenty-eight and the cost of confining an inmate in 1932 was approximately $260 per year.

There had been no executions at the facility since capital punishment was outlawed in Kansas in 1907. As a whole, the place was a big gray mass of smelly black smudged stone full of misfits of which some were prisoners and others hacks or guards.

Within a week of his arrival, Underhill allegedly fell in with a group of dangerous inmates who had long been planning an escape from the institution. The plotters included a pair of murderers, Orville Haines and Jim Morris as well as five other convicts, Glenn Belfield, Lee Myers, J. B. Knight, Francis Sharp, and Alva Payton, who were all serving lengthy sentences for robbery. Apparently the group had convinced an ex-locksmith assigned to the prison machine shop to manufacture three homemade shotguns and a zip-pistol for them which they hid in a hollowed out space in the interior wall of the twine plant. Several weeks before the break, the plotters had an outside connection attach a customized wooden box filled with a rifle and ammunition to the undercarriage of an automobile owned by E. H. Vanosdale, the prison's recreation director. The following day Vanosdale unwittingly drove the carload of contraband through the prison gates and into the hands of the plotters.

The day the breakout was planned to take place an inmate named Stanton Zuck who was serving a jolt for robbing the Golden Diamond Shop in Wichita approached a guard stating he wanted to see the Warden in regards to an upcoming bustout. When taken before Prather, the snitch spilled the beans providing him the details of the escape. According to the squealer, the group was planning to snatch the warden's car and take him hostage the following morning. Zuck continued his story saying the desperate convicts intended on killing three guards and a pair of trustees in order to give them an easy approach to the warden's vehicle.

Prather reacted to the news by dispatching a goon squad to round up the in-

Warden Kirk Prather. Courtesy Kansas City Star

mates in question while another group of officers confiscated the cache of weapons, which was discovered behind a freshly mortared brick wall at a warehouse located behind the twine plant.

The angry Warden had all eight conspirators, including Underhill, tossed into Cellhouse #2 (the hole) while Kansas Governor Harry W. Woodring rewarded Zuck with a parole for his " Honesty and faithfulness." In a statement to the press, Prather claimed the informant had saved the lives of at least twenty-five men. How he came up with that particular inflated number is unknown.

Underhill would spend the next few weeks chained to a wall in a small, dark, moldy cell furnished with only a slop bucket and a water jug in the prison's notorious punishment block. His only companion was his sinister thoughts. On the outside, his sister Dorothy began a letter writing campaign bombarding Warden Prather with pleas to transfer Wilbur back to "population" due to her belief Wilbur had not in any way been involved in the escape attempt. Saying her brother had merely "Taken the fall" while the real mastermind behind the planned breakout went free. Eventually her prayers were answered when Prather acceded; releasing the outlaw from segregation and transferring him back to "C" Block and assigning him to work at the tailor shop. Within a week of Underhill's release from the hole a "Letter to the Editor" article written by his mother appeared in the pages of the *Wichita Eagle*, implying her son had been officially cleared of all suspicion as to his culpability in the escape attempt. Whether her assertion was based on fact or wishful thinking is a matter of pure conjecture. Apparently, Warden Prather never commented on her claims, at least not for public consumption.

On the afternoon of November 11, censors looking at a letter Wilbur had written noticed the correspondence was double-spaced leaving large gaps between the lines. Holding the paper up to the light, they observed several words written in invisible ink (in this case urine), which appealed to a certain party to smuggle in a gun for his use in a planned escape. Underhill was again sentenced to the hole for an undetermined period. This time poor Wilbur had the added pleasure of being taken out each day for a period of several hours to the rock pile where he was issued a sledgehammer and instructed to reduce a stack of large boulders into smaller ones. News reports claim at the end of ninety days Warden Prather journeyed to the dungeons informing Underhill he would be released back to "population" if he gave his word to behave, the prisoner responded by spitting in his face.

After nearly a year of being housed and treated like a chained beast, the Warden reluctantly reassigned him to "C" block where he rejoined his mates and was granted a few simple privileges such as being allowed to write a single page (back and front) letter to his folks each Wednesday and Sunday as well as receiving correspondence from those on his approved list. Twenty-seven of these letters were recently made public after somehow surviving the past seventy-odd years reposing in a cardboard box in the attics and basements of several of Wilbur's descendants. Through these communications, we are able to have a rare insight into his life in prison through some of 1932 and much of 1933. From these letters one sees a man who is witty, domineering, moody, and temperamental yet not nearly as dimwitted as writers have portrayed him in the past.

Back in population, it appears Underhill temporarily gave up any idea of escape, instead turning his attention to gaining some financial assistance for his mother and sister, Dorothy, who were currently living in extreme poverty back in Kansas City, Missouri. It didn't take him long to come up with a scheme. He wrote in a letter dated November 20, 1932, "Dorothy you can make some money writing of my career in crime...contact *True Crime* and *Liberty* magazines... Get two or three old detective magazines and look through them to get an idea how to write mine.... make it sound worse than it was or the magazine may not take it...were only writing this to get out of it what we can...write about my escapes from Okmulgee and McAlester where I jumped off the bridge and stripped off my convict clothes and had civilian clothes on underneath and calmly walked across the prairie in plain view of six guards. I outran the dogs and they lost my scent in the business part of town then continued on foot across the mountains to Wister Junction, tell how the guards rode horses passing only a few feet from where I lay hidden, make it strong where I beat the bloodhounds, my hardships, no water or food for days. Leave things out of what happened in Picher, Oklahoma as I don't know anything about that, it might be incriminating." (Dorothy did eventually have several articles published in *Liberty* magazine)

The following week, a group of twenty University of Kansas School of Journalism students were allowed to visit Wilbur in his cell...He wrote, "I heard I made a good impression on them, they admitted they thought I was a cold-blooded killer, but when I told them I hadn't done anything worse than push little ducks in a pond, they changed their opinion...goes to show you that if my accusers actually knew me they would not write me up so bad."

On Christmas, the cons were given access to holiday parcels from home as well as a gift from the state of Kansas, which included one orange, an apple, and a bag of nuts along with a chicken dinner. Wilbur received packages from his sisters and mother (homemade biscuits and fudge) along with a present from a California girl named Alta he had been corresponding with. He also picked up a dose of the flu, (There was reportedly a serious outbreak of influenza occurring inside the walls at the time) which landed him in the prison infirmary for several days of which he wrote, "I think I got pneumonia as well. I lost several pounds but I'll gain it back in a few days as I am eating hospital food. The meals are specially cooked and there is most everything on the table."

After his release from the hospital, he received a visit from his nephew Hugh Baine (visitation was every day from 8:30 to 3:30 pm except on Sunday when visits were restricted to one hour, each individual visitor was only allowed to visit once every thirty days) of which he wrote, "I like Hugh but Frank is a pure turkey. (Wilbur and Frank had had a falling out) Hugh's a good kid…he's awful young to be so nervous…he ought to take some tonic or get a girl…maybe he's a misogynist (A woman hater)…gee, ain't I bright using such a word? Tell him not to go on the bum (hopping freights or hitchhiking across country looking for work). Things are bad everywhere. At least at home he can eat. I've lived like that and look where I'm at." He closed his correspondence with, "Dorothy, hope to see you and ma on the 16th. Thirty days is a long time to have to wait…I sure suffered at Mac when I couldn't see ya. If I don't get a letter from you or mom at least once a week I get uneasy and restless…When I see you I feel like a horse in a new pasture until you leave then I feel like crawling off and dying…Sometimes I dream about being at home, there ain't a day goes by I ain't building 'Air Castles' about home. I can hardly think of you without bursting into tears."

On January 22, 1933 he wrote Dorothy, "Well I'm glad you got the ten bucks I sent…mom put a dollar in my account which I blew on peanuts and smokes…I'm a peanut hound, they say all monkeys are…please go buy that 'Pretty' you were looking at…The Warden loaned me the ten bucks against my one dollar a month earnings."

The following week he ranted and raved about the movies he had recently seen, "We saw a good picture here called *Emma*. Marie Dresher (Dressler) was the leading character and believe me she was good (his favorite actress was Alice White, a twenties flapper starlet)…she played in *Passionate Plumber* here a week ago with Buster Keaton and they were a knock out…" (Wilbur loved the movies as a distraction to prison life) In a later correspondence he stated, "Sure had a good movie yesterday called *The Wet Parade,* there was a lot of timber sheiks in it… *Ben Hur* will be the name of the show next week. That's an old picture isn't it?" In another note he wrote, "They had a good show here, *Tarzan The Ape Man* …I liked it… I would like to see that show, *The Employees Entrance* it's about stenographers and sales girls selling kisses to hold their jobs." He also spent a great deal of his spare time listening to the radio (each cell block was equipped with a radio). He wrote Dorothy, "That Jones Store Revue sure has a good program. I listen to the radio all the time…I am usually done with my work by nine and fly to the radio. I'm like the old woman living next door, I don't want to miss a thing." In the same letter, he commented on his mother's recent spill on the ice where she had broken her arm… "I sure hated to hear you were hurt. The Underhills sure have their share of bad luck…I almost fell on the ice the other day. Boy, I sure cut some capers trying to stay on my feet. If I hadn't been foot heavy I would of busted something." He then changed the subject commenting on a lady he was writing in Joplin. "She threw a fit when I told her she was pretty. Said no one had told her that before…She is cute isn't she…I think she tried to flatter me for she said every nice thing about me…about my eyes, mouth, personality, build, etc…I do believe if I hadn't got in so much trouble she and I could of done things in a big way." Around this time, Wilbur was stricken with an infected eardrum, which would torture him the rest of his life to the point he had to wear a bandage over it during bouts of cold weather.

Responding to his mother's accident, he decided to take up a collection from his fellow cons in order to pay the doctor's bills. Strangely, when he asked Warden Prather for his permission, the Warden answered in the affirmative. He joyously wrote his mom saying, "I sent you $104.50, that should keep you a while." He relates to his sister an account of a dream he had the previous night saying, "You were calling me so loud and I tried to answer but just couldn't. Then I woke up and looked at the bars and knew it was a dream."

In a letter written the next week, Dorothy asked her brother about Warden Prather, Wilbur responded, "Mr. Prather is a very kind and considerate man, he grants me nearly all my wishes…like always, those who know me don't hate me." He then breaks into a long narrative musing about hatred and persecution writing, "I've had hatred in my heart and it makes one

Wilbur's favorite starlet, Alice White. Author's private collection

gloomy and disagreeable…I've been done dirty so much that some of my actions was forced on me…I'd gladly be a good a citizen as any man if I were set free…I know I could make good if set free." Changing the subject, he comments he is again ill and swigging cough syrup, saying, "What I really need is a big plate of fried potatoes, eggs and bacon, that would do more good than this swill." Adding, "Have you heard from Ernest lately? He could come home if he behaved himself." (Ernest had been busted for using "dope" in his cell in the Missouri State Penitentiary only days before he was scheduled to appear before the parole board) On another subject, he wrote to his mother, "Hugh has a detective magazine which tells of the methods white slavers use to snare their prey. Have Dorothy read the article."

In a note written in mid-March, he orders his sister to "Take some of that money and buy yourself some new clothes, a full layout, skirt, hat, hose, and 'pink things' (Wilbur was obsessed with woman's pink undergarments) .He also commented on his supposed wife Ethel, saying, "Ethel is a pretty good gal…she's a cute 'trick,' but if she really loved me she would come see me. Anyone can talk love…when prison bars separate lovers it often separates their love." When discussing Frank he comments, "Forget Frank like he forgot us. You do what old Wilb says honey, keep him away from the house."

Meanwhile, back in the free world, the depression deepened, another ten million workers joined the ranks of the unemployed. Newly elected President Franklin Roosevelt declared a bank holiday in order to stop the ongoing financial panic, assuring Americans "The only thing we have to fear is fear itself." In order to protect depositor's funds and ease investor's fears his administration created the Federal Deposit Insurance Corporation. When banks reopened a week later, he encouraged anxious citizens to trust financial institutions claiming "It is safer to keep your money in a bank then under your mattress." Addressing the nation in a series of live radio "Fireside chats" he proclaimed a "New Deal" for the country's unemployed creating the Works Projects Administration, Civilian Conservation Corps, and Agricultural Adjustment Act in order to provide jobs and ease economic suffering. Just a scant hundred miles west of the Kansas prison, huge mile high dust storms dubbed "Black Blizzards" would soon make their appearance battering the drought strickened plains.

In sports, Primo Carnera (The Italian Alp) knocked out Jack Sharkey for the heavyweight crown, Babe Ruth hit a home run in the first ever major league baseball All-Star game played at Chicago's Cominskey Park and the New York Giants won the World Series. The Worlds Fair opens in Chicago and *King Kong* is the box office smash of the year. On radio, humorist Will Rogers keeps folks laughing despite the hard times while "Jack Armstrong: All American Boy," "The Jack Benny Show" and "The Shadow" are the year's big "hits" hitting the airwaves and in May a little known crook named John Herbert Dillinger is paroled from the Indiana State Prison where he has served nine years for attempted robbery.

Living in the shadows of the cold rock walls of the Kansas State Penitentiary, Wilbur Underhill who had spent only a scant few months of his adult life in the free world, turned his thoughts to one of the few activities of normal society he had knowledge of, romance. Upon receiving a letter from a girlfriend he writes to Dorothy, "My pen is getting clogged…it's either clogged or my hearts aflutter from the letter Alta sent me…imagine a big yokel like me with a heart a flutter…She began her letter calling me her dearest heart smasher, leaving the impression she has several of them…she says she likes me best cause I'm a bad man. Now ain't that pitiful? She writes like she's been up the Van Dugan River too many times…Here I am telling you what Alta said and it doesn't interest you at all." He adds, "I was thinking about Lucille (His previous spouse from Heavener, Oklahoma) we would have been married 6 years on March 14. I sure loved her…I guess she never thinks of me…I can't hate her for quitting me…I guess she figured I would never be out and she was too young to go through the years alone… did you ever hear from Sarah (Sarah Riddle) If you have her address I'd like to have it. I heard she was living around Seminole, Oklahoma…I suppose you thought I like fat girls when you saw Sarah and Ethel, but I don't care for fat girls, I like tall and slender ones…Lucille wasn't fat" Later in this correspondence he discusses the changing weather and his beloved jigsaw puzzles, writing, "I'm glad spring is here…I like to hear the birds sing…the only birds I usually hear is these jailbirds and all they sing is the blues…I see where some doctor has found a new disease which he named the 'jig saw itch' …claims it's caused by the dye on the puzzles…I've heard of lots of itches but the 'jig saw itch' takes the berries. I sure love to work em though, they make time fly…keeps one from getting the blues which are terrible on ones nerves…I worked one yesterday called 'Pickets Charge at Gettysburg' in 7 hours and 20 minutes…this guy I'm celling with ain't too hot on working 'em. He tries to make all the pieces fit where they don't belong…We were working a puzzle the other night and he was trying to put a piece depicting a mans head on a horses backside…He sure gets hot when I laugh at him. P. S. Thanks for the candy bars as I ate them as soon as I got them. That is a queer name for them…maybe they were made especially for me."

(He was referring to the candy bar named O'Henry. Underhill's given name was Henry.)"

In late March, Wilbur writes his sister on the subject of food, as is a common obsession for underfed convicts, "Hugh left me a dollar yesterday. I was like a country boy come to town...I blowed it on candy, two cans of chili, and a bottle of pepper sauce and ketchup...It's a rare occasion when I have a whole buck to spend...I get real hungry for your lemon pie and biscuits...the more I think of the outside the better I do...if one lets his mind stay in here he becomes dull and ignorant and will gradually get to looking like most of these characters in here... In all my life, I have never seen as many half-wits... I'm not trying to run the joint down but facts are facts."

By April, he turned his efforts to making a stab at gaining his freedom through legitimate parole or clemency. Wilbur had written a letter to the Warden requesting an opportunity to go before the Parole Board. He received his answer in short order. "The Warden informed me the board would not call me out...that I could take it up with the new administrator (Prather was being replaced as Warden due to the outcome of the statewide elections where the Republican Al Landon had been swept into office.)...I am anxious to see what Miss Weeks (A church representative currently attempting to arrange a clemency hearing for Underhill) has to say...I'll wait and see what her plan is before I put any faith in it...She may be sincere but she hasn't reckoned with my reputation, perhaps she isn't aware of it...police departments in Kansas and Oklahoma are against me strong and will do everything in their power to keep me in...Old Wilb will never stand much of a chance at clemency...there's too many fighting me...There's not a citizen on the outside that would be more trustworthy than me....I don't see why I shouldn't be given a chance, but I will behave and do my best to remain a gentleman, a man can be a man regardless where he is" adding, "Didn't I try to get out of Mac on the square?...wasn't I there on a bum rap? Have Miss Weeks write the County Attorney in Miami, Oklahoma and ask him to dismiss that murder rap against me...if he will dismiss that charge I'll have something to have confidence in." He ended his letter saying, "Mom I'll do as you say, but I'll not try praying, for when I start that I'll become a Christian."

He wrote back a week later saying, "Well Deanie, I tried praying...Don't know if I got results or not but felt better the next morning...Thanks for your confidence...I've never had a true friend or anyone to take an interest in me...The ones I thought were my pals have all double-crossed me and never kept their word...I've been the fall-guy in all my dealings." As for his spin on religion, Underhill noted, "I do think there is a supreme power but I'm not versed enough to understand the bible. I've been protected throughout my life by something...take for instance when I was in McAlester, I was in solitaire 3 years 7 months and half the time I was hung up by my hands and at night I was in leg irons and handcuffs. No man there was ever hung up 45 days ...I stood it for six months. I begged to be let down but all I got was abuse and a thump on the head...what I went through has caused me to look at life the way I do...since the last of 1921 I have spent ten years in prison 7 and a half years in sol...I've suffered plenty...I'll make one more attempt to get my freedom on the square...If I fail I'll never try again." He continued his correspondence, "Just got back from the yard. We get the yard an hour and a half after supper and it's well worth the money. We came in a little early tonight cause it started raining...This time last year, I was in the blind cell nothing to do but listen to that little robin sing... they had them trace chains hooked up a little short on me...Dean (Dorothy), I believe your letters to the Warden helped me get out of that hole." He continued his ramblings writing, "Well, I'm freezing to death, I walked so much I'm hungry again...A T-bone steak and fried spuds wouldn't last long in front of me." He ended the note writing, "Yes I read about them finding that dead girl. (The body of a sixteen year old female had recently been found raped, murdered, and dumped in a ditch near KC) I think that is one of the most heinous crimes there is, I think it's awful to mistreat woman like that...that's one crime which deserves the death penalty...I may be considered a bad guy but rest assured old Wilb would never commit a crime like that"...changing the subject he writes, "I tried to raise some money for you but failed. My ear is aching again, I suffer so much there's got to be something done with it, if it stays like this cancer might set in."

In early May, he brings up the subject of clemency with his sister stating, "Have you seen Miss Weeks (Social worker) ...Looks like someone put the skids on her. I was confident she was taking on too much of a task. I've seen a lot of cases of these church people trying to do something for convicts and do nothing but build up false hopes...I read once that 'Hope is the dream of a man awake.'... I'm making a metal marker for George's grave...We sure had a good visit but when you leave I feel like crawling off and dying...I sure feel blue afterwards...tune in to 'Police Court' on WHB next Tuesday, they are going to be talking about a convict from Wichita with a life sentence, a cold-blooded killer who should never be granted clemency. I have no guilty conscience but I don't have to be slapped to know they are talking about me...He's probably a friend of Colver...such talk is an injustice to me."

One wonders how a man convicted of two murders and wanted for a third could ever hope to be granted a clemency hearing in the first place.

Somewhere around this time, Wilbur evidently lost faith in his plan to be released though legal channels and began considering another escape attempt. Realizing he would need help in the venture Underhill approached a lifer named "Big Bob" Brady inquiring if he was interested. Brady, who worked in the prison's kitchen, in turn recruited a trio of Oklahoma bank robbers, Jim Clark, Ed Davis, and Frank Sawyer into the scheme. Recognizing the fact they needed someone to finance the venture (pay for guns etc.) the group turned to the only inmate they knew who had access to ready cash on the outside, the incomparable Harvey Bailey. When contacted, Bailey readily agreed to join the group and provide the necessary operating funds.

All six of the men involved in the plot were hard-core habitual criminals. Five of the six plotters were listed as escapees from the Oklahoma State pen in McAlester. Oklahoma native Bob Brady, a quarter-blood Choctaw Indian, was first incarcerated at the age of fifteen on a charge of Grand larceny. He spent most of the 1920s in the Oklahoma prison on charges of robbery and forgery. Shortly after his release from "Big Mac," he was convicted of robbing the Bank of Texhoma, Oklahoma and sentenced to thirty-five years. He broke jail in 1932 and went on a crime spree, which included the robberies of the banks of Ada, Oklahoma (his hometown) and El Dorado Springs, Missouri. In October, he and a partner stole a car in Kansas and kidnapped the owner, finally releasing him in Texas. Later that year he was arrested in Des Moines, Iowa and extradited to Kansas where he was convicted of Auto Theft-Kidnapping and sentenced to life in prison as a habitual criminal.

Jim Clark (alias Jack Martin), who was assigned to the prison's mule barn, hailed from Muskogee County,

Oklahoma, where he was raised on a hardscrabble cotton farm located near the small community of Oktaha. He did a jolt in Oklahoma's Granite Reformatory before serving two terms in OSP, the first in 1928 for attempted robbery out of Hughes County and the second in early 1932 for cattle rustling out of Muskogee County. On May 25, 1932, Clark escaped from Road Camp #1 and soon joined up with Ed Davis and Frank Sawyer. In June 17, 1932, the trio was arrested near Nevada, Missouri and all three were convicted of the recent Fort Scott, Kansas bank robbery (A crime they did not commit). Clark, along with Davis, who had previously served two terms in "Mac" for armed robbery and the murder of a Marlow, Oklahoma policeman, were both given life sentences for their alleged parts in the Fort Scott job. Sawyer, who was listed by authorities as a murderer and escape artist who had busted out of "Mac" in 1930, was sentenced to 20 to 100 years. Harvey Bailey was an ex- bootlegger turned bank heist expert. He was suspected of being the brains behind some of the nation's largest bank robberies in the 1920s. A veritable superstar of the underworld, Bailey sported a reputation of being as slick as "Georgia clay in a rainstorm." He was currently doing a ten to fifty year jolt for armed robbery.

According to most sources, the plotters had either three or four automatic pistols smuggled into the prison inside a bale of hemp bound for the twine plant. On the afternoon of May 21, the conspirators consolidated their escape plans in a conference held in the prison yard. The plan was a simple one. The escapees hoped to kidnap the departing warden and several guards at an upcoming baseball game, which was to be held on Memorial Day inside the walls of the institution and use them as bargaining chips in order to gain their freedom. After nabbing Prather, they hoped to make use of a ladder Brady had commandeered from the kitchen to gain access to Guard tower # 3. Evidently, the plan was rather vague in specifics instead relying heavily on the assumption none of the guards would start shooting as long as the plotters held close to their hostages.

After returning from his next to last meeting with his co-conspirators in the yard, Wilbur wrote his sister saying, "Your most welcome letter received yesterday, but sorry you are feeling so blue. Cheer up pardner…Ain't that silly to say cheer up when there's nothing to cheer up for? They say sorrow is at its climax when joy is just ahead. Sounds like a lot of hooey…sorry mom's arm is hurting…I could ring that doctor's neck that didn't set it right. Dr. Hassig examined my ear and left instructions to use boric acid and alcohol and irrigate twice a day, but they been doing that for six months. The doc doesn't know his business or he could cure my ear…I've never met a doctor, lawyer or preacher that was any good. Well, I'll dummy up about it,

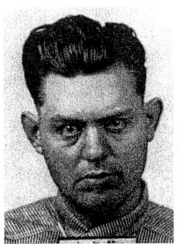

Bob Brady. Courtesy Kansas City Star

Ed Davis. Courtesy Kansas City Star

I don't care if it rots off…I tell you I detest everyone. I've seen so much crookedness I've lost faith in human nature. Outside of you and Mom, I don't care for anyone. I wish we three could go off some place and live and never go around anyone…" Next he puts on his Dear Abby hat, writing "Deanie, Always be your own boss, don't let anyone make a sap out of ya. You know what I mean don't ya? Don't listen to no soft line of jibe. Anyone who is sincere won't soft line you. You will find 99% of men don't amount to nothing. All they want to do is make a sap out of some young girl. I'm talking from experience and the things I've seen…Well, cheer up and write me some of those good letters. I think you are the prettiest little girl in the world."

In order to allow the reader full access to Wilbur's

Left: Jim Clark. Courtesy Lester Clark
Above: Harvey Bailey. Courtesy Kansas City Starr

mindset on his next to last day in prison his final letter is printed in full.

Lansing, Kansas
May 28th, 1933
Sunday eve
Dearest Mother and Dorothy,

      I got your letter of the 23rd. Also, the checkerboard puzzle but I can't work it. I had a puzzle like it with 12 pieces in it and worked it, but this one has 14 pieces it's a real puzzle. I rather expected a letter from you tonight, hope neither of you are sick. This leaves me feeling pretty good, physically I mean. My ear hasn't bothered me much the last couple of days. Mom, the reason I didn't write last Wed. is I answered one of the letters that I got some time ago. I never have answered Lida or Alta's letter. I guess Lida thinks I'm mad at her. Tell her I'm not mad. I love her. I think she a great woman. Well Dorothy, you spoke of Lyra going to try and get you

Frank Sawyer. Courtesy Kansas Department of Corrections

writing for some newspaper. I think that's a brilliant idea, you would make a good writer. You can express things so plain. If she really wants to help you, she could introduce you to the radio. Her name would put you over. If you could persuade Frank to go with you, both of you would be making money. He could make more in one week then he could in a year at what he is working at. He is supposed to be halfway smart and I can't see why he can't realize the opportunity he's missing. You're a good talker, try to get him up to your house and wake him up to the fact that you're both missing good money, that its necessary to help you, as it means as much to him as it does to you. He has a family to support and that he has a chance to take care of them in a big way. Well, do your best any way Deania. Well its time to go to the yard will finish when I come in...(Note: In this last meeting in the yard the plotters finalized their escape plans) Well I had my play now, so will try to finish my letter. This evening was pretty and I enjoyed taking a stroll. I looked for Frank to be over this am. Wouldn't his wife let him away? I bet he is hen pecked until he has as much backbone as a jellyfish. Miss Weeks was over today at the services but I didn't go. Neither did she trouble herself about calling me out. She certainly took out on us all of a sudden didn't she? Wonder if politics had anything to do with it. Well Mom I can't hardly think of a thing to say. My mind is so confused and when one is in that state of mind, they can't think of anything to say. But I do want you and Dorothy to know that I love you more than anything else in the world, I'd give anything just to be a free man to prove that I could and would be a good man. As much trouble as you two have been thru and stayed with me, I'd like to be given a chance to repay you, by being a good man. I guess it's useless to talk about such things, never the less it's sweet to think about. I let my mind dwell on the past when we was all together (happy and poor) but at the time I didn't realize what a man's freedom meant to him nor the misery it caused his people. I stumble into this life through ignorance and didn't wake up until I'd got too far in, then when I realized what it meant to us all, no one would help me or give me another chance. Life is that way though, no one cares about another's troubles. That is the lawmakers don't care. Dorothy, just this A.M. I was thinking back 11 years ago down on West 24th St, how you and George used to quarrel and you'd run behind me for protection. Ha. Those kinds of quarrels happen in every family. I like to think back to the times like that for I can never think ahead and see times like that. Remember how we all used to laugh at that picture where our whole family's picture was taken on the front porch at Neosho and at that picture where you and George and I was taken down on 20th and Sergeant. Well I'd better stop talking about it before I get the blues. I'll be hoping for a good letter from you and Mom tomorrow. Remember I love you both more than anything. With lots and lots and lots of love and kisses…Good Bye.

Wilbur Underhill #2337 Box #2"

Thirty-six hours after this correspondence was written Underhill and his conspirators made their move. All his previous letters had concluded with "Until next time," this final one signed off with a telling, "Good Bye."

Chapter Ten

The Great Escape

On the morning of May 30, 1933 the six plotters, armed with handguns, straight razors, and homemade shivs gathered near the backstop of the prison's baseball diamond just as the game between the American Legion Junior League teams from Topeka and Leavenworth began. The group became anxious as the game progressed and the warden failed to appear. Finally, in the fifth inning with the contest tied 2-2 Prather was spotted circulating in the crowd exchanging pleasantries with guards and inmates alike. On reaching the backstop, the player at bat smacked a home run igniting the cheers of 1800 convicts. With the crowd in an uproar, the plotters made their move, Jim Clark pounced on the unsuspecting warden wrapping a copper wire garrote around his neck tightening it to the point of cutting off his breath while Harvey Bailey shoved the barrel of an automatic pistol hard against Prather's spine telling him to "Do as we say or you're a dead man!" Suddenly, Underhill took hold of the wire encircling the Warden's reddening neck, ordering Clark to "Let me have that noose." Meanwhile, their fellow conspirators followed suit getting the drop on several guards. All was going well until Brady noticed the ladder he had hoped to use to scale the wall had been moved. Underhill, unperturbed by the distraction, ordered the hostages toward tower #3 which was manned by a rookie guard. On reaching their objective, Wilbur informed the Warden, "Here's our plan, tell that hack to chuck down his guns and the key to the tower or we'll kill you and all the guards in sight." When Prather hesitated, Underhill instructed Bailey to shoot one of the hostages. Knowing full well Wilbur meant business, Prather promptly ordered the tower guard to throw down the keys and guns. Then, according to several witnesses, Wilbur jabbed a gun barrel deep into the Prather's ribs ordering him to, "Dance a little jig for the boys, Warden," to which the head keeper tapped his toes a time or two and shuffled his feet in a half-hearted effort to appease the big thug while a gathering group of curious cons loudly chortled at the bizarre display. In the meantime a group of five other cons, Kenneth Conn, Lewis Bechtel, Billy Woods, Clifford Dopson, and Alva Payton, who had allegedly been involved with Wilbur in the aborted 1931 breakout, approached Underhill inquiring if they could join the festivities. Wilbur smiled while nodding okay.

Aerial view of prison showing baseball diamond in right foreground. Courtesy Kansas City Star

Upon gaining access to the tower through a small door located at the base of the structure the convicts and hostages sprinted to the top just as the prison's ear splitting siren blasted off. Taking hold of a rope used to haul coal for heating from the outside up to the tower, the crowd of cons and victims began sliding down one at a time toward freedom. Once outside the walls the two groups of prisoners split up, Underhill's bunch which was made up of the six convicts as well as three hostages including Warden Prather and guards L. A. "John" Laws and John Sherman, approached a small garage located adjacent to the prison where the automobile of Prison Farm Superintendent W. W. Woodson was parked. Just as the group arrived at the garage, an overzealous guard took a potshot with a thirty-caliber rifle, the round striking Harvey Bailey just above the knee of his right leg, splintering the bone. His comrades returned fire-wounding guard John Stewart before dragging Bailey into the vehicle, his leg bleeding like a stuck hog. With Clark taking the wheel, the five other convicts piled into the Dodge. Prather was stuffed on to the floorboard of the back seat while guards, Law and Sherman,

Number 3 guard tower-1933. Courtesy Kansas City Star

were forced to stand on the car's running boards with gleaming straight razors pressed hard on their exposed wrists. Underhill, still grasping the wire twisted around the Warden's neck while simultaneously pressing the business end of a pistol into his gut, shouted, "You show us how to get out of here and stay out of the mud," to which Prather nodded saying, "I'll get you to a good road. " Just then, Underhill somehow got his gun tangled up in his shirt and it went off shattering the car's back glass. Bailey turned and shrieked, "G-d damn it! Be careful you silly son of a bitch"

After driving several miles south of the prison on a gravel road in the direction of the community of Wallula, they came upon the slab (concrete) highway. Just as the vehicle hit the road, the Dodge sputtered running out of gas. Moments later a 1932 model Chevrolet driven by Ralph Pettijohn came tooling down the highway. When Pettijohn unwittingly slowed to inquire if he could be of assistance, he and his wife, her sister, and niece were jerked out of the rig and forced to stand on the side of the road while the carload of fugitives and captives changed vehicles. Accord-

Modern day view of Tower #3. Photo by Naomi Morgan

ing to Warden Prather, after the group switched cars they took to the dirt roads with Ed Davis now at the wheel. "I didn't talk for the first hundred miles fearing I would set them off. After crossing the Kansas River near Linwood, they drove to nearby Eudora where they stopped for gas. Underhill paid for the fuel with a twenty dollar bill he had somehow managed to squirrel away." Shortly after the pit stop, the fugitives ran headlong into a roadblock manned by three Douglas County lawmen led by Deputy Sheriff Fred Vogler. Davis pulled over and the convicts took up battle stations while making it clear they would kill their captives if attacked. After engaging in a short-lived stand-off, Vogler, fearing for the lives of the hostages, ordered the posse to "Hold your fire and let them pass."

For the next few hours, the fleeing vehicle kept to the dirt roads skirting the towns of Garnett, Iola, and Erie following a zigzag route toward Oklahoma. Roughly fifteen miles north of Parsons, Kansas the Chevrolet started to overheat. Spotting a car driven by a local dairy farmer named Ed Clum, which had been following them for sev-

Car taken from W. W. Woodson during breakout. Courtesy Kansas City Star

eral miles, Davis wheeled around and blocked the road. Sawyer and Brady jumped out and commandeered the vehicle, which contained Clum and his wife along with a nine-year-old boy. After piling into the captive automobile, the two-car caravan puttered along in a southerly direction until they reached a point just east of Parsons where the Clum car ran out of gas. Abandoning the vehicle, Sawyer and Davis jumped back into the Chevy instructing Clum to, "Not squawk and everything will be pretty," before leaving him and his party stranded in the middle of the road. According to Prather, the fugitives cheered up considerably when Sawyer produced a bottle of whiskey and a pack of Chesterfields he had stolen out of the glove box of the Clum car.

Meanwhile, the law enforcement community responded to the break by fielding several hundred lawmen

Mr. and Mrs. Ralph Pettijohn and niece. Inset, Milan Wood, whose car was later stolen by the second group of escapees. Courtesy Kansas City Star

and vigilantes throughout Kansas, Missouri, and Oklahoma manning roadblocks, crossroads, and bridges. Caravans of heavily armed officers began cruising the area's principle

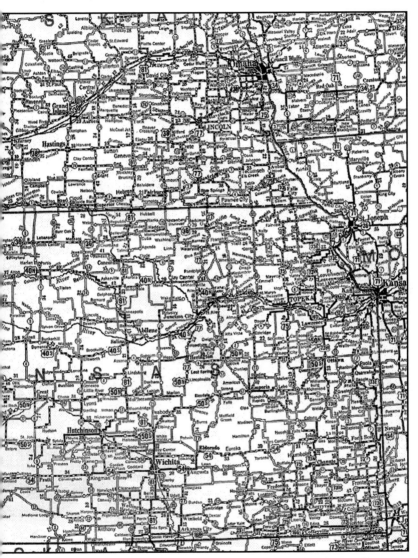

Road map of Kansas, circa 1930. Courtesy National Map Co.

highways in search of the fugitives. An all points bulletin was issued to police and sheriff's departments throughout the United States. The escapees were described as armed and dangerous. Officers were warned to shoot first and ask questions later upon encountering the villains.

After traveling another twenty-five miles in a southerly direction, the escapees stopped for gas in the small town of Edna located near the Oklahoma border. At roughly 7:45 pm, the Chevy suffered a flat tire just north of the community of Welch, Oklahoma. Davis pulled the rig off the road and the passengers all baled out sitting in the grass while the tire was being changed. At that point, Prather

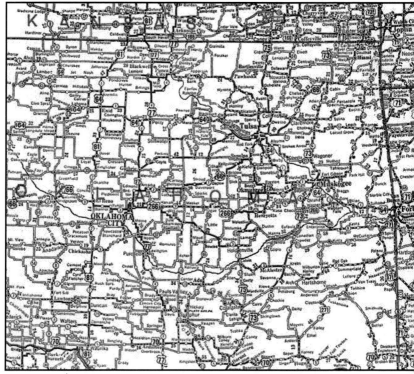

Road Map of Oklahoma circa 1930. Courtesy National Map Co.

claimed Underhill turned to him and remarked, "I don't know what to do with you guys, bump you off or what." The Warden later said he felt the hairs on the back of his neck standing at full attention at that moment.

Back on the road, Davis drove a few miles in a southerly direction before stopping at a point just north of the tiny crossroads prairie settlement of Pyramid Corners. Underhill ordered the hostages out of the car and into the enveloping darkness saying, "Here's where we bump you off." After a moment of intense silence, the escapees broke out laughing. Prather, unsure if Wilbur was truly making a joke or was serious in his threat to kill them attempted to break the tension by asking Underhill if he had heard from his family lately. The big convict sighed then retorted he hadn't for a while. After another moment or two of dead silence, Wilbur, staring intently at the Warden said, "Well, you have been a pretty good warden, best I've ever met. You've handled the prison pretty good." Adding, "Got any dough?" Prather replied, " Sixty cents." Wilbur dug into his pocket and pulled out a dollar bill saying, "Take this, you may need something to eat or smoke, if you can find a town." Prather replied he was "Hungry enough to eat a fencepost" to which Underhill chuckled and handed the Warden a cigarette before placing his right hand on his shoulder while pointing north with his left, saying, "Walk that way and you will find a town." With that said, the convicts climbed back into the car and sped into the night. Prather and the his companions trudged the three or four miles back to the crossroads settlement of Pyramid Corners where a passing traveling salesman gave them a lift into Welch. Once the Warden explained their predicament to the town marshal, Prather phoned his wife who was sitting on pins and needles back in Kansas. After eating a good meal provided by the town's citizens an individual named Earl Barrett from Morris, Oklahoma who happened to be driving through the area bound for Kansas City was hired to drive the hostages back to Lansing. On their arrival at the prison, the trio was welcomed with a tearful homecoming from their spouses and fellow workers.

In an interview given moments after their arrival back in Lansing, the Warden's wife informed newsmen she had felt positive about her husband's safe return due to her receiving a note from an inmate just moments after the

Warden Prather being greeted by his wife on his safe return. Courtesy Kansas City Star

breakout. The message, which she firmly believed originated from Wilbur Underhill, promised her husband would not be killed. "For that I thank him."

Warden Prather noted, "Although Wilbur was a dangerous dope addict who was unpredictable when on the stuff, he spared us due to my treating him and his family generously over the years." A red-faced John Laws contradicted the warden in his statement saying, "Underhill is yellow and wanted to shoot to kill. He sat next to the warden with a cocked pistol the whole trip. Davis, Brady, Clark, Sawyer, and Bailey were cool and collected. I give them credit for saving our lives. Underhill wanted to kill us just to get rid of us." John Sherman made no statement due to his being confined in the hospital for a knife wound he had suffered during the initial breakout. He was listed in good condition. News reports suggested both guards were ex-

Warden Kirk Prather along with guards L. A. Laws (far left) and John Sherman (far right) on their return from their harrowing ride. Courtesy Kansas City Star

periencing severe finger and leg strain due to their being forced to cling to the fleeing Chevy's sides while standing at attention on the vehicle's sideboards for over nine painful hours. When reporters inquired a second time why the mutineers didn't kill them, Prather responded, "I believe they would have if not for finding a bottle of whiskey. The more they drank the jollier they got." When asked the same question later that day, John Laws again gave a vastly different version of events saying, " When Underhill started drinking that liquor he got meaner with every swill, so in desperation I asked him to give me a shot and I drained the bottle thus saving our lives."

The Memorial Day jailbreak would set a record as the second worst in Kansas prison history, the most prolific taking place in 1923 when thirteen inmates tunneled under the wall of the powerhouse to freedom. News of the breakout would make the front page of every major newspaper in America. Within days of the mass escape, Kansas Governor Alf Landon signed an executive order deducting six months off the sentences of every man in the prison who had not joined the escape, saying, "Practically every prisoner in the place was in position

Newly appointed Warden Lacy Simpson. Courtesy Kansas City Star

to join the rioters but only five did. I believe good behavior must be rewarded." He also announced rewards totaling $350 for the apprehension of each of the escapees (Dead or Alive). In the wake of the breakout, newly appointed Warden Lacy Simpson issued orders to all guards instructing them to "Never under any circumstances give up your weapons to an inmate," adding, "Those who disobey this directive will be summarily dismissed from prison employment." He further ordered tear-gas bombs installed in each guard tower and reduced the scheduled work hours of the tower guards from twelve to eight hours per shift. Oddly, the rope and pulley system located in the watchtowers, which were used by the escapees to gain their freedom, were left in place and are still in use today. Needless to say, the annual Memorial Day baseball game at the prison was suspended indefinitely.

Warden Kirk Prather's administration ended with the escape attempt. Although he previously had hopes of being appointed the head warden of Leavenworth Federal Prison his dreams were dashed due to the bad publicity generated by the escape. The following year he ran unsuccessfully for Governor of Kansas as a Democrat against Republican Al Landon. In the latter 1930s, Prather would gain re-appointment as the warden of the Kansas pen. He served in that capacity for several years before retiring from public life. His life would be cut short when he dropped dead of a massive heart attack at age 56 in 1939.

****

As for the second group of escapees who had muscled in on the breakout at Underhill's invitation, they had since hijacked a blue model 77 Willys automobile belonging to a railroad inspector named Milan Wood. The fugitives took his wife, seventeen-year-old daughter, Louise and her teenage friend hostage while leaving poor Mr. Wood stranded on the roadside watching his family disappear into an uncertain future.

Over the next twenty-four hours, the press had a field day speculating what five hardened convicts were planning for a pair of innocent teenage girls. Thankfully, nothing occurred along those lines although one of the convicts did ask Louise Woods if she cared to sit on his lap, to which she replied, "You can shoot me, but I won't sit on your lap." According to Mrs. Woods, who was a semi-invalid, when she expressed a concern for the safety of her two teenage companions, one of the convicts turned to her stating, "We won't hurt you if you don't scream. Be thankful the other party of cons didn't nab ya, they're a bunch of real hard babies."

After driving some eighty miles south of the prison,

The two seventeen-year-old girls held by the mutineers, Cloris Wears and Louisa Woods, joined by an Aunt. Courtesy Kansas City Star

the convicts perpetrated a home invasion on a farm family named New just outside Pleasanton, Kansas. The fugitives spent the next few hours at the New farmhouse napping and tanking up on bacon and eggs before abandoning the hostages, driving away at approximately 10 pm in their stolen Willys automobile. Before departing, the convicts cut the phone line and stole Mr. New's car keys as well as a wooden chest full of tools and a double barrel shotgun.

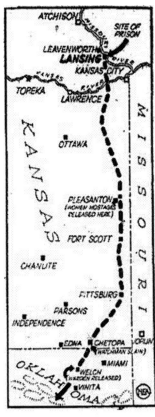

Map showing route taken by the second group of escapees. Courtesy Muskogee Phoenix

Soon after repairing the severed phone line with baling wire, the captives contacted the authorities and were driven back to Lansing by a local law enforcement officer. On their arrival back home on the afternoon of May 31, Mrs. Wood publicly thanked the convicts for treating her and her young charges in a "Kind and polite manner."

At roughly the same time as the second group of fugitives were driving away from the New family farm, Craig County Sheriff John York was assembling a large posse for a raid on an abandoned shack near Picher, Oklahoma which had once been used as a hideout by Underhill in the late 1920s. An hour after the raid's conclusion, which was a bust, lawmen were advised of a possibly related homicide which had taken place in the community of Chetopa, Kansas located roughly a dozen miles west of the scene of the raid.

According to police reports, truck driver John Rentz was delivering a load of strawberries to a local produce company located in an alley next to the Presto Tire shop and the local creamery in downtown Chetopa, Kansas at approximately 3 am on the morning of May 31 when his headlights fell upon a body lying in the roadway. Walking up to the prostrate form, Rentz noticed it was covered in blood. Repelled by the sight, he immediately rushed to a nearby residence seeking assistance.

Within the hour, Labette County Sheriff W. C. Miller and a deputy arrived on the scene. The County Coroner soon joined the officers. The body was quickly identified as that of Chetopa Night Policeman Otto L. Durkee. The initial investigation established bullets had struck the officer in the upper left breast as well as left thigh. His .45 caliber revolver was lying a few feet away; all six rounds had been fired. Investigators observed bullet marks on a nearby concrete curb and several adjacent buildings, one round was found imbedded in the front door of a neighboring shoe shop. The brass from three .25-20-caliber rifle rounds was discovered lying on the pavement across the road. What appeared to be drag marks and a blood trail

Mr. and Mrs. William New and daughter, shortly after being released by the fugitives. Courtesy Kansas City Star

led from the street into the alley.

When witnesses were interviewed an employee of Barr's Filling station, which was located one block from the crime scene, reported he had been visiting with Durkee at approximately 1:30 am when they heard a commotion up the street that sounded like dogs howling. According to the witness, Durkee, who had only been an officer for six weeks, excused himself walking down the road into the darkness to investigate. "A few minutes later I heard several shots. I figured he had shot at some stray dogs and thought nothing of it." A man living nearby stated he also heard shots that sounded to him like a burst from a machinegun. He strolled on to his porch and peered into the dark alley but was unable to see anything, although he heard what he thought sounded like a dog growling or perhaps a cow mooing. Several others heard the sharp reports but didn't bother to further investigate the odd occurrence.

When word was received of Warden Prather's description of the fugitive's tire blowout near Welch just hours before Durkee's slaying, investigators from the Labette County Sheriff's Department immediately leaped to the conclusion the officer had surprised the escaping convicts in the act of stealing tires from the tire shop and a gunfight had ensued. The day after the murder Chetopa Mayor H. W. Boon posted a $250 reward for the capture of Durkee's slayer or slayers. A wife and two children survived the forty-two-year-old Durkee who was a decorated veteran of the Great War.

Although detectives later cooled on the idea Durkee was slain by the escapees, no person was ever brought to justice for his murder and according to the current Labette County Sheriff, the case remains open to this day.

Three hours after the discovery of officer Durkee's bullet-riddled corpse, lawmen received news of a filling station robbery and hijacking, which had taken place in nearby Commerce, Oklahoma. The owner of the station, Jeff Weatherby, was robbed then forced to accompany the bandits on a five-mile drive to Miami where the hijackers released him. Weatherby identified the automobile driven by the hijackers as a blue Willys, which incidentally was the same model of vehicle the second group of fugitives were last known to be driving.

The following morning personnel armed with Browning Automatic Rifles from both the Kansas and Oklahoma National Guard were brought in to assist lawmen in the manhunt. Sheriff York informed newsmen he believed the two convict bands intended on rendezvousing in the wild Osage Hills, which had been used as hideout over the decades by such outlaws as the Dalton brothers, Al Spencer, and the notorious Poe-Hart Gang. He also warned area doctors and nurses to be on the lookout, since the escapees may well seek medical assistance to treat Harvey Bailey's wounds. Over the next few days, the escapees were reportedly spotted in a dozen different diverse locations across the state. Nowata County Sheriff Henry Lowery, convinced the fugitives were responsible for the burglary of a ranch house near Centralia, led a hundred man posse into the infamous Blue Canyon where they captured two unrelated suspects.

Adding to the area's general sense of unease, on the afternoon of June 1 a pair of convicted murders, H. D. Bradbury and Jim Stribling escaped from the Oklahoma State Penitentiary. The duo was captured near Stuart, Oklahoma after a short lived but intense manhunt.

On the same day, six well-dressed men robbed the Bank of Chelsea, Oklahoma of an estimated $2500. While making their escape in a dark blue Graham-Paige Sedan, the desperadoes were involved in a brief firefight with officers. Although area newspapers, in an obvious attempt to boost circulation, prematurely announced the Kansas escapees were behind the heist, lawmen vigorously denied the assertion. Over the next few weeks, investigators would become convinced the true culprits behind the Chelsea job were the notorious Eno brothers, Clarence and Otis, possibly joined by Ed "Newt" Clanton, Harry Campbell, Glenn Roy Wright, and others.

On the afternoon of June 3, a trio of roughly dressed individuals entered the N. H. Walton Hardware Store in Pawhuska attempting to purchase ammunition. When informed by the owner he did not carry that particular type of ammo, the three strolled down the street to another store. Walton, aware of the recent sightings of the Kansas escapees in the area telephoned police who dispatched motorcycle officer O. L. Henson to the scene. When Henson attempted to question the suspects as they exited the second store, one of the men responded by pointing a rifle he had been carrying close to his side directly at the officer's chest informing him to "Back off." The suspects then fled the area in a blue Chevy sedan with Kansas license plates. Henson positively identified the man who had gotten the drop on him as Wilbur Underhill. Although a large posse led by Sheriff R. B. Conner quickly descended on the scene, nothing more was seen of the suspects.

Meanwhile, Underhill and his companions drove deep into the infamous Cookson Hills of Eastern Oklahoma to the Cherokee County home of an acquaintance of Jim Clark's named Marion Pike. Pike, a middle-aged ex-con living in a one room shack near the backwater hills settlement of Peggs, had according to several sources ran a hideout for outlaws on the run for many years. After laying low for a few days, Davis and Wilbur drove Bailey to Oklahoma City where they stashed him at a safe house located at 21 SE 35th Street.

In looking around for a suitable nurse to tend to Bailey's wounds, Wilbur hired a sultry 35 year-old divorcee named Hazel Jarrett Hudson he had met at a speakeasy in the squalid Packingtown district of Oklahoma City soon after his hitting town. According to Hazel, her brother, Ralph Jarrett and a convicted bank robber named George "Dewey" Shipley introduced her to the outlaw who was going by the name of George Fitzgerald at the time. Over time, she and Wilbur would become romantically involved, rendezvousing at out of the way tourist courts and isolated abandoned houses. Hazel was the sister of the notorious Jarrett brothers of Nowata County Oklahoma. Two of her siblings, Floyd and Buster (Roger) were currently doing time at "Big Mac" while a third, Earl, was on the lamb after murdering a Federal Prohibition Officer. Brother Walter had been slain by the cops while Glen had died in prison. Lee (Levi) had lost his life in a car accident while running from the laws. At the time of his death, he was wanted on multiple counts of armed robbery as well as auto-theft and attempted murder. Another brother, Ralph, was presently on parole. An attractive brunette, Hazel was both widowed and divorced by the time she shacked up with Underhill. Her first husband, Albert Connor, had been a one-time member of the infamous Poe-Hart Gang who had terrorized the "Sooner" state during the First World War era. Connor was shot dead when he and Buster Jarrett were caught in the act of robbing a grocery store near Coffeyville, Kansas in 1923.

For the next few weeks Underhill spent his time between the Oklahoma City apartment and his haunts in the Cookson Hills while Clark and Brady took up residence at a rent house located in Shawnee. Frank Sawyer split from the group and was quickly recaptured and sent back to

"Big Mac" to finish out the term (A Life sentence for a 1920 murder) he owed the state of Oklahoma at the time of his 1932 escape.

Just a few days after Frank Sawyer's apprehension, US Customs agents arrested Billie Woods and Clifford Dopson in Junction, Texas. Although the pair quickly offered to plead guilty to the Chelsea bank robbery in an effort to stave off extradition back to the Kansas State Penitentiary, their efforts went for naught when the Chelsea bankers failed to identify them.

On the morning of June 15, the gang of five got back together at Bailey's rented digs in Okalahoma City to plan a heist. Joining them in their scheme was Dewey Shipley as well as Jess Littrell, best known for his involvement with

Wanted Poster sent from Wichita Police Department. Courtesy Michael Webb

the Poe-Hart Gang circa 1916-17. Littrell, who had recently been paroled from McAlester on a robbery-murder charge, was a close friend of both Jim Clark and Frank Sawyer. That evening Davis, Brady, and Clark along with Littrell and Shipley left the apartment headed toward Arkansas while Underhill remained with Bailey at the apartment.

The following morning the group knocked off the Black Rock Bank for roughly $29,000 in cash and bonds narrowly making their escape. Soon after the robbery, two out of work oilfield roustabouts, E. J. Wyatt and Thelbert Brady, were mistakenly arrested and charged with pulling off the heist. (*Note: Both individuals were eventually released from custody although Thelbert Brady, who was no relation to Bob Brady, would be promptly charged and convicted of the recent holdup of an Elks Club bingo parlor near Blackwell, Oklahoma)

On the morning of June 17, a posse of federal and state officers transporting a federal prisoner named Frank Nash from Hot Springs, Arkansas to Leavenworth Penitentiary were ambushed by several assassins armed with submachine guns in the parking lot of Kansas City's Union Station. When the gunsmoke cleared, three officers, a federal agent, and the prisoner laid dead. The public outcry over the event, which was dubbed "The Kansas City Massacre," was intense to say the least. The Justice Department's Bureau of Investigation (Soon to be officially dubbed the FBI) headed by J. Edger Hoover reacted by launching a nationwide manhunt for the killers. Within hours of the ambush, federal agents publicly announced the remaining escapees (Those still at large) from the Kansas prison breakout were on top of the suspect list along with Oklahoma's premier bandit of the day, Charles "Pretty Boy" Floyd and his sidekick, Adam Richetti.

Back in Oklahoma, Harvey Bailey was reportedly enraged upon hearing the news of his being named a suspect in the Kansas City affair. Putting his thinking cap on he convinced his pals to compose a letter to the *Daily Oklahoman* decrying their innocence as well as taking the blame for the recent Black Rock job stating they wanted no man to suffer for their acts. They also claimed the actual amount of loot taken from the bank was $4700 not $29,000 as was reported in the papers. (*Note: Apparently $1200 of the loot was in the form of heavy silver coins which in their haste to escape the area, was hidden by the hijackers in a hollow tree just outside town.) After writing a four hundred word detailed description of the robbery and escape they affixed their signatures (All except Bailey who signed with an X) and fingerprints to the correspondence. Whether the correspondence was meant to be a true act of compassion on their part for the two men who had been unjustly accused of the Black Rock job or merely an effort to establish an alibi for their whereabouts around the time of the Kansas City massacre is one for the historians to hash out.

Aftermath of the Kansas City Massacre. Courtesy Kansas City Star

The letter was postmarked Coalgate, Oklahoma, Monday, June 19 at 2:30 pm. Federal agents, studying the letter agreed it was the genuine article but claimed it held no significance germane to their investigation. Commenting on the letter, Oklahoma County Prosecutor Draper Grigsby said, "Why the Underhill boys are all ignorant illiterate criminals who couldn't spell most of the words in that letter if they tried all week." Adding, "Besides, it was drawn up in definite legal form and terminology. They had help."

On the afternoon of July 3, with the temperature hovering near the century mark, a late model tan colored two-door Ford V8 double-parked at a side entrance of the First National Bank of Clinton, Oklahoma. Five armed individuals, described by witnesses as unmasked and nattily dressed, dismounted the vehicle entering the institution. While two of the men took up positions at the entrances, the others began herding the dozen employees and customers present in the bank into the rear office of Bank President F. H. Crow informing the crowd "This is a holdup. Everyone keep your hands down, stay calm, and do as your told." Cashier Sam Richart was forced at gunpoint to fill a large white cloth sack with approximately $11,000 in cash and $4000 in bonds from the vault and cash drawers. Also snagged by the bandits in their search for cash was a loaded revolver conveniently placed in one of the money tills by the management in planning for just this sort of occasion. At the conclusion of the robbery, one of the bandits pointed to the pair of females in the bank saying "We'll just take you two girls with us." Forced to walk in front of the robbers as they made their retreat to the getaway car, eighteen-year-old Georgia Loving, an employee of a local ice company, and twenty-two-year-old Thelma Selle were informed "Were not going to hurt you. We will let you go on the completion of our business." Miss Loving was shoved into the back seat while her companion was compelled to stand on the car's running board. Both hostages were released unharmed just outside the city limits on an isolated stretch of Route 66. The robbery took less than ten minutes to complete. When interviewed shortly after the robbery, Miss Selle informed reporters one of the gang members had instructed her to "Be quite, we just want to carry you to the end of the street so they won't shoot at us."

Headlines from Clinton Daily News *regarding bank robbery.*

Incidentally, she had over $200 in cash in her pocket at the time of the robbery. Luckily, the hijackers neglected to search any of the customers during the heist. Less than an hour after the robbery the bandit's car, which had been stolen off the streets of Blackwell earlier that week was spotted being driven eighty miles per hour through the small Western Oklahoma town of Sayre located some fifty miles southwest of Clinton. Investigators surmised the robbery was the work of Harvey Bailey along with Brady, Davis, Clark, and Underhill.

An interesting side-note to the Clinton robbery involves a statement made recently by a relative of Jim Clarks concerning the loot. According to the family member, who was just a boy at the time, in the days following the Clinton heist he remembered his Uncle Jim, accompanied by a pair of men dressed in white shirts and straw "Panama" hats, arriving at their home located just south of Muskogee showing off a twenty-four-pound flour sack which appeared to be chock full of money. After spending the night, the trio jumped into their car and sped east toward the Cookson Hills.

On July 14, two of the second group of Kansas escapees, Kenneth Conn and Alvis Payton attempted to loot the Labette County State Bank in Altamont, Kansas. Midway through the robbery the bank's alarm went off and the streets began to fill with curious citizens. When the pair attempted to flee using a female hostage for cover a bank employee shot both robbers. Conn died instantly while a seriously wounded Alvis Payton was promptly returned to Lansing and lodged in the prison's infirmary.

Back in Oklahoma a large contingent of heavily armed Oklahoma City officers raided a residence located in the 1700 block of West Place. Arrested in the raid were Dewey Shipley and a man calling himself John Morris. Shipley, who was currently on parole from an armed robbery charge stemming from his involvement with the infamous "Blackie" Thompson in the 1923 hijacking of the First State Bank of Rush Springs, Oklahoma, was quickly extradited to Arkansas where he faced indictment on charges of conspiracy to rob the Bank of Black Rock on June 16, 1933. Although investigators were convinced Shipley had participated in the heist, he was eventually acquitted on a technicality and set free.

At 1:45 pm on the afternoon of August 9, a black Ford V8 Sedan with red-wall wheels pulled up to the curb parking on the south side of the Peoples National Bank of Kingfisher, Oklahoma. Three men later identified as Harvey Bailey, Jim Clark, and Bob Brady quickly dismounted the rig and began strolling toward the institution's front door. Bailey, who was carrying a newly acquired machine gun, paused just long enough to inquire of Roy Glover, who was parked nearby selling watermelons, the price of the melons. Reaching into his empty pocket the "Tommy Gun" toting bandit quipped, "I'll first have to go to the bank to get some change." According to witnesses, on entering the establishment Bailey took up a position just inside the front entrance, while Clark placed himself in the center of the bank's lobby, whereas Brady approached the cashier's window stating in a loud voice, "This is a stickup. Do as you are told and

Modern day view of the old Labette County State Bank building. Photo by Naomi Morgan

no one will get hurt." Meanwhile, Clark began herding the crowd of customers and employees toward the rear of the building while a sharp thinking bank clerk named Virgil Francis discreetly tossed a packet containing $3000 in cash under his desk and out of sight. The packet would go unnoticed and the bandits would ultimately depart the bank a little less prosperous than expected. Unable to enter the teller's cages through the door, Brady quickly scaled the barrier and began rifling the cash tills. Not finding as much loot as he hoped, the bandit inquired, "Is this all?" During the robbery, which took less than five minutes, a score of customers drifted into the bank and were instructed by Bailey to "Come on in and join the party, folks." Just as the bandits were finishing up their business, Bank President Burt Brigham asked Jim Clark, "What happens if my knocking knees buckle and can't support my weight?" Clark snorted then curtly replied, "They will hold out as this job is a short one." After looting the institution of approximately $6000, the bandits ushered every soul present in the building out the side door where their getaway car was parked before instructing bank employees, Burt Brigham, Virgil Francis, and Marion Mitchell to hop into the rig. After driving several blocks south, the robbers turned east then braked near the city park at a small bridge spanning Uncle Johns Creek where they ordered the hostages to "Get out in a hurry." Once shed of their excess baggage, the bandits fled east on old Highway 33 at a fast clip.

After gaining their freedom, the hostages began running back toward town. On spotting a farmer named Joe Jech and his young son sitting on a loading dock of a repair shop they began to shout, "We have been robbed and need to return to the bank." Eight year-old J. E. Jech, now in his mid-eighties, recalling the incident from a distance of seven decades past, recently stated, "I noticed the gentlemen and a well-dressed lady running toward us screaming at the top of their lungs. After explaining their predicament, we all hopped into my father's 1928 Chevy Sedan and began driving toward town. Mr. Brigham kept prodding dad to drive faster to which he answered, 'Do you want me to kill us?' On our arrival at the bank, Brigham, who was dressed in a fashionable pin-stripped suit, jumped up on a small wooden box and began addressing the crowd saying, 'Don't worry folks your money is insured. No one will loose a dime." Young J. E., who now had a heck of a story to tell his classmates when school resumed in the fall, relayed how he was scared out of his wits for the entire drive due to his belief the bandits were hot on their tail.

Within moments of the robbery's conclusion, lawmen arrived at the bank and began forming a posse. By three in the afternoon ten carloads of heavily armed officers and vigilantes led by Kingfisher County Sheriff Ed Martin began scouring the area roads in search of the hijackers while an airplane carrying a pair of lawmen was sent aloft from the airport in Enid. Around dusk, the bandit's abandoned getaway car was discovered by deputies mired in the middle of the Cimarron River bed at the site of an old crossing located approximately nine miles northeast of Kingfisher. The car, which was determined to be the property of a Ben F. Wice, had been stolen off the streets of Muskogee on the evening of July 27. After observing tire tracks on an isolated road located directly across from the ford, officers surmised the bandits had discarded the stolen rig after getting it stuck in the quicksand and walked across the river where a second car picked them up enabling them to make their escape. Later that night Bill Matheson, who operated a filling station located just a few miles east of where officers had discovered the abandoned getaway vehicle, informed lawmen he had serviced a customer who he identified by photo as Wilbur Underhill earlier that day. He added, "The man was accompanied by a woman." The following day several other area residents came forward stating they had also noticed a black Ford V8 occupied by a man and a woman parked near the river crossing around the time of the bank heist.

Back at the bank, two-dozen witnesses who had observed the robbery from either inside the bank or on the street were interviewed and shown mug shots from the local Sheriff's rouges gallery. Witnesses identified Bailey, Clark, and Brady as the robber trio.

Some controversy sprang from the Kingfisher robbery over the years having to do with whether Bob Brady was present at the event. Although some researchers have suggested Ed Davis instead of Brady, who was reportedly with his wife in Des Moines, Iowa at the time of the hijacking, was the robber who climbed over the bank cages, the fact remains a half-dozen eyewitnesses positively identified Brady as present in the bank at the time of the heist while not a single one recognized Davis as one of the raiders.

Soon after the Kingfisher heist, Harvey Bailey decided to visit his friend George "Machine Gun" Kelly at Kelly's father-in-law's ranch at Paradise, Texas. Unluckily for him not only was Kelly absent but the feds had been watching the place for some time hoping to capture the perpetrators of the recent Urschel kidnapping. (Note: Oilman Charles Urschel was kidnapped from his Oklahoma City mansion on July 22. After being held a week he was released upon the payment of a $200,000 ransom) When officers raided the ranch Bailey was caught up in the sweep. When searched he happened to have some of the marked kidnap money as well as part of the Kingfisher robbery loot in his britches. Although he vehemently denied any involvement in the

Urschel snatch, the feds promptly charged him with kidnapping. The irate outlaw was quickly lodged in the Dallas County Jail to await trial. On Labor Day Bailey sawed through his cell bars and taking a guard hostage forced his way to freedom. Commandeering a car, he fled north to Oklahoma. Several hours later, a party of officers captured him in Ardmore. After being transferred to the Federal lockup in Oklahoma City, he was soon convicted of kidnapping and sentenced to life imprisonment at Alcatraz Penitentiary. A Dallas County Deputy was subsequently convicted of aiding him in his jailhouse break.

In the months after his capture, Bailey would make numerous revisionist statements to the press and investi-

Harvey Bailey shortly after his capture. Courtesy
Daily Oklahoman

gators regarding the Kansas escape in which he attempted to re-invent his role in the affair by implying his motivation for joining the plot was mainly due to his desire to restrain Underhill's killing urges, to act as a "Guardian Angel" so to speak to the hostages. He stated, "I have been associated with plenty of tough characters in my time but Underhill was the worst man I ever knew. When I stopped him from killing the warden he sulked for three days. Every time we went through a little town and spotted an officer he wanted to stop and kill him." Ignoring his own culpability in the breakout, the wily bandit overlooked the fact he had personally held a gun firmly against the warden's spine during the opening act of the escape. We are led to believe in his case the weapon was merely a harmless prop with no serious mischief intended.

Chapter Eleven

Robbing Banks Ain't No Crime

A few days after Bailey's arrest in Texas, a large posse of Arkansas and Kansas officers began a surveillance of a farm home located eight miles north of Siloam Springs, Arkansas near the community of Springtown. The lawmen had received a tip from an informant, which indicated the remaining Kansas escapees would soon arrive at the residence, which they had reputably used as a hideout in the past. Around 2 am on the morning of August 17, a car sporting Oklahoma plates showed up containing two men and a woman. When officers demanded the occupant's surrender, the trio baled out of the automobile and attempted to flee on foot toward the home. Nearly two-dozen officers opened fire with a variety of rifles, shotguns, and a "chopper." When the gunsmoke cleared, an individual name Gene Johnson and his wife Jewell were discovered sprawled on the ground. Johnson, who was suffering from several rounds to the head and back, was draped over his wife's form in an obvious attempt to shield her from harm. He would perish the following day. The third subject had escaped running through a wall of lead finding sanctuary in a nearby stretch of woods. Bloodhounds quickly picked up his scent, which was marked by a well-defined blood trail that led toward the nearby Oklahoma border.

When Jewell Johnson, who was suffering from a gunshot wound to the arm, was interviewed, she admitted the Underhill bunch had used the residence for a hideout several times since she and her spouse had purchased the place on August 4th. She further stated the individual who had escaped the raid was Glenn Roy Wright, who was wanted for the May 14, 1933 murder of a McPherson, Kansas police officer named Charles Bruce as well as the slaying of a truck driver in Picher, Oklahoma. When the house was searched, a large quantity of ammunition and several rifles and shotguns were discovered as well as a dozen or more recently taken Kodak photo's showing Underhill, Ed Davis, and others. Although officers were able to stick to Glenn Wright's trail throughout the night, by dawn the fugitive was somehow able to shake loose of his pursuers just south of the little border community of Maysville.

****

On the morning of September 15, 1933, three well-groomed and fashionably dressed men brandishing automatic pistols entered the front door of the First National Bank of Geary, Oklahoma. The trio's spokesman demanded a crowd made up of a three employees including Bank President John Dillon and several customers move into the bank's lobby and stand in a single line at attention. After harvesting some $1497 from the tills, the hijackers exited the bank taking two bookkeepers and a cashier hostage. The hostages were forced to accompany the bandits clinging to the sides of a Ford V8 Sedan for approximately two miles where they were released. The automobile the trio used in the heist was discovered abandoned six miles outside Watonga that afternoon. The car had been stolen the previous day off the streets of Tulsa. Witnesses later positively identified the bandits as Bob Brady, Jim Clark, and Wilbur Underhill by photographs. At the conclusion of the robbery, the so-called Underhill-Bailey Gang broke apart. Clark, accompanied by Brady, took a short vacation prior to knocking off the First National Bank of Frederick, Oklahoma for an estimated $5000. The pair was captured later that day after a short gun duel with officers near Tucumcari, New Mexico and subsequently returned to Lansing. Ed Davis reportedly rejoined his wife striking out for the west coast.

Meanwhile, it appears Wilbur found sanctuary with his ex-cellmate, Charlie Dotson, at his home located fifteen miles southeast of Tahlequah, Oklahoma near the tiny settlement of Standing Rock, deep in the notorious Cookson Hills. The little crossroads berg was populated by perhaps a dozen souls and one business; a small store operated by an infamous whiskey maker and his cocky brother-in-law, Robert Trollinger (legal name Trolinder). Living nearby was Levi "Mount" Cookson, a noted bandit who had previ-

Glenn Leroy Wright. Courtesy Mike Roberts

ously served a term at the Oklahoma pen for his involvement in the 1918 robbery of the Bank of Gore, Oklahoma. Cookson, as well as many of the local folk were always happy to offer a hideout for any outlaw on the run, for a price of course. Legendary Cherokee County Sheriff Grover Bishop once called the isolated Illinois River settlement a nest of thieves and bootleggers. Just the previous year, four local lawmen and a trio of outlaws had lost their lives in a pair of deadly gunfights, which had taken place within a mile or so of the community.

Born in the southern part of the Cookson Hills near Marble City, the twenty-seven-year-old Dotson had already had a storied career for someone so young. He and his brother 'Bee' were once full-time members of the original 'Cookson Hills Gang' while still in their teens, having participated in several robberies with the likes of the legendary Ed Lockhart and Fred "Cottontop" Walker. While his brother was gunned down by officers at the conclusion of a high-speed chase in 1925, Charlie's blossoming criminal career was cut short when arrested and convicted of attempting to rob and kill a taxi driver on the streets of downtown Vinita, Okalahoma in 1924. The charge that day would have been homicide instead of attempted murder if Dotson's pistol had not misfired due to damaging

Robert Trollinger. Courtesy Muskogee Phoenix

the firing mechanism while in the process of vigorously striking his uncooperative victim over the head with it for several minutes.

On April 21, 1931, Dotson was given a leave of absence from the Oklahoma State pen due to his contracting TB, a common malady among prisoners in the nation's jails in the 1920s and 30s. Prison officials judged he was not long for this world. After visiting his kin near Marble City, the young man married a Cherokee County gal and moved to a farm near Standing Rock. However, due to his illness, Dotson was forced to spend several months in a TB Hospital in Shawnee, Oklahoma undergoing treatment after his release from the pen, there was apparently plenty of life left in the young man. Within a few months of his discharge from the hospital, Charlie, along with Robert Trollinger, Tom "Kye" Carlile, and Jim Benge were suspected of knocking off the First National Bank of Springdale, Arkansas. Although Dotson was never officially charged with participating in the robbery, he was questioned repeatedly over the next few years about his whereabouts at the time of the event. He was again hospitalized in the Tubercular Hospital for most of 1932 and some of '33. It appears he emerged from the hospital feeling better and ready for some action by mid-1933.

An interesting story often told around the hills concerning Dotson speaks of the time an oversized hillbilly cornered him at a barn dance being held near the village of Cookson threatening to "Slap the crap" out of him over some kind of girl troubles. Charlie, who was described as "puny" at best, reportedly turned and walked to his car, reached in and withdrew a nickel-plated .45 automatic pistol before strolling over to his tormentor where he quickly pressed the gun barrel to his head while softly whispering into his ear, "Go ahead."

On Underhill's arrival in the hills, Dotson re-introduced the outlaw to many of his ex-prison buddies. Two of those who would play a major role in Wilbur's future plans were Charlie "Cowboy" Cotner and his bad-tempered sidekick, Ford Bradshaw, both of rural Vian, Oklahoma, a small settlement located in the southern section of the Cookson Hills. Cotner was a career criminal who been paroled from the Arkansas State Prison in 1930 after serving most of a ten year jolt for the 1924 robbery of the First National Bank of Prairie Grove. His partners in the robbery were suspected to have been Charlie and Bee Dotson. Cotner was noted for possessing both a photographic memory and amazing rodeo skills.

Ford Bradshaw, who was often times described as smart, handsome, and a little bit nuts, literally epitomized the old phrase, "Live fast, die young, and leave a pretty corpse." He was prone to sudden outbursts of extreme violence when drinking. Fact was, he drank all the time. Ford was full-fledged member of the Oklahoma state prison fraternity and had done time with Underhill in both the Oklahoma pen as well as the Okmulgee County Jail in the latter 1920s. He had been in trouble since he was a teen. In 1927 while Wilbur was being tried in Okmulgee for the murder of George Fee, twenty-year old Bradshaw and four of his pals tore apart a café in nearby Hitchita, Oklahoma in a drunken brawl. When a riot call went out, the town marshal and an Okmulgee County Deputy arrived on the scene and arrested the youths. Upon being transferred to the county jail, Bradshaw and three others who were in the marshal's car, turned on the lawmen and beat him unmercifully throwing the officer out of the moving rig commandeering the car. The deputy who was following the marshal's automobile fired several rounds into the fleeing rig wounding two of the unruly lads causing the driver to loose control of the car and crash into the ditch. The suspects were transported to the Okmulgee County Jail where they joined Underhill.

In 1928, Bradshaw and a John Rogers who had been with him at the Hitchita riot, robbed a filling station in Muskogee. The pair was cap-

tured a few days after the heist both pleading guilty to armed robbery and sentenced to the state pen for five years. Just weeks after Ford's release from prison in 1931 he was discovered withering in pain on the pavement in front of a gas station on the streets of downtown Muskogee with a .38 caliber slug lodged in his guts. The ex-con refused to enlighten officers as to who had caused his predicament. Within a few days of his release from the hospital, he and Rogers were busted for transporting ardent spirits (bootlegging)

Ford Bradshaw. Courtesy Tulsa World

near Sallisaw. He did thirty days in the county jug and paid a big fine for that indiscretion.

In September 1932, an innocent young housewife named Susie Sharp was shot and killed in a failed car hijacking near a combination honky-tonk-whorehouse located just outside of Muskogee on the side of Braggs Mountain. Five men were charged with her murder including Bradshaw and his nephew-in-law, Ed "Newt" Clanton, a bank robbing ex-con hailing from Chelsea, Oklahoma, along with Thomas " Kye" Carlile, Jim Benge, and a vicious gunsel named Troy Love. Both Love and Carlile were escapees from the Arkansas State Penitentiary at Little Rock where Love was doing time for burglary and the attempted murder of a cop while Carlile was serving a stretch for the robbery of the banks of Leslie and Springdale, Arkansas. Carlile had long been associated with Charlie Dotson through their shared involvement with Ed Lockhart and the Cookson Hills Gang of the 1920s.

In the early morning hours of September 17, 1932, a posse set up a roadblock on an isolated dirt lane near Standing Rock in hopes of ambushing a car thought to be containing Carlile, Love, and an unidentified man (thought to of been Robert Trollinger) along with a youth named Bud McClain who later proved to be the rig's driver. When the fugitive's car approached the roadblock, the lawmen popped on their headlights and opened fire with Browning automatic rifles and shotguns killing McClain and severely wounding Carlile. Love leaped from the

Posseman Andrew McGinnis.
Courtesy McGinnis Family

vehicle armed with a high-powered rifle gunning down two of the officers. The leader of the posse, Muskogee County Deputy Sheriff Webster Reece, died on the way to the hospital while Tahlequah policeman Frank Edwards, expired as a result of his wounds some weeks later.

The following afternoon, a posse made up of several dozen officers surrounded Love and Carlile in a thicket where they had sought sanctuary and in the ensuing gunfight a posseman named Andrew McGinnis was shot in the heart and instantly killed while Deputy Sheriff Hurt Flippen was severely wounded. Flippen died the following day due to internal bleeding. After exchanging fire with the posse for several minutes, the fugitive pair made a mad dash toward a nearby tree line and was subsequently cut to pieces by machine gun fire.

Nothing was heard of Bradshaw until the evening of October 16, 1932 when he gunned down a man named

Telegram concerning Andrew McGinnis death. Courtesy McGinnis family

George Martin in a gambling dispute at a gin-joint located on the north side of Muskogee, Oklahoma. The victim was transported to a local hospital where he was pronounced dead on arrival, while Bradshaw and Clanton fled the area heading toward Tulsa in a black Chevy Coup.

At noon on November 7, Bradshaw, along with Clanton and Jim Benge robbed the American Exchange Bank of Henryetta, Oklahoma for roughly $12,000. On December 12, Ford and his little brother "Skeet" were arrested at a roadblock near Vinita, Oklahoma. The outlaw was transferred to Okmulgee to be tried for armed robbery of the Henryetta bank. Although numerous witnesses identified him as the lead bandit in the affair, Bradshaw was acquitted by a jury when in a bizarre twist of legal maneuvering Ford's lawyers was able to enter into the court record statements made by both the County Sheriff and several of his deputies uttered shortly after the heist in which they claimed the real robbers were Charles "Pretty Boy" Floyd and his sidekick George Birdwell.

The prosecution promptly claimed Bradshaw's acquittal had left a black mark on Oklahoma's system of justice. He further asserted the jury was prejudiced against banks and bankers to the point of taking up for sleazy, immoral bandits. He may have been on to something. By 1932, the great depression had deepened; America's economy had gone to "Hell in a hand basket." Unemployment had skyrocketed, farmers in the midlands had been victimized by three straight years of drought, and the country's once lush breadbasket was becoming a parched wasteland. Poverty and hunger stalked the streets of most major cities. Shantytowns, dubbed "Hoovervilles" in honor of the unpopular sitting President who most Midwesterners considered indifferent to their economic plight, sprang up in many metropolitan areas. In order to save what assets they could after the stock market crash, many banks began foreclosing on delinquent farm-loans and seizing equipment and liquidating or auctioning off the farmer's mortgaged assets in order to satisfy their losses. Farmers who normally operated year-to-year, crop-to-crop, living off bank loans was unfairly foreclosed on. In 1932 an average of 1000 families a week in Oklahoma, Texas, and Arkansas lost their farms to bank foreclosure. Ironically, after loosing their property, many farmers sought employment from the big land companies who now owned their property working as sharecroppers on the very land they had once owned. Numerous financial institutions simply folded up due to their being no FDIC (insurance) at the time and many depositors lost every nickel of their savings. These conditions added up to a public relations catastrophe for banks. Thus, when a financial institution in the area was robbed many normally law abiding folks simply turned their heads refusing to assist lawmen and prosecutors in their quest to capture and prosecute the bandits. Numerous Oklahoma citizens went as far as actively hiding out bank robbers. The average Joe's opinion at the time was, "Ain't no crime to rob a bank is it?"

****

Bradshaw's jubilation was tempered by his being transferred to Muskogee County to be tried for the murder of George Martin. When the witnesses from the scene of the crime all mysteriously disappeared, the desperado was able to make a $4000 cash bond and was released from custody until prosecutors could come with more evidence. Oddly, the bond money was wrapped in paper stating it originated from the American Exchange Bank of Henryetta, the very bank Bradshaw had just been acquitted of robbing.

By all indications, it appears that after renewing his

friendship with Bradshaw, Underhill made the Bradshaw farm, located a few miles north of the sleepy little Cookson Hills settlement of Vian his chief base of operations for the next few months. Ford's father, a convicted bank robber himself, was more than happy to see to his comforts. Any friend of Ford's, especially if there was a little green stuff involved, was a friend of his. Over the next few years, the farm would become renown as a major underworld hide-out reputably offering sanctuary to such gangland notables as Bonnie and Clyde, Charles "Pretty Boy" Floyd, Cliff Harbeck, "Bullet" Rolland, Jim Benge, "Kaiser Bill" Goodman, and "Machine Gun" Floyd Flippen.

Around this time, Clarence Eno and his brother Otis "Tony" Eno who had both been recently released from McAlester joined up with Bradshaw bunch. The brothers were old hands in the business of armed robbery, Clarence, the older of the two had done time in numerous penal institutions over the years including two jolts at the Oklahoma State Penitentiary, one at the Kansas State pen, as well as terms at both the Colorado and Kansas men's reformatories. Otis had been sentenced to the Colorado reformatory at age sixteen before graduating to the Detroit House of Corrections. He later served time at McAlester and Leavenworth Federal prison. He was married to Ford Bradshaw's sister

Charles "Pretty Boy" Floyd and friend. Courtesy Rick Mattix

Gypsy. Clarence had been a cellmate of both Charlie Dotson and Wilbur Underhill's at "Big Mac" in the latter 1920s.

Running low on funds, Underhill, along with Charlie Cotner and an unidentified individual, probably "Newt" Clanton, set out in search of a "tin can" bank to hijack while Dotson, Bradshaw, Robert Trollinger, and an ex-con named Joe Harris who had recently been released from the Oklahoma pen where he completed a stretch for auto-theft, took off north toward Nebraska.

On the afternoon of September 19, 1933 an automobile dealer named Max Reager and a his companion, Sam Pointer, were driving from their hometown of Sallisaw

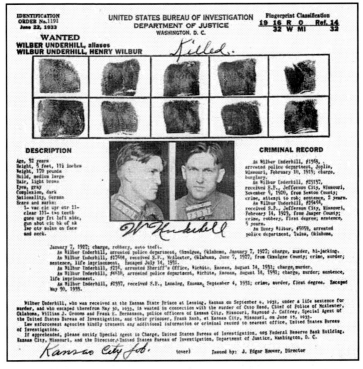

Wanted poster referring to Underhill circa 1933. Courtesy Michael Webb

to Oklahoma City on Route 266 when suddenly a trio of men driving a "rust bucket" ran them off the road. When Reager asked the men what the big idea was, the leader of the bunch whipped out a .45 automatic and ordered the pair into the nearby woods where he and his companions tied them to a tree before stealing their car and fleeing the scene.

The following day, Dotson's crew ransacked the First National Bank of York, Nebraska for over $9000 in cash and coin. After making a clean getaway, the four desperadoes made it back to the sanctuary of the Cookson Hills arriving at just about the same time as Wilbur and company were strolling into the Peoples National Bank of Stuttgart, Arkansas. According to witnesses, three armed men entered the institution, the leader of the crew placed himself in the center of the bank's lobby and commenced to shout to a flock of female bank employees saying "You've read about me, I'm Machine Gun Kelley," while waving a "Tommy-gun" toward the freighted women. The menacing individual then ordered bank employee Joan Morgan to open the safe. When the lady insisted she couldn't due to the safe being on a time lock, the machine gun toting bandit reacted by poking her hard in the ribs with the chopper while growling a threat to her life if she continued to be uncooperative. After quibbling with the clerk for a few moments, the bandit threw up

Otis Eno. Courtesy Tulsa World

his hands saying, "Piss on it, clean out the tills, boys."

After collecting roughly $1000, the trio forced the female witnesses, identified as Vera Newkirk, Estelle Gettle and Miss Morgan, along with a customer, W.H. Maynard, into the street before ordering the foursome to hop on the getaway car's running boards to act as human shields. After driving less than a hundred feet, Mrs. Gettle leaped off the fleeing automobile into a ditch where she landed unhurt. The other three hostages remained clinging to the car until the robbers released them a mile outside the city limits.

A posse consisting of a dozen area lawmen and another fifty deputized citizens hastily set up numerous roadblocks and vigorously patrolled the roads between Stuttgart and Little Rock throughout the night but came up empty. The bandits had made a clean break. The following day, Max Reager, the Sallisaw auto dealer whose car had been stolen, positively identified a photo of Wilbur Underhill as one of the men who had hijacked him and his pal. When the witnesses from the Stuttgart robbery were shown a prison mug shot of Wilbur the day after the bank heist they all agreed the photo bore a perfect likeness of the leader of the robbers who had done all the talking.

Just days before the Stuttgart heist, Oklahoma City Police Detective Clarence Hurt received information from one of his informants indicating Wilbur Underhill had been sighted in the company of Hazel Hudson at Dewey Shipley's old residence located on the 1700 block of West Park Place. Officers began a surveillance of the now vacant home as well as Hazel's own residence at 736 Southwest 31st Street, which she shared with her nineteen-year-old son and two daughters. The day after the Stuttgart raid, officers tailed Hazel and her son to the Park Place address. Moments after her arrival, a posse led by Hurt raided the dwelling but turned up nothing of any interest. Hazel and son were detained and questioned for several hours before being released.

On the evening of October 8, twenty-one-year-old Owen Gallamore was driving sixteen-year-old Bernice Thorton home from Sunday evening church services in his 1932 Model Chevy Sedan when he was flagged down by a pair of rough looking men dressed in dirty overalls just outside of Purcell, Oklahoma. On pulling over to the side of the road, the two unsavory looking characters muscled their way into the car forcing the youth to drive north at gunpoint. Just outside of the small community of McLoud, Gallamore and his gal were ordered to stop the rig and dismount the vehicle. The frightened pair was then taken to a schoolhouse and tied up with ropes. While harnessing the two youths, one of the men introduced himself as Wilbur Underhill and his companion as Ed Davis. The kidnappers remarked they were taking Gallamore's vehicle because they needed "A good car for a bank robbery."

The following day, October 9, two men armed with pistols entered the Farmers and Merchants Bank of Tryon, Oklahoma, one using the side door the other the main entrance. Inside the bank at the time was a cashier named Clarence Hall along with customers William Vassar, an attorney, and Arthur McConnell. Upon cleaning out the tills to the tune of $537.20 the bandits took the three witnesses hostage forcing them into their getaway car that was being driven by a woman dressed in bib-overalls. After driving several miles south of town on a gravel road, the hijackers released their captives unharmed. At noon, deputies discovered the getaway car parked in the middle of an isolated dirt lane near the small berg of Warwick located some dozen miles south of Tryon. Lincoln County Sheriff Buck Gillaspy reported the vehicle's gas gauge was sitting on empty. A check on the car's license plates turned up the fact the vehicle was the same one stolen from the young couple near Purcell the previous night. Area newspapers immediately announced Wilbur Underhill was the leader of the band of brigands who had robbed the Tryon bank.

An hour later and several hundred miles to the northeast, a new maroon Chevy sedan bearing Oklahoma plates carrying five individuals parked in front of the American National Bank of Baxter Springs, Kansas. Four of the men dismounted the rig while the fifth stayed at the wheel with the motor running. While one of the quartet took up a station at the door of the financial institution the other three entered the bank. The tallest of the trio announced it was a stick-up while the other two rushed behind the cages and rifled the tills gathering up about $3000. When informed the vault could not be opened due to being on a time lock, the robbers fled the establishment with their plunder pushing bank employees John Conrad and Eddie Whitaker in front of them. On reaching the getaway car, the pair of bankers was forced to ride on the running boards for a distance before being told to "Get off" by one of the bandits sitting in the rear seat. Unluckily for Whitaker when he attempted to leap off the moving vehicle which had slowed to a crawl in order to enable the hostages to dismount without breaking their necks, he discovered his tie was lodged in the closed car door, although he pleaded with the hijackers to open the door they refused leaving him no choice but to give the tie a good yank and tear himself loose thus ruining his expensive piece of apparel.

Within moments of the robbery's completion, Elsie Bland, an employee of the bank who was out to lunch at the time of the heist, entered the financial institution. Quickly realizing a robbery had occurred she sprinted across the street to a store and phoned the police. Unfortunately, only

Jailor Fred Nichols was able to answer the call of duty due to the majority of the town's police force having picked that day to be out of town. The bandit's fleeing rig was last seen racing south on Route 66 toward the Oklahoma border.

That evening Conrad and Whitaker as well as Ted Mason who had witnessed the robbery from across the street, identified Wilbur Underhill from a wanted poster as one of the hijackers. As was the norm with these heart-thumping events, it appears the so-called "Fog of Battle" syndrome set in, confusion reigned, and witnesses gave conflicting reports as to what they had observed. No sur-

American National Bank, Baxter Springs, Kansas. Courtesy Baxter Springs Heritage Center

veillance cameras existed at the time and authorities had to rely on contradictory eyewitness reports given by small town folks who had just received the monster scare of their normally dull, monotonous lives. But at the end of the day, police were able to say with some degree of certainty the bandit gang was made up of Wilbur Underhill, Charlie Cotner, "Newt" Clanton, Ford Bradshaw, and Clarence Eno (A single witness identified Robert Trollinger as one of the hijackers through a mugshot).

Meanwhile, O.P. Ray, of the Oklahoma Bureau of Identification had just completed his investigation of the kidnapping of the two youths near Purcell, Oklahoma, whose car was definitely linked to the Tryon robbery. Ray's conclusions differed from the newspapers. According to the investigator, the kidnapped youths had not only identified a photo of an escapee from Granite reformatory as one being of the hijackers but neither victim could identify Underhill through mug shots. Ray's thesis was further backed up by the findings of fingerprint expert C. M. Reber

Main Street, Baxter Springs, Kansas 1930s. Author's private collection

who stated none of the prints found in the Tryon bank and on the abandoned getaway car matched either Underhill or Davis. On top of that, none of the witnesses from the robbery were able to positively identify the pair as the bandits involved in the holdup. (One of the witnesses from the bank did tentatively identify Underhill from a mug shot but later reneged) It appears by all indications the newspapers had "missed the boat" on this particular story. In the 1920s and 30s news journalists had a habit of penning robberies on whoever was the "Flavor of the month" whether it be Underhill or "Pretty Boy" Floyd. The rational being, big name criminals sold newspapers while the small fry didn't.

The following evening, two men forced a new dark colored Chevy Sedan being driven by an Okmulgee, Oklahoma schoolteacher named Elizabeth Barnes who was accompanied by a friend off the road near Beggs, Oklahoma. After taking the pair hostage, the taller of the two, whom the ladies later identified as Wilbur Underhill, pointed a large pistol at Miss Barnes and asked his partner if they should silence the pair. The second hijacker, who was described as short, (Newt Clanton) told his pal to "Forget it, let's get on the road." The man then asked if they knew Okmulgee County Sheriff John Russell. To which the women replied they did not. The hijackers sped from the scene in Barnes's car leaving the ladies standing on the deserted roadside, their hats in their hands.

Chapter Twelve

The Bradshaw-Underhill Gang

At roughly the noon hour on October 11, 1933 four unmasked men, the leader armed with a machine gun and the others carrying pistols, entered the International Bank of Haskell, Oklahoma. Cashier W. E. Combs and Teller Denis Rainwater stood stunned as the leader carrying the chopper ordered them to "Get 'em up or I'll give ya the works." Observing a black man, Jay Harris, lounging on a bench in the bank's lobby, the bandits instructed him to "Stand up and face the wall," while two of the hijackers rushed behind the counter and rifled the tills for nearly $1200 in bills and silver. The man with the Tommy gun then ordered Combs to open the safe. Combs informed him that was not possible due to it being set on a time clock. Frustrated and cursing his luck aloud, the leader of the gang, who the bankers later described as a snazzy dressed, tall fellow with a bandage attached to his left ear and wearing a brown suit and black tie, ordered the two bank employees to march outside to the roadside curb. On his way out the door, Combs reached over and rapped his knuckles on the window while mouthing the words "Hold up" to a pair of elderly gentlemen standing outside the bank shooting the breeze. One of the bandits who Combs later positively identified as Ford Bradshaw placed the palm of his hand over the banker's mouth instructing him to, "Shut your yap."

When the group reached the road, the bankers were instructed to mount the running boards of the getaway car, which was described as a black 1932 Chevy, and "Hang on tight." After a few blocks, the hostages were forced off the moving automobile. The getaway car was last seen turning east at the four-mile junction racing toward Muskogee at speeds in excess of 80 miles per hour. Within an hour of the holdup, area lawmen had set up a series of roadblocks throughout Eastern Oklahoma. The hijackers, obviously familiar with the area's lesser-traveled roads slipped the dragnet.

Later that day Muskogee County Sheriff Virgil Cannon showed up in Haskell with a large mug book containing numerous pictures and wanted posters of area criminals. Both bankers picked out photos of Wilbur Underhill naming him as the gang's leader. They also selected pictures of Ford Bradshaw and Charlie Dotson naming them as two of his companions in the heist. Although Sheriff Cannon was convinced Bradshaw's pal "Newt" Clanton was the driver of the getaway car, another Cookson Hills

Site of the old International Bank, Haskell, Oklahoma. Photo by Naomi Morgan

desperado named Jim Benge would later admit to several acquaintances he was the wheelman on the Haskell job.

****

Add for International Bank of Haskell, Oklahoma, circa 1932.
Courtesy Haskell News

Less than a week after the Haskell robbery, one of the York robbers, Joe Harris, was arrested for public drunkenness on the streets of Muskogee. At the police station, he foolishly flashed a roll of dough large enough to choke a horse. When questioned where an unemployed ex-con got such a wad of cash he admitted he and several others had robbed a bank in Nebraska. Sheriff Cannon immediately got in touch with Nebraska authorities. York County Sheriff A. E. Carter arrived the following day demanding extradition, which the loose-mouthed bandit quickly agreed to. On his arrival in Nebraska, Harris pled guilty to robbing the York bank but refused to implicate his partners, The local Judge praised the defendant for not wasting the taxpayers money with an expensive trial prior to sentencing him to ten years at hard labor at the Nebraska State Penitentiary in Lincoln.

At approximately the same time as Joe Harris was taking the heat in a Nebraska courtroom; Sheriff Cannon received a tip from an informant as to the present whereabouts of Charlie Dotson. A trio of Muskogee County lawmen rushed to Tahlequah, Oklahoma where several Cherokee County officers joined them. The posse surrounded the home of Dotson's in-laws and on offering the little man the choice of surrender or certain death he promptly came out of the dwelling with his hands in the air. Both Combs and Rainwater picked out Dotson from a lineup, positively identifying the young gunsel as one of the robbers of the Haskell bank.

Meanwhile Sheriff Carter had been busy as a beaver trying to figure out who else was involved in the York robbery. Due to witnesses claiming the getaway car had sported Oklahoma tags, and the fact Joe Harris had been captured in the "Sooner" state, the Sheriff's department had reacted by flooding various Oklahoma law enforcement agencies with wanted posters which depicted drawings of the suspects in the case. Sheriff Cannon evidently studied these drawings and on observing Charlie Dotson shortly after his arrest, thought one of the sketches favored the little Indian. He promptly phoned York County authorities voicing his suspicions. The following day, Sheriff Carter journeyed back to Oklahoma by automobile accompanied by three witnesses from the robbery.

On the afternoon of October19, Carter and the witnesses attended a lineup held in the basement of the Muskogee County Jail, all three witnesses positively identified Dotson as one of the bank raiders. Carter quickly demanded possession of the prisoner and filed extradition papers with Oklahoma's Governor Murray. That same afternoon a phone call was received at the offices of the

News headline referring to Underhill's threat to spring Charlie Dotson by force of arms. Courtesy Muskogee Phoenix

Muskogee Phoenix, the caller, who identified himself as Wilbur Underhill, stated in no uncertain terms that if the Nebraska lawmen attempted to extradite Dotson they would never make it back to their homes alive. Later that evening, State Investigator O. P. Ray contacted Sheriff Carter at his hotel room warning him that according to his confidential underworld sources, Underhill had been overheard making threats on the Sheriff's life to his cronies ever since the newspapers had announced Dotson's eminent extradition back to Nebraska. Muskogee Police Chief Ben Bolton promptly arranged round-the-clock protection for Carter for the remainder of his stay in Muskogee. Carter, who could have been described as an old-west style lawman, scoffed at the arrangement saying, "I know how to handle these sugar-coated punks." By listening to the crusty lawman's statements one could easily discern he evidentially didn't know much about Wilbur Underhill who although was guilty of having a great many nasty character traits, being a punk was not among them.

When Dotson's extradition hearing was held on Friday, October 20, two-dozen armed guards were stationed at every entrance to the courthouse. Dotson vigorously denied he was involved in either the Haskell and York jobs. Over a dozen witnesses showed up from Cherokee County swearing, they had seen the pint-sized outlaw in Tahlequah on the day of the York robbery. The trio of witnesses from Nebraska testified Dotson was the leader of the gang, which had robbed the bank in York on September 20, 1933. In the end, Judge Crump refused to release the defendant on habeas corpus and denied him bond on the Haskell robbery charge due to the fact he was an ex-con and a prime suspect in several other robberies. The Judge granted extradition to Nebraska on the condition Muskogee County Prosecutor Phil Oldman and Oklahoma's Governor agreed.

Oldman reportedly made a pact with Carter stating if Dotson was acquitted on the York robbery case, he would immediately be sent back to Oklahoma to face the music for his part in the Haskell job.

The following morning Dotson was transported north in a caravan made up of four cars carrying eight heavily armed Oklahoma officers as well as Sheriff Carter and a Federal Marshal while the witnesses from the robbery traveled home via passenger train. On reaching Independence, Kansas, the sheriff and his prisoner boarded an airplane bound for Lincoln, Nebraska. According to Carter, when the plane reached an altitude of approximately 4200 feet, Dotson turned to him with a smirk on his face saying, "There are two things I always wanted to do, first, witness the Kentucky Derby, and second jump out of an airplane." Carter quickly quipped, "Be my guest."

Meanwhile, Underhill's pal, Ford Bradshaw, along with his baby brother, "Skeet", were involved in a particularly cruel incident in the little Arkansas River town of Webbers Falls, Oklahoma where the pair senselessly shot down a pair of colored men while hooraying the town. Afterwards "Skeet" was captured by a posse of Muskogee County lawmen while Ford escaped the dragnet by hijacking a car occupied by a male schoolteacher and two underage girls. One of the girls, Amy Walters, telling of her experiences a half century later, explained; "Bradshaw asked Bob (the schoolteacher), who was driving, to take a country road which would get us around the roadblocks. Bob did as instructed. Ford stated if we were stopped he would shoot it out with the cops and we might be killed." On conversing with the outlaw, Amy asked him if he knew her brother, which he did. Afterwards, the badman began treating her more kindly telling her, "I can't let anything happen to my pal's sister." Around midnight, Bradshaw instructed the driver to stop at a drive-in café in Henryetta and get some food. After ordering four beers and hamburgers, the girls informed him they didn't drink. The outlaw retorted "That's OK," and guzzled down all four beers with gusto before instructing the driver to "Get moving." Later that night, Ford had the driver stop and pick up a female passenger at her home near Beggs. At dawn the outlaw released the hostages giving them five dollars apiece and threatening to come back to "See ya" if they informed anyone of their adventures. He then drove off with his lady friend leaving them standing in a cold drizzling rain on an isolated mountain road.

The following day two of the Eno brothers, Clarence and Otis, along with Charlie Cotner and "Newt" Clanton knocked off the Merchants National Bank of Nebraska City, Nebraska for $6135. Again, several hostages were placed on the getaway car's sideboards and released on the edge of town next to Highway 75. The authorities immediately suspected the hold-up was the work of Wilbur Underhill until witnesses were unable to identify any of the four robbers as Wilbur when shown his photograph.

Meanwhile, Underhill and his sweetheart were apparently spending their time romancing between the Bradshaw farm and Charlie Cotner's nearby residence when not staying at various rented digs around Oklahoma City. A story dating from this time period which is told by a reliable old-timer now in his 90s who lived near the Bradshaw farm in the early 1930s implies he saw Underhill around the place on several occasions. He went on to say, "Underhill had a strong personality, when he spoke everyone listened. He made no effort to hide his identity." Adding, "One day I was sitting on the Bradshaw porch hanging out with one of the Bradshaw grandkids when Ford, his good-looking girlfriend, (Boots Moody) and Underhill walked outside when the Eno boys pulled up in a brand new bright blue Chevy. Underhill began tongue-lashing Clarence for buying a blue rig saying, 'Always get black cars, witnesses never notice black." Incidentally, Bradshaw's chum, Charles "Pretty Boy" Floyd, who hailed from nearby Sallisaw, stated in a 1932 interview with reporter Vivian Brown, he preferred brown colored rigs due to their blending in with the dirt roads he normally drove.

At approximately 1 pm on the afternoon of October 30, three well-dressed men entered the Galena, Kansas National Bank. One individual, who was later identified as Charlie Cotner, approached Banker T.O. Moeller who thinking he was a customer asked how he could assist him. Cotner suddenly whipped out a sawed off shotgun from under his long coat saying "Don't make a sound or a move." Another of the individuals, later known to be Clarence Eno, produced a sub-machine gun and covered assistant cashier A. H. Moorman while a third man suspected to have been Ford Bradshaw pulled a pistol, dashed behind the counter and began harvesting the money from the cash drawers. When ordered to open the vault, Moeller replied it was impossible due to it being on a time clock. Satisfied with what loot they had garnered, (roughly $2500) the trio ordered the two bankers to slowly walk outside and step up on the running boards of their waiting Chevy Sedan. While the group was making

Charley Floyd and wife in 1931.
Courtesy Rick Mattix

their way toward the door, a seventy-year-old female customer entered the bank and was ordered to sit in a chair and stay still. While the gang's getaway car headed out of town with its two unwilling passengers clinging to the sides, the elderly woman phoned the telephone operator and gave the alarm. A few blocks down Main Street, Chief of Police Charles Hatfield, getting word of the hold-up, burst from his office when he spotted the bandit's car driving past his position. Although Hatfield was armed with a scattergun, he was unable to fire due to his fear of hitting the hostages.

Positioned across the street, Roy Deem, the manager of the Chicago Meat Market, sighted the bandit's fleeing rig and took down the license plate, Kansas 5-9238. Deputy Sheriff Bert Elliott, standing in front of an automobile repair shop with Virgil Fisher, also spotted the escaping outlaws. The pair jumped into Elliott's car and began pursuit. Chief of Police Hatfield accompanied by Juvenile Officer R.R. Tillman flagged down Elliott and joined them in their rig. The officers, soon re-enforced by Ottawa County Okla-

Looking north on the main drag of Galena, Kansas, circa 1930s.
Author's private collection

homa Sheriff Dee Watters and Deputy Gerald Hodge, engaged in a running gunfight with the robbers for nearly twenty miles until the officers finally lost sight of the bandit's speeding vehicle.

Suspicion was cast on Wilbur Underhill for the Galena heist when one of the bankers told lawmen the outlaw's mug shot vaguely resembled the man who had walked behind the counter rifling the cash draws. Contradicting his statement, the second banker as well as the elderly witness from the robbery and Chief Hatfield all disagreed with his identification.

Nothing was heard of the bandit gang until noon on November 2 when four nattily dressed individuals strolled into the Citizens National bank of Okmulgee, Oklahoma. Inside the bank at the time were Vice Presidents J. H. McElroy and Crittenden Smith, along with Assistant Cashier Oscar Kirk, and Clerks H. S. Garst, Lillian Frye, Eunice Hunt, and a Negro janitor named P. H. Benson as well as several customers. According to witnesses, two of the four men approached the main cashier's window while the others stood back near the front and side entrances.

One of the bandits, known to have been Ford Bradshaw, announced it was a robbery, telling the employees to stand up and move to the rear of the bank. Everyone froze in place except Mr. Smith who rose from his desk and told the speaker "That's carrying a joke too far fellow." Suddenly, the second man, later identified as Underhill, who had accompanied Bradshaw to the forefront stepped forward and menacingly shoved a .45 pistol into the banker's face stating, "This is no joking matter, pal." He continued, saying, "If you think this is a comedy, try not following orders and see what happens." Smith immediately responded, "That's all I wanted to know," before ushering the other employees to the rear of the building against a wall. Just then, Bradshaw and Eddie Clanton rushed behind the counter and began looting the cash drawers.

Meanwhile, the fourth bandit, suspected to have been Charlie Cotner, standing just inside the front entrance, described as wearing a blue suit and polka dot tie, greeted nearly a dozen customers entering the bank during the heist, instructing them to "Line up there with the rest of 'em." Sitting unseen behind a nearby partition, Switchboard Operator Eunice Hunt quietly slipped under her desk and out of sight. She later remarked that although she couldn't see much, she could hear everything going on. She did get a fleeting look at the leader of the gang who she stated was a tall, snaggle-toothed individual who snarled when he talked.

Around this time, Underhill grabbed Cashier Kirk and led him to three safes that were in plain view. Ordered to open the safes, the cashier at first refused until Wilbur firmly instructed him, "Don't get fresh, do as you're told if you don't want to get bumped off." After cracking open two of the boxes, Kirk informed the big bandit, "The third one is on a time clock, I can't open it. I swear." Underhill reacted by threatening to "Blow you're brains across this building." Kirk responded, "Go ahead and shoot if you must, but I cannot open it." Just then, Ed Clanton approached the red-faced Wilbur whose veins were popping out of his neck, saying, "I don't think he's lying about that safe, lets get the hell out of here." A stony silence fell over the scene while Wilbur, with a scowl on his face, considered whether to split or pop a cap in the uncooperative banker. Suddenly, the phone at Mrs. Hunt's desk began to ring. Hunt later stated she literally began to shake in terror fearing the bandits would discover her hidden under the desk and punish her for her subterfuge. Luckily, for her the robbers merely ignored the ringing and the cringing telephone operator. After spending a few more seconds glaring at the banker, Underhill acceded the point and the group began to withdraw from the bank carrying $12,776.04 in cash and silver along with a single $1000 Liberty bond in two pillowcases. Strangely, the bandits failed to rob any of the assembled witnesses or employees during the heist.

On completion of the robbery, Underhill selected Kirk and McElroy as hostages and ordered then to walk in front of them to their waiting 1933 model black Chevrolet. While they were making their way to the front exit, Underhill asked Kirk to tell ex-Sheriff John Russell, hello (Russell had transported Wilbur to the Oklahoma State Penitentiary in 1927). On reaching the getaway car, the bankers were ordered to mount the sideboards, one on each side of the car, which was being driven by Clarence Eno who had remained at the wheel during the actual robbery.

According to witnesses, when Eno began to pull away from the scene he first collided into the car parked in front of him then backed up smashing into the automobile

Citizens National Bank, Okmulgee, Oklahoma. Photo by Naomi Morgan

stationed behind him before finally maneuvering his way into the street. After driving a few blocks, the bankers were ordered off the car. McElroy stated he "Didn't need to be told twice." Upon their release, the hostages raced into the nearby Long-Bell Lumber Yard to report the hold-up.

In a statement made the following day, Okmulgee County Sheriff John Lenox expressed the opinion; "It is probable that Underhill robbed the bank in order to finance Charlie Dotson's judicial appeal which is currently underway in Nebraska."

****

On the evening of November 5, a caravan of cars occupied by a host of machinegun wielding thugs blasted the front windows of a farmhouse located near the Bradshaw farm before motoring into nearby Vian where they spent the next hour driving up and down the main street hooraying the town, hurling threats at pedestrians and firing several dozen rounds into the police headquarters and various storefronts. When a pair of the town's cops attempted to confront the drunken hooligans, they were quickly driven off by machinegun fire. The officers wisely fled into a store where they barricaded themselves and called Muskogee for re-enforcements. The lawmen later positively identified the three individuals sitting in the lead car as Wilbur Underhill, Ford Bradshaw, and Charlie Cotner.

An hour later, a dozen officers from Muskogee and surrounding counties arrived in town. By that time, the caravan of thugs had withdrawn back into the nearby Cookson Hills. Come morning, the posse, now swelled to some sixty officers aided by a pair of bloodhounds, began a massive manhunt in the vicinity Quarry Mountain, which is located approximately a dozen miles northeast of Vian.

After searching the heavily timbered area for several hours, the posse brushed up against the desperadoes producing a short firefight in which no one was injured. The lawmen chased their tails for three days before finally throwing in the towel retreating back to civilization.

Chapter Thirteen

Brothers In Crime and a Trip To The Alter

$\mathbf{A}$cting on a tip from one of his informants, Underhill's old nemesis, Joe Anderson, now Chief of Police of Oxford, Kansas, contacted Creek County, Oklahoma Sheriff Willis Strange with intelligence, which pointed to the whereabouts of the elusive outlaw. Anderson's information indicated Underhill along with Ford Bradshaw was using a residence in the oil field town of Bristow, Oklahoma as a hideout. Apparently the lawman had also been informed the pair was shacking up with a twenty-eight-year-old divorcee named Hazel Winn (alias Hazel Wind), a well-known underworld moll who was acting as their front, renting homes for the gang as well as shopping for their groceries and operating as a courier. Winn, who hailed from nearby Kellyville was suspected of being the woman Bradshaw had picked up several days earlier when he was riding about the countryside with his hostages after the Webbers Falls incident. Anderson, along with a large party of officers from Galena and Baxter Springs, Kansas arrived in Bristow on the afternoon of November 9.

Since being contacted by Anderson, Sheriff Strange,

along with Deputy T.O. Davis and members of the Bristow Police Department had been questioning area residents and business people in an effort to discover the bandit's hideaway. The officers had also been passing out photos of the fugitives and their girlfriends who were fairly well known in the area. By the time, Anderson and the Kansas officers hit town Strange had a line on the outlaw's present location. Evidently, a local pool hall "character" had informed the Sheriff, Miss Winn was keeping company with some fellows at an apartment house located on West Fourth Avenue. When lawmen showed the landlord photos of Underhill he admitted he had observed him entering the apartment several days previously. He identified Hazel Winn as the individual who had originally rented the furnished "digs" on October 1. That evening, Deputy Davis and Anderson along with four Kansas officers began a round-the-clock surveillance of the apartment. Noticing a man and a woman moving about inside and figuring they should strike while the iron was hot, Davis phoned Sheriff Strange at his office in Sapulpa requesting re-enforcements. The Sheriff replied he and a force of deputies along with a contingent of Sapulpa city cops were on their way, adding, he would bring the county's "Type-writers" (Machineguns).

Sheriff Willis Strange. Courtesy Sapulpa Herald

At dawn, eighteen

officers raided the apartment smashing the front and back doors down with sledgehammers. Discovered sound asleep in the front bedroom was Clarence Eno and Miss Winn. A sawed-off automatic shotgun was found propped up next to their bed. Otis Eno was lying on the living room couch, a high-powered rifle was leaning on a nearby coffee table and his sixty-one year-old mother Mary Eno, was deep in her slumbers in the back bedroom. All four suspects surrendered peacefully offering no resistance. When Otis, who was suffering from a self-inflicted gunshot wound, (he had accidentally shot himself in the left foot with his rifle a week before the raid) was moved off the couch, a pile of quarters and half-dollars fell out from the sheets. Searching under the couch cushions, lawmen found four bags containing $1859.05 in mainly silver. A brand spanking new Pontiac automobile was discovered in the garage adjacent to the apartment house. The vehicle was registered to old lady Eno. When searching the car's trunk, a dozen rifles, shotguns, and pistols were discovered along with a great deal of ammunition.

Although officers were a bit disappointed not to find either Underhill or Bradshaw in the apartment, the Kansas officers were overjoyed with the capture of Clarence Eno who was wanted in their state for the robbery of the Baxter Springs and Galena banks. Sheriff Strange, commenting to the press stated, "We didn't get Underhill, but we did nab one of his Lieutenants." When Okmulgee County authorities were contacted, they immediately asked for the return of Clarence who had been positively identified by photo as one of the robbers of the Citizens National Bank. When contacted by Sheriff Strange, the authorities in Nebraska stated they would attempt to extradite Clarence due to his suspected participation in the October 24 Nebraska City bank job. Craig County Oklahoma officers also expressed interest in questioning both Eno brothers about the June 1, 1933, Chelsea bank robbery.

By 8 am, the prisoners had been transferred to the Creek County Jail in Sapulpa. The attractive Miss Winn was again charged with harboring wanted felons (she had been arrested twice in the past year for harboring the robbers of the banks of Peru and Sedan, Kansas). The following day, Otis Eno was transported to the Tulsa County Jail to face charges of auto-theft while Clarence was driven to Okmulgee under heavy guard where he was charged with robbing the Citizens National Bank. Mary Eno was released from custody due to her advanced age and health problems.

In truth, arresting the Eno brothers was a real feather in the officer's caps. No family, besides the Barkers of nearby Tulsa and possibly the prolific Jarrett family of Nowata County, Oklahoma had made such a lasting impact on the recent criminal annuls of the southwest. The family, which hailed from Stone County, Missouri, located deep in the Ozark Mountains, was made up of the father, Lewis Sr., mother Mary, several girls and five boys. Among the boys, Lewis Jr, was the eldest, followed by Virgil, then Earl, Clarence, and Otis. All five had done stretches in various prisons throughout the country for crimes ranging from attempted murder to bank robbery. In 1926, three of Mother Eno's lads, Lewis, Virgil and Otis were suspected of murdering Joplin Chief of Detectives Jessie Laster on an isolated road just north of Joplin. Although Virgil and Otis were both able to establish credible alibis and were cleared of suspicion, Lewis remained a viable suspect in the case for many years.

That evening, Baxter Springs, Kansas Bankers John Conrad and E. J. Whitaker arrived in Okmulgee accompanied by Cherokee County, Kansas Sheriff Dave

Hasenphaugh. Both bankers positively identified Clarence Eno from a lineup at the county jail, as one of the robbers of their place of employment. Several witnesses from the Okmulgee bank heist, including cashier O. H. Kirk, identified Eno as the driver of the getaway car involved in the Citizens National Bank heist. A witness from the Galena, Kansas robbery also identified him as one of the perpetrators of that crime as well. The following morning, Okmulgee County Jailor Bush Rayburn was having a pleasant conversation with Clarence when the inmate suddenly grew quiet. Staring out the barred window at the courthouse lawn he slowly remarked, "You know if I get the chance, I'll bust out of this tin-can."

After spending a week locked in the Tulsa County jail reading comic books and chewing bubble gum (his favorite hobbies), Otis was set free through a habeas corpus hearing in the common pleas court as to the auto theft charge. No sooner had he been granted his freedom then Deputy U S Marshal Tom Dean arrested him on the courthouse steps for his suspected participation in the June 1st 1933 Chelsea, Oklahoma bank robbery. Dean, who was a town constable in Chelsea at the time of the bank heist, had traded shots with the robbers and had recognized the badman from a photo ran in the Tulsa newspaper.

A week after his arrest, Otis was given his preliminary hearing on the Chelsea armed robbery charge in which a $2000 bond was set. His attorney took a shot in the dark requesting the return of the $1859.05 in mostly silver and small bills seized by the officers in the Bristow raid. The authorities had previously offered the loot to the Okmulgee bank's insurance company if the bank could identify it. When they failed to do so, the judge unexpectedly declared Eno's claim was as good as any. Thus, Otis was able to make his bail due to his unexpected windfall.

After the Bristow raid, Underhill, either feeling the heat from the cops or simply tired of his association with the bloodthirsty Bradshaw and his faithful minions, decided to move his operations west into the Central Oklahoma oilfield district driving a new tan Ford V-8 vehicle Hazel and Blanche Cotner (Charlie Cotner's sister) had purchased for him at a Ford dealership in Okemah, Oklahoma. The pair motored to the farm of Wilbur's purported cousin, George " Wash" Nash, who as well as raising a few pigs and a crop of cotton, sometimes operated a hideout for underworld figures near Konawa. His son, Houston, was married to the sister of C. C. "Champ" Patterson, who had recently been captured while attempting to rob a bank in Boley, Oklahoma with "Pretty Boy" Floyd's partner, George Birdwell. Patterson was wounded in the fray while a banker as well as Birdwell and a man named Glass were slain. C. C. was later convicted of murder and sentenced to life at

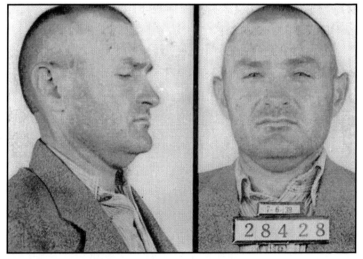

C. C. Patterson. Courtesy Oklahoma State Penitentiary

the Oklahoma State Penitentiary where he spent the next seventeen years until he was paroled in 1949.

The oversized (6'2", 220 lbs.) droopy-eyed, heavily-joweled Houston Nash, who was described by lawmen as a bootlegger and gambler, had several minor brushes with the law in his youth but avoided any major difficulties with the justice system until one hot afternoon in September 1933 when he was arrested for pointing a gun barrel out the window of his car directly at O. P. Ray, the head of the Oklahoma Bureau of Identification, near the state's capital building in Oklahoma City. Nash was charged with concealing a deadly weapon and released on a $500 bond. Exactly why he committed this bizarre act is unknown.

Young Nash's best friend was a thirty-four-year-old divorced out of work bank clerk and World War veteran

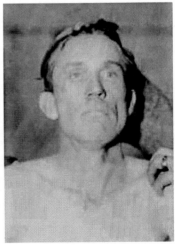

Left: Hazel Underhill. Courtesy Daily Oklahoman.
Above: George Birdwell in death. Courtesy Michael Webb.

named Bruce M. Brady, who happened to be the older brother of "Big" Bob Brady, who had participated in the Memorial Day prison break with Wilbur. The elder Brady had recently been arrested in Oklahoma City on a charge of suspicion of burglary out of Ardmore as well as an auto theft charge from Blanchard, Oklahoma. The day after his capture Brady posted a hefty bond in order to gain his temporary freedom.

On the morning of November 18, 1933, Wilbur and his sweetheart, accompanied by Bruce Brady and an unidentified young girl dressed in a white fur coat, boldly parked in front of the Coal County Courthouse. Wilbur and the kid sat in the car while Hazel along with Brady strolled past the office of Sheriff Walter Clark entering the clerk's office where they made application for a marriage license made out to Henry Underhill age 35, and Beatrice Hudson age 32, both of Tishomingo, Oklahoma.

When Brady, who had an odd habit of tilting his chin while half-closing his eyes when speaking, asked where they could locate a Justice of the Peace, the clerk replied, "Down the street at the barbershop." The pair then moseyed out the courthouse door stopping just long enough to nod "Howdy" to Sheriff Clark and a deputy who were standing in the hallway shooting the breeze. On reaching the barbershop the proprietor, Charles A. Magness, who was also a part time Justice of the Peace and Minister of the Coalgate Church of Christ, informed the couple (Underhill had since switched places with Brady assuming the role of groom) he'd get right to them as soon as he finished shaving a customer. During the short informal ceremony Magness jokingly asked Wilbur if he was related to the famous gangster, Underhill assured him he was not. On completion of the nuptials, Underhill inquired, "How much do I owe you?" The good reverend replied, "How much is

APPLICATION FOR MARRIAGE LICENSE

STATE OF OKLAHOMA, Coal County, ss.   IN COU]

I, ~~Henry Underhill~~ _____ the undersigned, hereby apply

to Mr. ~~Henry Underhill~~ _____, aged _35_ years whose resider

State of_ ~~Okla.~~ _____, and Miss ~~Beatrice Hudson~~ _____

years, whose residence is ~~Tishomingo~~ _____, State of _ ~~Okla.~~ __

the same do solemnly swear that I have personal knowledge of the facts herein stated, that the 1
of said parties are truly and correctly set out above, that neither of said parties are disqualified or
into the marriage relation, nor are they related to each other within the degrees prohibited by law

and reside at ___ ~~Tishomingo~~ ___, County of ~~Johnson~~ _____

                                                    ~~Henry Underhill~~

Subscribed and sworn to before me this __1 8__ day of_ ~~Nov.~~ _____

                                                    ~~Patsy Greene~~

(Seal)   By _____.

I, the undersigned, _____ of _____

above application as being of the age of_____ years, do hereby consent to _____

Dated at Coalgate, Oklahoma, this_____ day of_____

STATE OF OKLAHOMA, Coal County, ss.

Before me, _____

and State, on the_____ day of_____, 19____, personally appeared_____

to me known to be the identical person who executed the within and foregoing instrument, and ack

the same as_____ free and voluntary act and deed for the uses and purposes therein set fort

WITNESS my hand and official seal, the day and date above written.

My commission expires_____, 19____.

MARRIAGE LICENSE

STATE OF OKLAHOMA, COAL COUNTY, ss.   IN COU

TO ANY PERSON AUTHORIZED TO PERFORM AND SOLEMNIZE THE MARRIAGE CEREM

You are hereby authorized to join in marriage Mr. ~~Henry Underhill~~ _____

County of ___ ~~Johnson~~ ___, State of_ ~~Oklahoma~~ _

and Miss ~~Beatrice Hudson~~ _____, of _ ~~Tis.~~

of ___ ~~Johnson~~ _____, State of ~~Oklahoma~~ _____

And of this License you will make due return to my office within thirty days from this date.

WITNESS MY hand and official seal, at__ ~~Coalgate~~ _____

of__ ~~November~~ _____ A. D. 1933__.

(Seal)   ~~Patsy Greene~~

                                              By _____

Recorded this _18th_ day of ~~November~~ _____, 1933.

By _____ Deputy. ~~Patsy Greene~~

CERTIFICATE OF MARRIAGE

STATE OF OKLAHOMA, Coal County, ss.

Marriage license of Wilbur and Hazel Underhill, notice Bruce Brady witnessed the document by signing his middle name 'Merrill' instead of his first name. Courtesy Coal County Clerk of Court

she worth?" According to Magness, the outlaw reached into his fat wallet and handed him a bill of large denomination before strolling out the door of the barbershop. Afterwards, Wilbur and party again waved to the Sheriff who was now standing on the courthouse lawn as they drove out of town. On reaching the city limits, Brady began laughing aloud commenting how clever they had been outwitting the dumb "hick" cops. Speaking of dumb, Hazel had unwittingly instructed the good reverend to send the license to her mother at an address in the Capitol Hill district of Oklahoma City. (*Note: There exists some controversy whether in fact Hazel was legally divorced from her second husband, Sam Hudson, at the time of her marriage to Underhill)

How the authorities finally put two and two together and figured out the groom was actually the notorious outlaw is unclear. Some sources imply a Coalgate resident who knew Underhill by sight had spotted the outlaw sitting in his car outside of the courthouse and after waiting a week or more informed police of his observations. Another report infers Wilbur's attorney, Clarence Sowers, snitched the outlaw off in response to Wilbur writing him a letter informing

COURT HOUSE RECORDS

Civil Cases Filed in Dist. Court
Anna S. Drahos vs. M. H. Ramsey; Foreclosure.
Aetna Life Insurance Company, a corporation, vs. Silas Floyd Duncum; et al. Foreclosure.
R. H. Crim vs. The Board of County Commissioners Coal County, Oklahoma, Reduction of valuation of taxes.

Marriage License Issued

Bill Profit, 22, Tupelo, Miss Audie Dean, 18, Tupelo.
Jack Shirley, 26, Wapanucka, Miss Lou Reed, 19, Wapanucka.
Henry Underhill, 35, Tishomingo, Miss Beatrice Hudson, 32, Tishomingo.
Cecil Holder, 21, Coalgate, Miss Ruby Norris, 18, Coalgate.
Oscar Standridge, 22, Coalgate, Miss Fay Morrison, 18, Coalgate.
D. W. Hall, 23, Centrahoma, Miss Anna Burris, 19, Coalgate.

Court House record of marriages listing Wilbur's marriage in the Coalgate Record and Register

him of his wedding a week after the event while a third version of events implied the authorities were tipped off to Wilbur's marriage the moment Rev. Magness attempted to file the license at the county clerk's office. Regardless of where the information originated, on receipt of the tip Federal Department of Justice agents swarmed to the Coal County Court House uncovering the marriage license. When the investigators questioned Reverend Magness, he subsequently informed them the bride had requested the document be sent to the Capitol Hill address. Officers were promptly assigned to conduct a round the clock surveillance of the home in question. Although the actual name of the residents of the address has never been made public, two basic facts are known. First, the marriage license could not of been sent to Hazel's mom as she had implied due to her dying the previous July, and second, the dwelling's occupants were definitely linked to a pair of miscreant quasi underworld connected brothers named Lonzo and Seedell Johnson who were also put under police surveillance.

Meanwhile, at 1:45 in the afternoon of November 23, four bandits armed with machine guns, sawed-off automatic shot-

C. A. Magness. Courtesy Robert D. Magness Sr.

guns, and pistols boldly strolled into the State National Bank of Frankfort, Kentucky pillaging the institution of $9519 in cash as well as $5500 in negotiable bonds issued from the Franklin Title and Trust Co. The leader of the hijackers who reportedly stood at the rear of the bank's lobby during the raid with a "chopper" cradled in his arms was de-

CLARENCE R. SOWERS
LAWYER
SUITE 904 CENTRAL BLDG.

WICHITA, KANSAS

December 8, 1933.

Mrs. Almira Underhill,
220 South Bales,
Kansas City, Mo.

Dear Mrs. Underhill:

I received a nice letter from Wilbur and was very pleased to hear from him. I enjoyed reading it very much and I was glad to hear that he got married.

I hope that things will shape themselves out so that Wilbur can live happy the rest of his life and can spend the rest of his days as a respected citizen. I know that he wants to do that and would do that if given a chance.

I should like very much to see him.

I honestly believe that he will make a good husband.

I enjoyed very much Dorothy's letter and I want to wish you all my kindest regards and the best wishes for the coming season.

Tell Frank that I often think of him and hope for his success.

With sincere regards, I am,

Yours very truly,

CRS:SMB

Letter dated December 8, 1933 from Attorney Sowers informing Almira of her son's recent marriage. Courtesy of Michael Webb

scribed by witnesses as "Six-foot tall, 175 pounds, and sallow complected." According to bank employee, Stanley Berry, the man kept telling his companions to "Take it easy, we have plenty of time." Berry further stated the fellow appeared to be an "Old hand at the game."

On exiting the bank, the robbers entered a large Plymouth sedan forcing five bank employees to mount the sideboards to act as human shields. At a point roughly half a mile from the scene of the heist, the leader of the group growled for the hostages to "Bail off." The following day officers recovered the fugitive's getaway vehicle abandoned in a cornfield located seven miles northwest of town. It was discovered the car had been stolen the previous week from a local high school football coach. An area farmer came forward stating he had witnessed the Plymouth along with a Ford V8 drive past him the afternoon of the robbery. He further claimed he witnessed the two cars park on the edge of his field stating, "Several men got out of the sedan and transferred to the Ford." The farmer was able to get a good look at one of the men saying, "He wore dark clothes and was bareheaded. Tall fellow, rough-looking, very rough-looking."

In the aftermath of the robbery, Frankfort Police Chief Crawford Lee allowed how the bandits were likely Harry Pierpont and John Hamilton, both members of the John Dillinger Gang. Turns out the lawman was as wrong as he could be, Wilbur Underhill would one day admit to his role as leader of the hijackers. The identity of his companions has never been discovered although rumor has it, Underhill's pal, Charley Cotner, may have been involved in the heist.

****

At approximately 10 pm on the night of November 25 Okmulgee County jail trustee Otis Schuler, who was awaiting trial for robbing the Liberty Café in nearby Henryetta, Oklahoma, grabbed hold of jailor Don Loomis pinning his arms behind his back while another trustee, Earl Williams, who was doing thirty days for petty theft, pressed an ice pick hard against the officer's neck. Knowing he was bested, Loomis quickly gave up his key ring to the pair. The duo then locked the jailor into an empty cell and running down the hall began opening all the cells except the ones leading to the Negro section, calling on their fellow inmates to join them. Only Clarence Eno and James Quinn who was being held on a federal bootlegging charge joined the pair. On their way out the door, Lawrence Weisner, a recent escapee from the state insane asylum at Vinita began begging the escapees to let him accompany them. Weisner, who had been deemed legally insane by a District Judge after kidnapping and robbing an elderly couple at gunpoint, was known in the jail as an overly zealous religious "nut," attending prayer services held at the jail every Sunday by the Baptists and hanging copious amounts of religious literature on his cell walls, as well as spouting Jesus' "Sermon on the Mount,"

Stairwell inside the old Okmulgee County jail in which Eno and his confederates fled. Photo by Naomi Morgan

to all who would listen. Eno turned and stared at the fanatic for a moment before instructing Williams to let the "Damn preacher go."

After rushing down four flights of stairs, the escapees paused just long enough to loot the empty Sheriff's office of several loaded shotguns and rifles before rushing into the street. After splitting with Quinn and the "Preacher," Eno, Williams, and Schuler hijacked a carload of teens from in front of a local drive-in café and taking the kids hostage, began driving west out of town. Unluckily for the fugitives, a pair of Okmulgee city cops sitting in their patrol car witnessed the hijacking and immediately began pursuit.

At a point, roughly three miles northwest of town, the hijackers halted the stolen car and bailed out fleeing on foot across the prairie into the swampy Deep Fork Canadian River bottoms. Not realizing the hijackers had escaped from the county jail, the officers fired a few shots in the fugitive's direction before giving up the chase and driving back to town. Two hours later, a passing taxi-driver heard a series of faint screams emitting deep from the bowels of the jail. He contacted the Sheriff who on investigating the "odd noises" discovered Loomis a prisoner in his own jail. The Sheriff phoned the Fire Department instructing them to blow it's ear-shattering siren four long blasts. Within minutes of giving the alarm, fifty citizens, including twenty National Guardsmen had gathered on the courthouse lawn. While the guardsmen were stationed around the jail in order to prevent any further escapes, a large posse of armed officers and deputized citizens drove in a caravan to the spot the escapees had last been seen and began tracking the fugitives.

Back at the jail, officers were unable to release the jailor due to the escapees stealing the cell keys. After a locksmith had spent several hours attempting to unlock the cell, a welder was called in to cut the bars with a blow-torch finally releasing the poor man.

After searching through the night, the hungry and exhausted posse stumbled back to town with nothing to show but empty bellies and sore feet.

Chapter Fourteen

Running With the Devil

Meanwhile, Wilbur, shuttling between his several hideouts, apparently took time out from his nefarious activities to enjoy a brief period of marital bliss as well as get re-acquainted with several old friends, including the notorious Elmer Inman. The Missouri born Inman who had recently been paroled from the Oklahoma State Penitentiary was a thief of epic proportion. The son of a railroad brakeman, he spent his childhood on the move living in such diverse locations as Mountain Grove, Missouri, Corning, New York, and Shawnee, Oklahoma. While in his teens an uncle employed him as a watchmaker apprentice at his jewelry store in Stroud, Oklahoma where he was not only trained in the art of repairing timepieces but the science of gemology (gem appraisal) as well. It was an education, which would serve him well in the future. In 1916, he was hired as a diamond buyer for a concern located in Arkansas City, Kansas where he promptly embezzled the business for over $7000 of its inventory. The debonair rouge was soon arrested, convicted, and sentenced to ten to twenty years at the Kansas State Penitentiary in Lansing for grand theft. By 1921, the smooth talking Inman had wiggled his way into being appointed a trustee. Soon afterwards, he was selected by Warden J. K. Codding to act as his personal chauffer. The choice proved to be an error in judgment the Warden would live to regret. Inman immediately began a secret liaison with the Warden's naïve young daughter.

In August, Elmer finagled a conditional parole due to his influence with his boss, the Warden, who obviously would not of thought as highly of his prized flunky if he had known of his nighttime rendezvous with his precious daughter. First chance he got, Inman gathered up his sweetheart, stole a car and motored to Holdenville, Oklahoma where the lovebirds took their nuptials. Shortly afterwards the pair was arrested, Inman was thrown back into the pen for parole violation (auto theft) and his marriage annulled by the Governor. His blushing bride begged the state's chief executive to reverse his decision calling their affair a classic case of "eternal love." The authorities turned a deaf ear to the foolish girl's pleadings. Her father, aghast when he heard news of the marriage, was soon forced from office due to the ensuing scandal. After his outing into the free world and short-lived romantic fling, Inman was tucked safely into the innards of the prison with a smile firmly pasted on his face.

After his parole from KSP in the mid-1920's Inman became one of the chief operating officers of the firm of Inman-Terrill-Barker Inc., which soon evolved into the most prolific gang of professional burglars ever to hit the state of Oklahoma. Over the next eighteen months, Elmer, along with legendary arch-criminals Ray Terrill and Herman Barker (Ma Barker's psychopathic eldest issue) robbed an astounding number of businesses in a three state area. The gang's mode of operation was to drive a tow-truck up to the front entrance of a business, smash the door, then roll out the cable, attach it to a safe and simply winch the iron cashbox onto the truck bed before driving to a secluded spot and cracking the safe at their leisure. Business proprietors from one end of the "Sooner" state to the other let out a huge sigh of relief when the gang was broken up in 1927. After being arrested and escaping from several county jails as well as a moving train transporting him to McAlester, Elmer was finally sentenced and successfully delivered to the Oklahoma prison for a term of seven years. Upon completing his hitch at "Big Mac" in September of 1931, he was transferred to Rogers County to stand trial for the 1926 burglary of the City Meat Market. On the evening of October 25th he and "Newt" Clanton's brother, Herman, (Who would one day be charged with robbing the State Bank of Chetopa, Kansas with "Skeet" Bradshaw) along with "Slippery" Willy Elms escaped from the county jail. Inman and his fellow escapees were recaptured five days later near Coffeyville, Kansas. Inman eventually pled guilty to the Claremore burglary and was sentenced to two years in the state slammer along with an extra year for escape.

On his release from McAlester in early 1933, Inman traveled back to Oklahoma City where he joined a pair of his old prison pals and began pulling off some B&E jobs for his daily bread. Inman's new gang was made up of Jack Lloyd, a thirty-year-old five-time looser from Johnson County, Oklahoma along with an incorrigible Missouri born thief named Ralph (Alias Raymond) Roe who along with his two brothers, James and Robert Lee, had been one-time associates of Chester Purdy's in the mid-1920s.

Ralph's criminal history included a commitment to the Oklahoma State Boys Training School at Pauls Valley at the age of twelve followed by a short incarceration at a California Reformatory from which he escaped. Next on the agenda was a one-year stretch at the Tucker Prison Farm in Arkansas, then a stint at Oklahoma's Granite Reformatory. In 1927, he was sentenced to a twelve-year hitch at McAlester for the armed robbery of a café in Paden, Oklahoma. Penitentiary officials described him at the time as twenty-one-years-old, six feet tall, 170 pounds, fair complexion, hazel eyes, and chestnut hair. While at OSP, he was disciplined along with Purdy and Underhill several times for making "Choc" beer, a potent form of "Indian home brew." Roe's younger sibling, Robert, was arrested in Perry, Oklahoma in April 1931 in connection to the slaying of a Lawrence, Kansas patrolman named Melvin Howe. Robert was in turn shot and killed by officers a few weeks after his apprehension while attempting to escape from custody.

After his parole from McAlester in June 1933, Ralph was arrested in Ardmore, Oklahoma in the aftermath of an auto accident. Roe, who was suspected of involvement in a recent aborted kidnapping in Arkansas as well as an area burglary, was held several days for questioning before he was allowed a hearing before a judge. After being charged with reckless driving and suspicion of possessing burglar tools, (a crowbar and hammer) he posted a $500 bond and immediately skipped bail.

In early November Roe and Inman leased a bungalow located at 606 West Dewey Street in Shawnee, Oklahoma from a prominent real estate broker and elected state representative named Joe H. Smalley. Roe signed the lease, "R. H. Reynolds," and Inman, "Joe Sullivan." The resi-

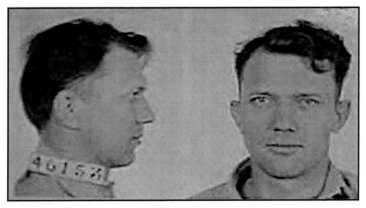

Ralph Roe. Courtesy Rick Mattix

dence would be used as a hideout as well as a gathering place for Inman's underworld companions over the next several weeks.

In the morning hours of Friday December 8, two men, one later identified as Elmer Inman the other as Ralph Roe, purchased a truck in Ada, Oklahoma then drove it to a machine shop where they had a heavy-duty cable winch installed on the rear bed of the rig.

At 1:30 am on the morning of December 12, fifty-eight-year-old Constable Jackson Smith was ambling down the deserted main street of Harrah, Oklahoma heading toward the Barnsdoll Filling Station to fetch a bucket of coal for his home stove from a bin located in the rear of the establishment. Just as he arrived at the station, which was situated directly across the street from the First National Bank, he looked up noticing a tan Ford Sedan with its headlights turned off coming his way. Wondering what a rig was doing out and about at such an hour, he stopped and glared at the car, which was occupied by two gentlemen.

Elmer Inman. Courtesy Tulsa World

The vehicle pulled into the station and one of the men hollered out to Smith saying, "Hey Pop, got a quart of oil?" Smith who was trusted with the keys to nearly every business in town replied in the affirmative and began filling their request when suddenly the men leaped from the car aiming pistols his way. One of the individuals, later identified as Wilbur Underhill, covered the lawman with a large automatic pistol while the other grabbed Smith, abruptly pulling his hat down over his face and spinning him around before binding his hands with electrical tape. After stealing a pair of pearl handled revolvers he was toting, Smith was forced into their car and blindfolded.

The kidnappers, along with their hostage then drove to a point just east of town where they were met by a truck mounted with a winch, which was being driven by an unknown individual accompanied by Houston Nash. When one of his captors asked the watchman if the floor of the bank was wood or concrete, he lied saying "Concrete." Smith was then shoved back into the car and both rigs made their way back to the front of the bank. On the caravan's arrival at the financial institution, Smith was left in the running automobile while the driver and passenger fanned out in the street to keep a lookout. The truck then backed up to the front door, the passenger got out and hooked the winch line to the door of the bank and with a roar of the engine snapped it cleanly off its hinges. Two of the robbers then entered the building hooking the cable hook to the bank's large safe, which sat on a brick pedestal. The driver then put the winch in gear and with a roar moved the safe that weighed an estimated 7000 pounds a few feet until it fell off its base, snapped the cable and crashed through the wooden floor into the basement. According to Smith, who was able to peer under a corner of his loose fitting blindfold, "On hearing the crash, the driver of the winch truck took off like a bat out of hell driving toward the edge of town." The others jumped into the idling Ford and pursued their comrade catching up with him about a quarter of a mile outside of the city limits. After a great deal of arm-twisting, they talked their frightened cohort into returning to the bank in order to attempt to winch the safe from the basement. On the second try, the cable again broke and the bandits gave up fleeing town with the constable tied up in the rear seat. About dawn, Smith was released in a field near Earlsboro, minus his billfold, which contained a five-dollar bill.

The following morning a boy on his newspaper route noticing the front door of the bank was wide open rushed to the home of banker O. G. McClurg breathlessly notifying him of his discovery. A crowd quickly formed around the open doorway staring into the large hole in the floor containing the oversized safe. Citizens of Harrah hadn't seen so much excitement since a pair of youthful bandit's had raided the same bank on the morning of March 11, 1931. On that occasion, one of the hijackers was slain by a well-aimed shotgun blast fired by an alert vigilante while his companion was able to make his escape minus the loot, which was discovered in the dead bandit's pockets.

Several posses from the area were formed and began setting up roadblocks. They were later joined by a large group of lawmen from nearby Oklahoma City. But no trace could be found of the robbers. At nearly 5 am an exhausted Jackson Smith was discovered collapsed outside a radio station near Earlsboro. Local lawmen transported him back to Harrah and his over-wrought family. Although the night watchman would later identify Wilbur Underhill as one of his kidnappers, Oklahoma County Deputy Bill Eads initially informed newsmen the heist was probably the work of "Amateurs."

Officer Jackson Smith. Courtesy Keitha Fudge

The following afternoon the same brown Ford V8 used in the Harrah raid parked next to a roadside curb near the First National Bank of Coalgate, Oklahoma. Three well-dressed men stepped out of the car and casually strolled through the bank's front door. One of the men, described as swarthy and short in stature, stopped just inside the bank's entrance while the other two who was described as "Taller" entered the lobby.

Inside the bank, Cashier Oliver Browning was at his station at the main counter servicing a customer named Frank Collettea, while Assistant Cashier Lillian O'Connell was doing figures. Browning noticed the men enter the building but paid little attention until he observed one of the individuals was carrying what looked like a machinegun. Suddenly a large man armed with a pistol announced in a loud voice, "Don't anyone stick em up, just stay still." Adding, "We got the lowdown on this place, we want some money you have." He then elbowed his way past Collettea ordering Browning to "Open the safe." Just then, a customer named Milt House walked into the lobby hoping to get a check cashed. He was immediately ordered to "Join the others and get your face against the wall."

Ford V8. Courtesy Muskogee Phoenix

As for opening the safe, Browning retorted, "Can't, it's on a time lock." Suddenly the other large bandit armed with the chopper approached the Cashier menacingly waving the gun, the muzzle directly pointed at Browning. He stopped a foot from the frightened banker's face and snarled, "Open it up." Browning, knowing the fellow wasn't fooling, immediately complied. Turning the safe's lever, it popped open. Ironically, the robbery was taking place at exactly the moment the safe was set to open. After cleaning out the cashbox and tills for roughly $2800 in cash and a little over $300 in silver, the robbers marched the four witnesses out the front door to their getaway car which was parked on the corner of Main and Ohio Avenues. On reaching the automobile, the bandit carrying the "Tommy gun" who was later identified as Wilbur Underhill, instructed Mrs. O'Connell to, "Sit your duff in the rear seat" while ordering Frank Collettea, Milt House, and Oliver Browning to "Mount the running boards," adding, "Do as we say or we'll kill ya." The hostages were let off at a point two miles northwest of town on Highway 19. The quick thinking Browning took note of the car's license plate that checked out to a 1929 Chevy owned by S. B. Strickland of Duncan, Oklahoma. Mr. Strickland had reported the plate stolen the previous week

Although the bank had no alarm system, several citizens who had watched the entire event immediately reported the hijacking. It seems as though Emma Morgan, who operated a newsstand located in a room attached to the rear of the bank, was cracking pecans when she noticed the commotion next door. Looking through a crack in the thin wall that separated her shop from the financial institution she observed the ongoing heist. Running to the Jones Café, she attempted to find the proprietor, Bill Jones, who was also the town marshal. Unfortunately, the lawman was out of pocket. Next, she hustled to the Mayer Hotel where she instructed the desk clerk to phone the Sheriff. After she had done her civic duty, Mrs. Morgan, now joined by the hotel owner and her daughter, scurried back to her shop where the three ladies had a front row seat to the biggest event in town.

Several hours later and forty miles distant, a Konawa, Oklahoma policeman spotted a car that matched the description of the one used in both the Coalgate and Harrah raids leave the slab (paved) road pulling onto a dirt lane just south of town. The officer tried to follow the rig but lost it near the Canadian River bottoms. He then went back to town and phoned Jake Sims, the Chief of Police of nearby Seminole. Sims, an ex-US Department of Justice agent, in turn contacted officers in Coalgate as well as A. B. Cooper, an investigator for the Burns Detective Agency who had been hired by the Oklahoma Bankers Association to track Underhill. Sims began organizing a posse made up of his self, Cooper, Federal Agent Tyler Birch, Pontotoc County Sheriff Clyde Kaiser, and several Pontotoc and Seminole County officers.

The following day, the posse set out in a two-car caravan in an attempt to scout the vicinity where the suspicious automobile was last seen. Just before dusk the vehicle containing Agent Birch and the deputies suffered a flat forcing them to stop and change the tire while the other squad car containing Sheriff Kaiser, Cooper, and Sims was able to continue. At a point five miles south of Konawa, Sims spotted the getaway car in the front yard of the George Nash farm parked next to a tool shed. The license plate-OK224124 matched that given by a witness to the Harrah robbery. Observing old man Nash standing in the back yard, the lawmen quickly descended on him verbally assaulting him with a barrage of questions. While this was going on,

Underhill, suffering from a bad cold, high fever, and his usual accompanying earache, was sound asleep in a bedroom located toward the front of the residence. Awakened by all the commotion, the outlaw, dressed only in his long-handled underwear, grabbed a pair of Lugar pistols and a bag containing the bulk of the loot from the Coalgate job off a nearby table and slipped out a window making his way to his car. While the officers were clustered in the rear of the home engrossed in conversation with George Nash, Underhill started the car and by the time the officers realized what was going on the fleeing Ford was spinning gravel headed toward freedom. An angry Sims, caught unaware by the sudden development, asked Nash, "Who was that? The old man, who was difficult to understand due to his not having a tooth in his head, mumbled, "Wilbur Underhill."

Just as the second carload of lawmen turned into the Nash's driveway, they spotted Underhill's speeding Ford heading right toward them. Suddenly the fugitive's car veered off the road into a cow pasture traveling about a hundred yards before crashing through a barbwire fence and upon entering the main road accelerated into the coming darkness. The officers quickly turned their rig around taking off in pursuit of the badman but their automobile promptly bogged down in a mud hole. Back at the Nash farm, Sims and Cooper began searching the house. When Sims entered the bedroom where the outlaw had been sleeping, he discovered a machine gun, Underhill's clothes, and a bottle of cold remedy. Laying on a table in the living room was $5 in nickels and dimes. The frustrated officers could do nothing but wring their hands in frustration. Actually, the raid was reportedly ill planned at best. According to news reports, several members of the hastily assembled posse had showed up unarmed, forgetting their guns at home.

Meanwhile, the elder Nash, knowing he was in deep trouble, stopped stonewalling the officers and promptly began answering their questions, advising officers Underhill was supposed to meet his son Houston and Bruce Brady, whose notorious younger brother had recently been apprehended in New Mexico, that night at the farm. Lawmen settled down to a stakeout hoping to nab Brady and Houston Nash if they showed up.

Around 9 pm, the pair, unaware of Underhill's escape, came driving up to the house. The moment they dismounted their rig, the posse surrounded them with guns drawn. The men gave up peacefully. When questioned both men pleaded ignorance claiming they had no idea of any meeting with Underhill. Upon their detention, the two men were taken to Coalgate to face a lineup. Sims, who stated the elder Nash had been "cooperative," released him from custody.

When none of the witnesses from the robbery were able to identify either man, they were set free on a Habeas Corpus hearing. Upon the suspect's release A. B. Cooper along with Coal County Sheriff Walter Clark, Agent Birch, Deputy US Marshal Allen Stanfield, and several Pontotoc County officers, set up a surveillance of the Nash farm. That night ex-Sequoyah County Sheriff John E. Johnson, now assistant Superintendent of the

Officer Jake Sims. Courtesy Seminole Producer

Oklahoma State Crime Bureau, in an interview with a reporter from the *Daily Oklahoman* stated the trio who robbed the Coalgate bank was made up of Wilbur Underhill, Ford Bradshaw, and Ed Davis.

The day after the Konawa raid, officers observed the younger Nash arrive at his father's home where he stayed only a few minutes before motoring west on a dirt road. After driving less than a mile, he stopped and got out of the car with a burlap bag and began walking into the woods. Suspecting the youth was attempting to hide something, Cooper, accompanied by a pair of Pontotoc County officers, approached the suspect who reacted by making a mad dash in the direction of his parked car. When one of the lawmen fired a warning shot over his head Nash abruptly stopped, throwing his hands up in surrender. Searching the area, lawmen discovered a half dug hole containing a burlap bag filled with $258.65 in silver coins. Nash was arrested and transported to the federal lockup in Muskogee. The money was returned to the bank in Coalgate. Back at the Nash farm, George Nash was questioned as to where the loot came from. He clammed up and soon joined his son in the slammer. Both were charged under the federal statutes governing the harboring of fugitives as well as state charges of carrying concealed weapons. Later that same day, Bruce Brady was arrested by a squad of G-men at a hotel in Ada and charged with harboring. Bonds of $10,000 each were set for the trio.

That night federal officials once again intently interrogated the three as to any information they had in their possession concerning Underhill's movements. While George Nash refused to further cooperate, his son informed interrogators that Underhill had often times used a junkyard in Konawa as well as an apartment in Ada as hideouts. He further declared an employee of the salvage yard had purchased ammunition and supplies for Underhill on several occasions in the past. Although agents watched both the junkyard and now vacant apartment for several days, nothing came of the surveillance. Young Nash also told officers he had first met Wilbur through Bruce Brady in late November declaring, "I was only interested in writing the outlaw's life story. I offered him a 50% royalty on the venture." The big man further claimed, "Underhill came to my home the night of the Coalgate robbery driving a brown four-door Ford sedan. Moments after he arrived, two men introduced to me as Gene Clark and Ed Davis (*Investigators later suspected the individual introduced as Davis was in reality Ralph Roe) driving a black two-door 1933 Ford joined us. I asked him, 'Did you rob the Coalgate bank?' He replied 'Hell yes.' When I asked him how much he got, he said, 'Over a grand apiece.' He then went to my father's place to spend the night." Adding to his statement, Nash said, "The next morning I drove out to see Wilbur. He was sick in bed and asked me to go to an address in Oklahoma City and get his wife. I picked her up about four and on our way back drove past my father's place and noticed three cars parked on the road. I knew the officers had made a raid so I took her to Bill Haven's Tourist Camp where she caught a bus back home." When Bruce Brady was questioned, he refused to make any sort of statement written or otherwise instructing the cops to "Go shove it." Although Brady would soon be released on bond, within months he would be returned to jail facing an unrelated federal counterfeiting charge.

A few hours after Brady's apprehension, a nineteen-man posse raided a nightclub in Joplin, Missouri after they had received a tip suggesting the outlaw had been spotted loitering in the establishment's parking lot. Kansas City officers also initiated a 24-hour surveillance of the home of

Almira Underhill and began shadowing the movements of her and her daughter Dorothy.

Meanwhile, several hundred miles to the north, three large men strolled into the First National Bank of Syracuse, Nebraska looting it for $1500. There were reportedly twelve witnesses in the bank at the time of the hijacking. Although a pair of bystanders identified Wilbur Underhill from a photograph as was one of the bandits, the other ten witnesses positively identified Wilbur's ex-partners in crime Ford Bradshaw, Clarence Eno, and Robert Trollinger as the actual raiders. The robbers made their getaway in a new blue Chevy Sedan with Illinois license plates and white wall tires.

Chapter Fifteen

Epitaph For a Badman

Meanwhile, Ralph H. Colvin, regional director of the U S Department of Justice's investigative wing, (The forerunner of the FBI) taking note of Underhill's activities decided to put on a full court press in an all out effort to capture the badman.

Shortly after becoming aware of Wilbur's marriage at Coalgate, Colvin, who had been the lead investigator in the recent Urschel kidnapping case, and Agent Frank Smith,

Agent Frank Smith. Courtesy Tulsa World

a survivor of the Kansas City massacre, began assembling a task force which included twenty-nine federal agents along with a contingent of officers from the Oklahoma County Sheriff's office and a party of Oklahoma City policemen which included Detectives Mickey Ryan, D. A. "Jelly" Bryce, and Clarence Hurt.

The thirty-six-year-old Clarence Hurt, who had led the raid on Hazel Hudson's Oklahoma City residence, was a formidable force in his own right. Joining the Oklahoma

City Police Department as a patrolman in 1919, he rapidly worked his way up the ranks to the position of Assistant Chief of Police by the age of thirty-two, becoming the youngest chief in the department's history. In 1926, he was loaned out to the Department of Justice seeing service as an investigator during the infamous Osage Indian murder case. In 1931, he joined the detective bureau as a supervisor. Jelly Bryce joined the force after impressing Hurt with his marksman ability at a shooting match. Bryce had a reputation as a "Triggerman," gunning down several fleeing felons during his first year with the department.

A week after the Konawa raid, task force members re-interviewed George Nash, who after sitting in the Muskogee jail for a few days decided he didn't cotton to that sort of existence and began singing like a church house choir giving the officers a wealth of information. He informed his interrogators, "I first met Underhill several weeks ago at my son's home in Ada. He was introduced to me as George Hudson. Houston asked me to put him up at my house for the night. On the way home, he asked if I needed anything from town. We drove to Streetman's Store in Konawa where he bought me $3.50 worth of groceries.

The Oklahoma County Sheriff's Department circa 1933. Courtesy of Stanley Rogers

He had a .45 pistol tucked in his belt and the rear of his car was piled high with blankets. When he left, he gave me $15.00.... He came back the morning of the Harrah robbery with a couple of pals and again on the night of December 13. He stayed all night and most of the next day and was very sick from a bad cold. My son-in-law drove to Konawa and got some soothing medicine for him. When the officers drove up he got in his Ford and drove off." When crowded as to the identities of the two men accompanying Underhill the morning of the Harrah raid, the elder Nash claimed one was unknown to him while the other was a shadowy ex-school teacher from Pittsburg County named Eugene Clark, alias Glen Davis.

On receipt of the information concerning Underhill's ill health, agents took a shot in the dark fanning out questioning area doctors and druggists showing them photos of Underhill.

Clarence Hurt. Courtesy Jack Hurt

The day before Christmas investigators finally got a break in the case. A Seminole physician identified a photo of Underhill as a man he had treated at a beauty shop in town. According to the doctor, the morning after the Konawa raid, he had received a phone call from a local druggist inquiring if he would make a house call to an apartment above the Blue Bird Beauty Parlor located at 207 East Oak Street in order to treat a man with a severe cold and ear infection. It appears that the operator of the shop, a thirty-three-year-old three-time divorcee named Eva Mae Nichols, had contacted the pharmacy in search of a doctor to treat a "friend." The physician continued, saying the man had given his name as George Hickson. The authorities immediately began a loose but apparently ineffective surveillance of the beauty shop, which was located in a two-story downtown brick building. Miss Nichols lived in a second story apartment above the shop with her sister.

A short investigation of Miss Nichols, who was described as plump but attractive, turned up the fact she was apparently a well-respected business women known for her wit, intelligence, and drive. She and her sister, Lena, who worked and lived together, were both obvious "thrill seekers" having a penchant for dating unsavory types. Eva, who had left home at the tender age of seventeen traveling alone

Modern day view of the site of the Blue Bird Beauty Parlor. Photo by Naomi Morgan

to New York City to attend beauty school, was apparently a headstrong and free-spirited lass. She was a bit of an enigma, although she obviously enjoyed living on the wild side she in turn willingly took on the responsibility of supporting her younger siblings after the death of their parents. Not your typical gangster's moll.

According to FBI reports the investigators were not operating totally in the dark, they had an ace in the hole in the form of a mole operating inside the Underhill mob. An informant, whose identity is still unknown to this day, (Name is blacked out on FBI reports) approached the feds in mid-November offering his services for a fee. FBI agent Frank Smith, who was appointed the snitch's handler, evidently offered him a $500 cash reward as well as his assistance in gaining the $350 reward offered by the state of Kansas for the badman's capture if he could put the outlaw on the

Downtown Seminole, 1930s. Courtesy Seminole Producer

spot. The informant, who was dubbed "Jack Hughes" for contact purposes, was provided some spending money and presented with a car for his use compliments of Uncle Sam.

On the evening of December 29, Agent Smith was phoned by "Hughes" who stated he and Lon Johnson had just visited Wilbur Underhill at a residence located at 606 West Dewey Street in Shawnee. "Hughes" requested Smith instruct the Shawnee police to immediately arrest him and Johnson in order to avoid any suspicion that he was involved in any raid made on the place. This was done. When Smith arrived at the city lockup in order to confer with his stool pigeon, "Hughes" advised him he and Johnson had stopped by the Dewey street address at approximately 7:30 pm but found no one at home. At roughly 8:30 pm, the pair again visited the residence, this time Underhill's automobile was parked in the driveway. According to the informant, he and his companion entered the residence and spoke with Wilbur who was in the company of his wife and Ford Bradshaw.

Agents conferred with Shawnee Night Chief Frank Bryant who instructed his investigators to search the utility deposits on file at city hall. The deposits for the residence in question were found to be under the name of J. H. Reynolds. When the owner of the home, Hatler Smith, a prominent insurance agent, was rolled out of bed and questioned he informed officers the cottage was rented to a man of the same name. He

Eva Mae Nichols. Courtesy Daily Oklahoma

further instructed lawmen he had not set eyes on the individual. Instead, a politician turned real-estate agent and part-time bond merchant named Joe Smalley had made the actual lease arrangements. When Smalley was contacted, he stated he had let the property in early November to a pair of individuals who signed the agreement as J.H. Reynolds and Joe Sullivan. After some arm-twisting, he admitted the character using the name of Sullivan was in reality Elmer Inman. That name rang a bell. Smalley explained his actions by stating although he had known Inman for many years he was unaware the slick gangster was wanted at this time for any crime. It later came to light; the house had been under observation for nearly two weeks by Shawnee Police detectives who suspected the residents were engaged in bootlegging activities. At half past midnight a squad car carrying Agent Frank Smith and Detective Clarence Hurt accompanied by the informant drove past the residence in order to ascertain if there was any activity-taking place. The officers spotted a light in the back bedroom with sounds of a drinking party emitting from the place. Upon receiving information of this new development, Agent Colvin contacted the members of his task force instructing them to "Saddle Up!"

At roughly 2 am on a cold, wet, foggy morning, a large party of heavily armed federal, county, and city officers rendezvoused at the central police station located in downtown Shawnee. Colvin informed the group "I think we have our man, now lets set the trap!" To ensure the lawmen would not be shooting at one another or into surrounding homes, Colvin gave explicit instructions as to where each officer would be stationed during the ambush. Afterwards, the group set out in several automobiles parking a block and a half from the house in question. Setting up in front of the residence directly across the street was federal agents T. N. Birch, G. H. Franklin, and J. M. Edger all equipped with shotguns, positioned nearby was Oklahoma County Deputy Sheriffs George Kerr and Don Stone. Next to them was Shawnee Night Chief Frank Bryant, armed with a machinegun. Standing on the porch of a dwelling located directly east of the targeted residence were Oklahoma County Deputies Bill Eads and John Adams. Federal Agents Colvin, Frank Smith, K. D. Deadrick, and Paul Hanson, along with Oklahoma City Detectives Clarence Hurt, A. D. Bryce, and Mickey Ryan were assigned to cover the rear of the residence. Colvin and Bryce were armed with machine guns, while Smith, Ryan, Hanson, and Deadrick had shotguns. Hurt was equipped with a tear

Several members of the posse, Agent R. H. Colvin, top left, Clarence Hurt, top right, Jelly Bryce, kneeling right. Courtesy Jack Hurt.

gas gun as well as his trusty "chopper."

Hurt, accompanied by Colvin, crept to the window of a bedroom located on the northeast corner of the rear of the dwelling while the others took up positions to their rear. Although the darkness and heavy fog limited their vision, officers could make out a faint light glowing in the room. The pair peered into the window. Colvin pressed the barrel of his machinegun against the screen while Hurt readied his gas gun. They both observed Underhill standing at the foot of the bed clothed only in his long underwear while his scantily dressed wife sat on the edge of the mattress.

When a dog started barking in the distance, Underhill looked up and began walking toward the window. A couple of feet from the window, he suddenly stopped locking eyeballs with Officer Hurt. Hurt yelled, "This is the law Wilbur, stick 'em up!" The outlaw replied, "Okay," then whirled about grabbing a wicked looking automatic Lugar pistol which was attached to an ammo drum with a capacity of thirty-one rounds, off a nearby nightstand. Hurt reacted by firing a single round from his gas gun, the missile crashing through the screen and glass before bouncing off Underhill's stomach. Colvin squeezed the trigger of his machine gun loosening a full clip of .45 rounds that smashed into the bedroom's walls and shattered a glass mirror. Hazel fainted, dropping like a stone to the floor, a maneuver that probably saved her life. The officers standing behind Hurt and Colvin opened up with machine guns and shotguns pumping a ferocious volley of lead into the room. Hurt stated he quickly ducked and weaved to get out of the line of his comrade's fire. Meanwhile, the second male suspect, currently lying in bed with a female companion in an adjacent bedroom was struck in the left arm and shoulder by rounds piercing the wall between the rooms. The female, later identified as Eva Mae Nichols, jumped up running toward the front door screaming hysterically when suddenly she crumpled to the floor in a bloody heap hit squarely in the stomach by a pair of steel-jacketed .45 caliber rounds. Amazingly, she found the strength to gain her footing and rush out the front door and on to the front yard where she abruptly pitched forward to the ground when a machinegun round struck her in the foot.

Hurt maintained he saw Wilbur fall to the floor then jump up and rush into the bathroom where he stopped momentarily to return fire before darting into the living room and on to the front porch. On hearing the sudden explosion of deafening gunfire emitting from the rear of the residence and observing the blinding detonation of a myriad of muzzle flashes lighting up the inky-black night like a fourth of July fireworks display, the posse stationed in front of the house took their safeties off and stood at the ready searching for a target. The moment they caught sight of Wilbur sprinting out the front door, Bryant, Eads, Adams, and Stone began hosing down the outlaw with shotgun and machine gun rounds. Sideswiped by the fierce volley of lead, Wilbur fell to the muddy earth with a thud where he lay still. Temporarily holding their fire, lawmen began to warily approach the badman when suddenly like Lazarus from the grave he leaped to his feet and dashed madly into the shadows between two neighboring houses.

Meanwhile, Colvin, hearing the firing coming from the front of the home was just rounding the corner when he nearly bumped into the fleeing Underhill. The G-Man responded by, in his words, "Tattooing" the fugitive's back with a machine gun burst. At about the same time, a pursuing Frank Bryant, dropped to one knee and unleashed a full drum of submachine gun rounds into the fleeing man's direction. To both his and Colvin's astonishment, the horribly wounded bandit just kept running till he again disappeared into the foggy night. Colvin later explained, "I don't know how he did it. The bastard just wouldn't stay down."

Back at police headquarters the switchboard suddenly lit up like a Christmas tree, citizens living near the scene of the shootout reported someone was setting off illegal firecrackers, others described their windows being broken by rock throwing juvenile delinquents while yet another citizen reported a prowler running through his yard clothed only in his underwear.

Moments after Underhill had pulled his Rasputin act, Deputy Kerr, standing staring in the darkness, heard the voice of the second male subject emitting from inside the tear gas filled house begging to be allowed to come out and surrender. Kerr ordered him to crawl out the bedroom window while instructing the posse to hold their fire. The suspect, who had taken slugs to the shoulder and elbow,

The scene, shortly after the gun battle, arrow points to the back window where officers spotted Underhill. Courtesy The Daily Oklahoman

responded, "I can't but I'll crawl out the front door." Kerr replied, "Go ahead," then covered the outlaw with his weapon as he wiggled on his belly on to the porch where he was handcuffed and transported to the Shawnee Municipal Hospital. Although he refused to answer questions from officers, he did identify himself not as Ford Bradshaw as previously thought but Ralph "Raymond" Roe. He expressed great anxiety over Miss Nichols condition, saying, "She is innocent of all our doings...I got her into this and now she's gonna die...She's a good kid who strung along with us asking no questions even when she saw all those guns."

After waiting a few minutes for the tear gas to dissipate, Colvin and a group of officers entered the residence where they discovered an unconscious but unhurt Hazel Underhill sprawled on the floor next to the bed. Lawmen were amazed to find her unscathed while the walls of the bedroom were literally shredded. Officers picked her up

606 West Dewey Street. Bloody mattress Roe and Nichols were lying on shown in foreground. Courtesy The Daily Oklahoman

and carried her into the front yard where suddenly she jerked away from them and began clawing at her burning eyes and gasping for fresh air. When questioned, Hazel was reportedly incoherent. Colvin suggested she was inebriated. Mrs. Underhill was then transported to the city jail and locked in a cell where she immediately flopped on a cot and fell into a sound sleep. Eva Nichols, floating in and out of consciousness was transported to the emergency room located at the Municipal Hospital where she occupied a room adjacent to her wounded lover. On her arrival at the medical center, she asked for her ex-husband who lived in nearby Seminole. Both wounded suspects were placed under heavy guard.

Back at the scene of the raid, the posse fanned out

Above: Oklahoma County deputies in the act of arresting a pair of Kansas bank robbers at a rural roadblock circa 1930s. Courtesy Stanley Rogers

Left: Officer Bill McKenzie. Courtesy Daily Oklahoman

splitting up into several small groups and began a house-to-house search while two-dozen other officers from surrounding counties soon joined the manhunt. Operating on the misguided notion that suggested the desperado had somehow gotten possession of a set of wheels and was seeking a friendly face, a contingent of Oklahoma County sheriff's deputies raided Lon Johnson's SE 23rd Street address at approximately 4 am. Although Underhill was not found, lawmen arrested Lonzo Johnson's little brother, Seedell, on charges of harboring a fugitive from justice. Although the youth vigorously denied ever meeting Underhill, tire tracks matching those of plaster casts taken from Wilbur's Ford were discovered in the Johnson's dirt driveway.

Meanwhile, ten miles east of the Johnson residence the bleeding and dazed fugitive, in a superhuman effort, ran several blocks before stumbling face first onto the rain soaked ground. He laid there for several minutes in order to gain strength and get his bearings before racing east across the Jefferson School yard finally com-

The used furniture shop where Underhill was captured. Courtesy The Daily Oklahoman

ing to the Shawnee Creek drainage ditch where he collapsed and laid low for an hour or more, unable to move due to numerous patrol cars criss-crossing the area. Around 5 am, he attempted to start an old feed truck he had spotted nearby but failed. Cursing his luck he stumbled in a southerly direction until he hit an alley located between Main and Seventh. His journey on foot while suffering from numerous painful wounds which would have killed a normal man came to an end when he reached the back door of the McAlester Furniture Store located sixteen blocks from where he had began his dash for freedom. He could go no further.

At roughly 6 am, officers came across a large pool of blood on the banks of the Shawnee Creek drainage ditch. The officers decided to stay put and wait for the arrival of bloodhounds from the state penitentiary in McAlester.

An hour later Bill McKenzie, a motorcycle cop who was temporarily acting as a dispatcher at police headquarters, was contacted by R. A. Owens, the manger of a second-hand furniture store located at 509 East Main, with startling news. Owens reported a large man clothed only in his underwear had broken into the back door of his establishment. McKenzie, suspecting the intruder was Underhill rushed out to the station's parking lot where he encountered Oklahoma County Sheriff Stanley Rogers who had just arrived on the scene. Rogers, accompanied by his son who happened to be home on Christmas vacation from medical school, quickly gathered a posse, which included radio dis-

Sheriff Stanley Rogers. Courtesy Oklahoma County Sheriff's Department

patchers Jack Roberts and John Whalen along with Oklahoma City Detective John Cassidy and Oklahoma County Deputy W. E. Agee. The small group hurried to the scene in a two-car caravan, lights flashing. The younger Rogers, McKenzie, and Agee took the front door of the establishment while the sheriff accompanied by Cassidy, Roberts, and Whalen took the rear. The officers, seeing several shadowy figures moving about, kicked in the locked front door while the officers located in the rear entered the already open back door. They quickly discovered an individual lying in a blood-soaked bed with a Lugar pistol lying on the floor next to him. The store's manager and his wife were standing frozen in position in the far corner of the room.

Sheriff Rogers reported he approached the individual who he recognized as Wilbur Underhill and after checking out his wounds, leaned down telling him, "You're in a bad way, boy." Underhill haltingly replied "Ya, I'm shot to hell, they got me five times. I counted the slugs as they hit me. When I set sail they really poured it to me." Rogers stated "His back was peppered with shotgun wounds and he had been struck by .45

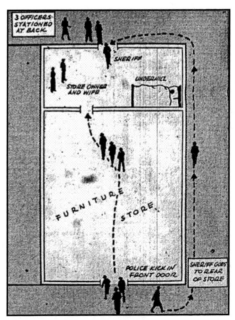

Diagram of store where Wilbur was discovered. Courtesy The Daily Oklahoman

slugs in the head, right arm, back, and right leg," adding, " How he got through that hail of lead and ran sixteen blocks suffering from those terrible wounds is beyond understanding."

Officer Bill McKenzie, describing the badman's capture in a story for the *Shawnee Morning News* stated "We found Underhill lying motionless on a blood-soaked bed. His blond hair was dyed red from blood, (actually the outlaw had recently had his hair dyed a reddish-brown tint at Miss Nichols beauty shop) he could hardly breath, choking and gasping. His face was wracked with pain. I noticed the top half of his left ear had been shot off. He was also suffering from exposure to the cold due to his long run clad only in his underwear and socks. We expected to have to kill him. It was a relief to discover him lying helpless and offering no resistance." The dying fugitive was transported to the Municipal Hospital to join his partner and Miss Nichols. According to McKenzie, the wounded outlaw repeatedly howled in pain and begged the ambulance driver to slow down due to his fear of falling off the stretcher as the rig made several sharp turns on the ride to the hospital."

When the proprietor of the furniture store, who maintained his living quarters in the rear of the building, was asked why the fugitive had picked his establishment to collapse in, he responded, "I don't know. We were awakened when he forced his way through the back door into our bedroom just moments before the cops arrived. I never seen him before in my life." Owens later changed his tune, claiming Underhill had awakened him by pounding on the back door asking for a drink of water. After admitting the fugitive into his apartment, he claimed he put him to bed and offered first aid out of the compassion of his heart. It also appears the storekeeper, rather than immediately contacting the cops, waited nearly an hour before seeking their assistance. A story soon began circulating inferring the store had been used in the past as a warehouse for stolen goods. (A fencing operation.) There appears to have been some credence to this claim. According to FBI reports, Owens was an ex-con who had done time with Wilbur in McAlester. The report went on to read, "Evidently Underhill knew exactly where he was headed when he fled." Due to Owens cooperating with the authorities, the feds decided not to further pursue the matter.

Back at the scene of the raid, officers began searching the Dewey Street house for evidence. The residence was described as looking like a war-zone, all the home's furniture was turned over except the dining room table, which

Posse of Oklahoma County deputy's commanded by Sheriff Stanley Rogers after a successful raid circa 1933. Sheriff Rogers, fourth from left standing, as well as Deputies John Adams, far left standing, W. A. Agee, third from left standing, and Don Stone, sixth from left standing, were all involved in the apprehension of Wilbur Underhill. Courtesy Stanley Rogers

sat upright, on it sat a half-empty quart bottle of whiskey. Broken glass and debris covered the floors; the walls and ceilings were shredded by gunfire and splattered with blood. The cottage's woodwork and doors were reportedly splintered. Officers estimated over two hundred rounds had been fired in the shootout. A packet containing $5300 in negotiable bonds issued by the Franklin Title and Trust Company of Frankfort, Kentucky that was identified as part of the loot from the November 23, 1933 robbery of the State National Bank of Frankfort was discovered in one of the bedrooms. The bonds were in $1000-$500-and $100 denominations. A large quantity of ammunition and four pistols, a Lugar automatic with a folding stock, two Colt .45 automatics, and a .38 caliber revolver were also found in the search. When officers searched Wilbur's Ford which was parked in the garage, they discovered a .30-.30 rifle, a sawed-off .12 gauge Winchester pump shotgun, a short double barreled shotgun with a pistol handle, and a tin pail full of roofing nails for use as a deterrent for pursuing squad cars (Not exactly James Bond-like, but effective).

Chapter Sixteen

Home Sweet Home

Back at the Shawnee Hospital, doctors observed Underhill had been struck by four .45 caliber steel-jacketed bullets, one slug entered his back slicing through his liver destroying his bladder and a kidney, while a second struck him in the left front corner of his forehead plowing a groove around his head cutting off the top of his ear, a third struck him in the right forearm, and a fourth had plowed into his lower right leg. He was also suffering from numerous buckshot wounds to the left arm, lower back, buttocks, and legs. His condition was deemed as non-re-

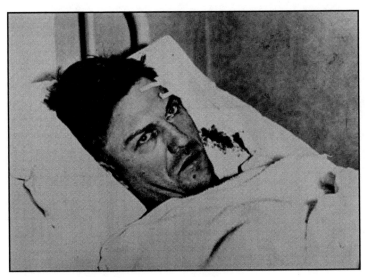

Wilbur Underhill shortly after the gunfight. Courtesy Rick Mattix.

coverable. He was patched up and put in a private room on the second floor guarded by a quartet of heavily armed G-men. Ralph Roe's wounds were evaluated as non-life threatening; he was treated and transported to the city jail. As for Eva Mae Nichols, her condition was judged critical and doctors doubted she would make it.

Underhill lapsed in and out of consciousness for the next thirty-six hours. When awake, Agent Colvin and Detective A. B. Cooper vigorously questioned the outlaw. The bandit partially cleared his conscious admitting his participation in the robberies of the banks of Clinton, Coalgate, and Harrah, Oklahoma, as well as Baxter Springs and Galena, Kansas, Frankfort, Kentucky, and Stuttgart, Arkansas but denied playing any role in the robberies of the Kingfisher, Okmulgee, and Haskell banks nor would he admit

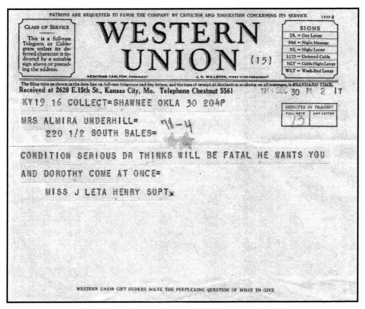

Telegram received by Almira Underhill from A. B. Cooper informing her of her son's condition. Courtesy Michael Webb

the identities of any of his confederates. When specifically asked who assisted him in the Coalgate job, he responded, "A couple of hicks." Underhill claimed he was in Shawnee to unload the hot bonds, which were found in the Dewey street residence. When crowded about his suspected involvement in the Kansas City massacre, he stated, "When that job was pulled I was in Oklahoma City with Harvey Bailey taking care of that wound in his leg." (*Note: Strange Underhill would go to the trouble of giving a deathbed statement establishing an alibi for Bailey on the day of the massacre while Bailey would in turn spend the rest of his life making harsh statements as to Wilbur's role in the Kansas prison escape and aftermath) Wilbur also requested Cooper contact his mother as to his condition, which he did later that day by telegram (collect). It appears the feds took little solace in Wilbur's rambling confession. In Colvin's official report to FBI Director J. Edger Hoover he noted, " Due to the subjects dire physical condition it was impossible to secure a continuous or coherent statement of his past activities."

Meanwhile, the news of the West Dewey Street gunfight spread like wildfire. By mid-day Saturday, only a few hours after Underhill's capture, the street in front of both the residence and the furniture store was bumper-to-bumper with rubberneckers causing a massive traffic snarl. Crowds of souvenir hunters literally looted the home of its furnishings, even picking up shards of glass, wood splinters, and pieces of the carpet. Wilbur's watch and clothing along with Hazel's mink coat went missing. Hatler Smith, the owner of the residence was reportedly more than a bit perturbed to see his property in shambles. The looting stopped only when R. H. Colvin threatened to arrest anyone stealing objects from the home on federal obstruction of justice charges. A few blocks away, a huge crowd of curious citizens swarmed police headquarters hoping to catch a glimpse of any of the prominent figures in the case. When a barefoot Ralph Roe emerged, his arm in a sling and clothed in Wilbur's missing suit in the company of Shawnee Chief of Police F. A. Budd and a half dozen G-men who were moving him from the city to the county jail, the unruly crowd had to be roughly pushed back by city cops in order for the officers and the prisoner to make their way to the waiting vehicles.

At 5:40 Sunday morning, New Years Eve day, Eva Mae Nichols, surrounded by her ex-husband, brother, and sisters, died of her wounds. Before she expired Eva gamely informed others of the final distribution of her property as well as requesting her burial be exactly at sunset. Her body was transported to a Seminole undertaking establishment. The following afternoon her funeral was held at the Methodist Church. Later that day with the sun setting in the west, she was buried at the Maple Grove Cemetery in Seminole. Her tragic death was officially noted simply as "Death

Scene at the shootout site the morning after. Courtesy Shawnee Morning News

by misadventure." There was no official inquest held and law enforcement officials went to great lengths to avoid commenting on her demise. When interviewed shortly after the funeral, her ex-husband, a postal employee named Bert Eppler, claimed he had briefly met with her only a few hours before she was caught in the crossfire, stating, " She was a good-time Charlie who never knowingly wronged anyone in her life."

A few hours after Miss Nichol's death, a grief stricken Almira Underhill accompanied by her daughter Dorothy and their ever-faithful Attorney Clarence Sowers arrived from Kansas City by automobile. The gray haired matriarch gave a quick press conference publicly thanking Chief Budd for returning Wilbur's suit and tie from Roe and Hazel's fur coat back from the looters of the Dewey street residence. She then thrust her chin up and hardening her face proclaimed, "My boy couldn't of done the things they say he did! There has never been a disgrace in our family before. (She must of possessed a very selective memory) I dreamed of his death the night before he was killed and plainly heard his voice crying

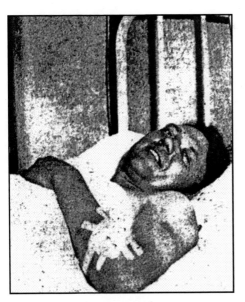

Ralph Roe just hours after the shootout.
Courtesy Daily Oklahoman

'Mamma' throughout the night." According to witnesses, the old lady swooned the moment she entered her son's hospital room. Wilbur reacted by bluntly informing her, "I ain't dead yet!"

That evening, Muskogee County Sheriff Virgil Cannon arrived with Haskell bankers W. E. Combs and Denis Rainwater. Both men positively identified Underhill as the leader of the quartet who robbed their bank on October 11. No sooner had Cannon and party exited then Sam Pointer and Max Reager, the pair Underhill had allegedly taken hostage and tied to a tree near Meeker before stealing their car for use in the Stuttgart robbery, walked into the room and also identified the outlaw. An hour later, the bankers from Baxter Springs, Kansas, accompanied by Cherokee County Sheriff Dave Hasenphaugh were also invited to eyeball the prisoner. Oliver Browning, the cashier of the First National Bank of Coalgate, joined the crowd as well. Also escorted into the room by Detective A. B. Cooper for a short visit was his now fully rested and sober wife. According to Cooper, who remained in the room in

Grave of Eva Mae Nichols Seminole, Oklahoma. Photo by Naomi Morgan

order to eavesdrop on the conversation, the pair exchanged a few personal comments before the hard boiled bandit instructed her to "Make sure I get a proper burial, now go on home, they got nothing on you." After sobbing for a moment or two, she blew her nose and regained her composure before replying, "I know they don't, but I'm going to stick with you." Cooper then broke in saying, "Let's go honey."

On her arrival back at the city jail, reporters interviewed Hazel who was clad in a spiffy brown skirt and flaming orange jacket. Acting every bit the classic tough as nails gangster moll, (which in reality she was) Hazel announced, "I'm not talking to you birds. I'll not put Wilbur on the spot, see?" She continued talking though, adding, "He's a good boy and was trying to do right, but the cops kept hounding him." Thrusting her left hand toward the assembled pack of news hungry journalists, she bragged about the oversized, gaudy diamond ring she was sporting on her ring finger, saying, "Look at that rock boys, that shows Wilbur took good care of me don't it." When reporters inquired how her and Wilbur had gotten acquainted she responded, "Through my brother." Asked about Roe and Eva Nichols, she claimed, "There no friends of mine…I don't know how long Wilbur knew Roe." Commenting on the shootout she asserted, "The bullets began coming through the window and went right past me into Wilbur. The window glass got into my hands and eyes. My dress is full of glass splinters that cut me when I touch it." Asked if she knew their marriage would likely come to a tragic end? Hazel responded, "Sure I knew it would have to end sometime." She went on to say, "There's only one thing I'd like to get cleared up in this whole mess, who was the dirty dog who put the finger on us?" Asked, "What about the report that says you tipped off the authorities to the hideout?" she glared at the questioner with blood in her eye before answering, "You'll have to ask the cops." Another journalist inquired if she had fainted when the bullets started flying as was reported. She snorted before replying, "Are you kidding?"

****

Reacting to the news of his pal's capture, the unpredictable Ford Bradshaw and his companions Charlie Cotner and others decided to show the world what they thought of the event by once again raiding the sleepy little town of Vian on New Years Eve. They shot out the windows of several downtown businesses and the police station. The peaceful citizens thereabouts becoming somewhat accustomed to the so-called "Cookson Hill Gangs" occasional violent forays into town, headed for their underground storm shelters or simply laid low till the storm passed. After shooting the village up the boys headed for Muskogee where Bradshaw viciously assaulted several individuals before becoming engaged in a surprisingly bloodless machinegun duel with the ever deadly and overly efficient Deputy Sheriff Grover Bishop near Tahlequah. Afterwards, getting his fill of blood lust, Bradshaw and company went to ground.

On New Years day, Underhill's condition was listed as critical and worsening. The doctors insisted the outlaw was defying death, saying, "His insides are shredded, he's just barely hanging on." Nurses attending the badman told reporters he had turned abusive, swearing at the attending physician, calling him a "Dumb old cluck" when the "Doc" refused to give Wilbur painkilling drugs for his wounds. When asked if he needed to speak to a minister or priest, the contrary badman growled, "Not hardly." On being informed his mangled arm may have to be amputated the killer responded, "Why, it's doing better than the rest of me." All the while, his mother and sister remained at their bedside vigil, clothed in black and drowning in a river of tears. Later that day officers discovered the winch truck used in the Harrah robbery abandoned in a garage in Ada located just forty miles south of Shawnee.

The same day Hazel was officially charged with har-

Hazel Underhill and Detective A. B. Cooper. Courtesy The Daily Oklahoman

boring and moved to the federal lockup in Oklahoma City where she joined Bob Brady's wife Leona who had arrived at the institution under a bizarre set of circumstances. Apparently, Mrs. Brady, who had been busy dodging the cops for several weeks, was involved in a traffic accident the previous week. When questioned by police she gave them a phony name. She was issued a ticket for reckless driving. The following morning she showed up in court pleading guilty to the charge. When the Judge levied a six-dollar fine, the spunky Mrs. Brady instructed his honor, "My momma needs that money more than the city." She was promptly sentenced to ten days in the Oklahoma City slammer. The following day Detective Clarence Hurt, who happened to be visiting the jail, recognized the unlucky woman. That evening she was hauled before a federal magistrate and charged with harboring her husband. Also held in the facility at the same time was the girlfriend of another Kansas escapee, Jim Clark. Joining them on the men's section of the jail under a $1000 bond was twenty-five year old Seedell "Sleepy" Johnson and his brother Lonzo, both charged with harboring fugitives from justice. Strangely, Joe Smalley, who had arranged for Roe and Inman to rent the cottage on Dewey Street, was never prosecuted in the case although he was later convicted of bribery and embezzlement in an unrelated incident.

Meanwhile, newspapers throughout the country were having a heyday reporting the gory details of the shootout giving the story wide coverage even making the front page of the *New York Times*. Over the next few days, journalists wrote a great deal of inaccurate information and outright lies about Underhill's capture and life in general. One report stated Underhill had been planning to join up with "Pretty Boy" Floyd and John Dillinger in order to form a "Supergang." Another claimed the outlaw had been struck by sixteen .45 slugs instead of four. Others stated the doctors had removed the slugs. (According to most reports they did not) Several papers falsely reported Underhill had robbed the bank of Canton, Kansas in the summer of 1933. Rumors of a snitch in the case ran rampant. Some news reports suggested Miss Nichols' ex-husband, hearing news of her affair with Raymond Roe had turned informer in a fit of jealousy while another account claimed either the Johnson brothers or Bruce Brady were the stool pigeons. Other stories suggested Underhill had purposely shot Eva Mae during the shootout suspecting she had put the outlaw on the spot by either informing police of his whereabouts or carelessly allowing the cops to tail her to the Dewey Street address. It appears some of these rumors may have been spoon-fed to the media by the feds in order to protect their informant. For example, although several news reports suggested Miss Nichols was followed to the cottage by the laws, now declassified official FBI reports deny this assertion.

On January 2, Doctors rushed Wilbur into emergency surgery in an effort to correct a blockage of what was left of his bladder. Before Wilbur went under anesthesia, he informed Dr. J A. Walker, "Doc, I am more afraid of that needle than I am a bullet." Afterwards a hospital spokesman said the bandit was "White as a sheet and fighting peritonitis." Meanwhile, the hospital began receiving dozens of "Masher" letters addressed to Underhill from female admirers from as far away as Canada. Several of the notes, heavily scented with perfume, even went as far as proposing marriage, which was just what the dying outlaw needed, more wives! The hospital also began receiving dozens of crank calls asking for a "Mr. Underhill."

That evening Oklahoma State Penitentiary Warden Sam Brown arrived at the hospital in an ambulance manned by three machine gun wielding guards, demanding Underhill be turned over to him so the badman could finish his life term at McAlester for the murder of George Fee. Agent Colvin immediately claimed he had dibs. The pair engaged in a heated turf war until the US Prosecuting Attorney in Kansas City wired an official indictment of Wilbur for his suspected role in the Kansas City Massacre. The document trumped any claims the state had on the outlaw and the chastised but extremely "Pissed off" Warden withdrew to McAlester with his tail between his legs.

On the morning of January 5, Underhill suddenly sat up in bed asking a nurse what floor he was on and how would one got to the highway. She immediately reported the conversation to one of the feds on guard who in turn informed his superior. To the amazement of the doctors, the outlaw began to rally in the afternoon eating solid foods and talking lucidly. According to official FBI reports, the bandit repeatedly requested agents for the use of one of

News headline from The Seminole Producer.

their guns in order to protect himself from his gang who he claimed would knock him off to keep him from squealing. R. H. Colvin, alarmed by recent underworld rumors suggesting Wilbur's psychotic pal, Ford Bradshaw and his gang of cutthroats were planning on busting the badman out of the hospital, combined with news of Underhill's recent health gains phoned his boss, J. Edger Hoover in Washington suggesting the prisoner be moved to a more secure location. Hoover, fearing the loss of his prize pigeon would create a public relations disaster for the fledgling FBI as well as put a damper on his own soon to be storied career, quickly agreed.

At approximately 8:30 am on Saturday January 6, an ambulance and a pair of vehicles loaded down with Oklahoma State Penitentiary Warden Sam Brown (He finally got his way), accompanied by a bevy of machine gun toting prison guards along with Colvin and several heavily armed G-Men pulled up to the main entrance of the Shawnee Hospital. Colvin instructed Almira her son was to be moved to McAlester for safekeeping. Later reports claim she became hysterical on receiving the news, informing Colvin the trip would kill him. After being allowed to spend a few moments telling her fair-haired boy farewell, she was sent on her way and Wilbur loaded on to a stretcher and wheeled to the waiting ambulance with little fanfare (Note: The media was not informed of the badman's transfer for another hour). The caravan then sped off toward the big house, the ambulance in the lead and the two escort vehicles following closely behind. About midway through the seventy-mile trip, the officers were thrown into a frenzy when a small plane buzzed the caravan several times. At 11:30 am, the procession arrived at the prison. While Underhill was being unloaded at the prison hospital, he turned to Warden Brown with a sardonic sneer on his face, commenting, "I'm ready to come back home."

A few hours after the wounded fugitives return to OSP, Warden Brown told a crowd of reporters Wilbur had stood the trip well and had been moved to "Big Mac" in order to finish his life term. He also stated the prison offered a more secure environment than the Shawnee Hospital which was a bizarre statement considering 163 inmates had escaped from the Oklahoma prison system in 1933 alone.

Examining the prisoner shortly after his arrival, prison physician, Dr. J.A. Munn, expressed little hope for his survival. At approximately nine that evening Underhill lapsed into unconsciousness and at 11:42, with only a pair of hos-

Telegram from Agent Colvin to Director Hoover. Courtesy US Department of Justice

pital attendants at his side, he rolled to his right side, shuddered and died.

While her husband was undergoing his death throes in McAlester, Hazel Underhill was being given the third degree by a team of federal officers led by Agent Frank Smith at the federal detention center in Oklahoma City. After several hours of intense questioning, the tough moll dropped her rough façade. Tears burst from her eyes as she informed interrogators of their movements since her first meeting with Wilbur in early June 1933. Near the conclusion of her detailed statement, she told investigators, " On the Friday before Christmas I met Wilbur at the Hollywood Tourist Camp near Norman. I got in his car and my son drove mine (Wilbur had recently bought her a 1933 model Chevrolet Tudor Coupe automobile). We drove to Ardmore then on to a farm of a friend of mine where we spent the night. We then drove to Wichita Falls, Texas spending the night at the Kamp Hotel. We did some Christmas shopping, mailing some parcels back to his kin in Kansas City. We then returned to the farm after stopping in Gainesville for supper at a diner. My son met us and I returned to Oklahoma City after making arrangements to meet Wilbur on the night of the 29th near Shawnee at the XYZ filling station." She continued saying, "My son drove me to meet him on the 29th. We met and my boy (Marvin) drove my car back to Oklahoma City. We drove to a house in Shawnee occupied by a man named Roe and his girlfriend. I did not know these people. I was skeptical about going to this house but Wilbur said it was all right. Later that night Lon Johnson came by the house and spoke to Wilbur then left. I don't know whether anyone was with him or not. Later on we were occupying a back bedroom while Roe and the woman were in the other, suddenly I heard a command, 'Come out Wilbur,' or something like that. Wilbur started toward the door, the next thing I knew the house was full of gas, and there was considerable shooting going on." Later that day Hazel's son, Marvin Connor, gave his own expansive statement to officers, which dovetailed his mothers.

Chapter Seventeen

A Funeral Fit For a King

At almost the exact moment Underhill was greeting his maker, several carloads of police led by Seminole Police Chief Jake Sims were pulling up in front of the Sun Rooming House located at 610 North First Street (now Phillips Avenue) in Seminole, Oklahoma. Sims had received a hot tip involving the whereabouts of Wilbur's running buddy, Elmer Inman, who Harrah night watchman Jackson Smith had recently identified by photo as one of the individuals who had kidnapped him after the aborted bank heist. Unfortunately for the cops, an underworld character named Grace Cunningham, who had chosen that moment to walk through the lobby on her way to buy some beer, spotted Sims. She turned and rushed back to a her room where she was currently entertaining Inman, an unidentified man, and Lena Nichols, the sister of Eva Mae, who had been slain in the company of Wilbur that past week. "Cops" she shouted the moment she burst through the doorway. Inman, along with Cunningham and the other individual, grabbed their suitcases and ran to the businesses back door then quickly jumped into a late model Ford V8 (Newspaper reports claimed the car was Wilbur's familiar Ford, which seems unlikely since it was currently in the possession of the Shawnee police) speeding into the night leaving poor Miss Nichols, who was passed out on a couch to face the heat. Not noticing the outlaw's exit, the minions of the law crashed through the door of the fugitive's room only to be greeted by a now wide-awake and hysterical Miss Nichols along with an overwrought Lillie Foster, the establishment's manager. At that same moment, two lawmen, Deputy Sheriff Charlie Dove and Special Agent Bob Short, who were late joining the posse, spotted Inman and company making their getaway. The officers rushed back to their squad car and gave pursuit into the snowy night. Traveling north on Highway 48 at breakneck speeds, the fugitive's Ford hit a large washout in the road near the community of Little, which is located seven miles north of Seminole. Splashing into the high water, the speeding rig immediately stalled out leaving the suspects exposed like deer in the headlights. The unidentified man bolted out of the car fleeing into the woods while Inman turned and fired several rounds at his pursuers with a pistol. The lawmen returned fire with shotguns shattering the back window of the car with buckshot, shards of glass raining down on the suspects, several pieces striking Inman in the face and eyes leaving horrible gaping lacerations. Inman and his female companion then baled out of the car running into a patch of nearby timber while Short and his companion continued to blast away with their scatterguns.

On approaching the disabled vehicle, officers discovered a great deal of blood on the seats and floorboard. The officers searched the immediate vicinity but came up empty-handed. Within a half-hour of the shootout, re-enforcements began to arrive and the search was on, bloodhounds were brought in but due to the recent rain and snow, they failed to stay on the scent. Inman and his lady friend sprinted over a mile to a farmer's house and began pounding on the door shouting they needed assistance due to being involved in an automobile accident. The farmer and his wife hustled them inside and built a roaring fire in order to dry them out. Elmer's torn face was bandaged with a strip of bed sheet. After resting a spell, Inman, his face still bleeding profusely and unable to see out of one eye, offered the man $5.00 to take him to a gas station in the oilfield community of Bowlegs located some five miles south of Seminole. Being hard times and all, the farmer readily agreed.

Arriving at the filling station at approximately 2 am, Inman used the pay phone calling a relative who lived nearby. When his kinfolk refused to give him a helping hand, he then dialed for a taxi. Problem was, just as he was making his second call, so was his not so loyal relative. Unluckily for Elmer, the moment the taxi arrived so did Jack Ketzler, a special officer working for the Empire Oil Company in Seminole. Elmer, described by Ketzler as blood-soaked and covered in mud, and his lady-fair offered no resistance as they were placed under arrest. An automatic pistol was recovered from the fugitive's person.

A few minutes after Inman's apprehension, Jake Sims and two Seminole County officers arrived at the gas station taking custody of the prisoners and transported them to the county jail at Wewoka where they joined young Miss Nichols. According to officers, Inman, his eyeball swollen to epic proportions, declared he would tell the officers anything if they would get him to a doctor.

After receiving treatment for his wounds, (a dozen shards of glass were plucked from his eye and chin) the outlaw declared he had split from the Underhill gang two days before Wilbur's capture due to his engaging in a quarrel with Ralph Roe over the affections of Eva Mae Nichols. Elmer claimed Underhill had taken sides with Roe in the matter. Both Elmer and Eva's sister Lena loudly proclaimed from their separate jail cells that Roe was responsible for Eva's death due to his using her as a shield in the shootout. Inman, with a venomous look in his one good eye snarled, "Roe is a punk and a lady-killer, and I'm going to take care of him." How the pair ever came up with this theory is unknown. Lawmen publicly speculated the unidentified man who had fled Inman's car after the shootout north of Seminole was an escaped convict out of Cherokee County, Oklahoma named Bob (Coy) Terrill who the newspapers incorrectly identified as Inman's ex-crime partner and the infamous Ray Terrill's brother (In reality, Ray Terrill's only male sibling was a much younger half brother named Jesse Patton).

Inman was initially charged with the robbery of the Harrah bank when Constable Jackson Smith identified him as one of the bandits through a mug shot. The charge was dropped the following morning when Smith was unable to pick Inman out of a lineup saying, "It was dark and I was blindfolded most of the time." The Federal Prosecutor then charged the outlaw with harboring a fugitive (Underhill).

The same day, "Jack Hughes" filed a request with the Attorney General of Kansas claiming the $350 reward offered for the capture of Wilbur Underhill. A letter accompanied his request from Federal Agent R.H. Colvin endorsing the claim. The following day, Colvin's boss, J. Edger Hoover, fired a letter to his underling chastising him for overstepping his bounds and demanded a full explanation. Although Colvin attempted to enlighten the director how the informer was directly responsible for Underhill's apprehension, Hoover would have none of it. Apparently, the Director was steamed how the newspapers

Coy Terrill. Courtesy Muskogee Times-Democrat

had reported local law enforcement had accomplished Wilbur's actual capture. A statement that while technically true was not a very honest assessment of the facts of the affair. It was also reported that Hoover felt giving an informant too much credit for cracking a high-profile case might detract from the greater glory of the bureau. Whether the mysterious "Mr. Hughes" ever received any cash reward for his efforts is unknown.

****

At dawn the morning following Underhill's demise a phone call was placed to Almira Underhill at her hotel room in Shawnee by Warden Sam Brown informing her of her son's death. The stoic woman immediately called a press conference. A dry eyed Almira with the ever present Dorothy by her side, informed journalists she had warned prison officials the trip to McAlester would prove to be too challenging to her boy's condition. She went on to state, her son was simply misunderstood in life and a tragic victim of circumstances. "In a strange way, I'm glad he's dead," adding, "It will be kinda comforting having him where I can wait on him like he was a little boy." It would be the last news conference she would ever give. Perhaps the gray haired matriarch had finally tired of being in the limelight. Afterwards she arranged travel by rail to McAlester in order to claim Wilbur's body. Taking a taxi to the train station, she stopped at the Shawnee Municipal Hospital and thanked the doctors and nurses for their kindness shown to her over the past week. She also picked up her son's effects including the large silver cameo ring Wilbur had handmade at the Kansas State Penitentiary, which had been taken off his finger in the emergency room during triage.

On her arrival in McAlester the women visited the

funeral home where Wilbur's body was being prepared picking out a moderately priced gray steel coffin and instructing the mortuary to bar the public from viewing his corpse saying "There will be no circus evolving around my son." She then gave the undertaker his suit she had retrieved from the authorities in Shawnee and placed the cameo ring, which had a photo of her inside on his finger. Almira also arranged to travel back to Joplin by rail on the same train her son's body would be transported.

On the morning of January 8, Underhill's coffin, accompanied by his mother and sister was greeted by a crowd of several hundred at the Kansas City Southern Rail Station in Joplin, Missouri. The body was whisked away to

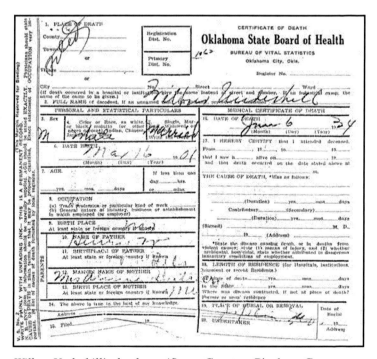

Wilbur Underhill's death certificate. Courtesy Pittsburg County Genealogical Society

the Frank Sievers Undertaking Company. Later that evening the casket was moved by hearse to the home of Wilbur's sister, Mrs. Anna Lewis at 1502 McKinley Avenue where relatives kept an all-night vigil.

The following day, Federal Judge Edger S. Vaught reduced Hazel Underhill's bond from $10,000 to $2500. Her attorney, an Ex-Carter County prosecutor named James Mathers, who had recently defended the infamous George "Machine Gun" Kelley in his kidnapping trial, made her bail and arranged to repossess the Chevrolet Wilbur had bought for her. That afternoon the pair sped to Joplin where they joined the family at the Lewis home.

Speaking to a reporter from the Joplin Globe, Dorothy, engaging in a war of words with Oklahoma prison authorities said, "We hold no resentment toward anyone except for those who moved Wilbur to prison just as he was improving...the trip directly caused his death." On receiving news of this harsh statement, a representative of the Oklahoma penal system came out swinging, emphatically declaring, "In no way did Underhill's transfer hasten his death."

Ernest Underhill with mother and sister, Dorothy. Courtesy Michael Webb

Meanwhile Almira requested her son

Ernest, who was doing a life term in the Missouri pen for murder, be allowed to attend the funeral. Warden J. M. Sanders agreed to a three-day supervised pass, providing it did not cost the state anything. Prisoners at the institution took up a collection for train fare and expenses. Ernest arrived in Joplin accompanied by a prison guard just hours after Hazel steamed into town. His keeper, Luther Laster, took the convict on an auto tour of his hometown, which he had not seen since the funeral of his brother George three years ago.

The family stated it was only the third time Almira had set eyes on her son in twenty-one years. Reporters from the Joplin Globe were granted a lengthy interview with the prisoner. Taking front stage, he began his dialogue by carping about not being paroled from prison due to his brother's bad reputation. He then allowed he had no one to blame for his misery but himself, adding, "I don't agree with what Wilbur did. I really believe he is better off dead." He then publicly thanked his fellow cons for paying for the trip, stating, "I've worked in the prison's shirt factory for twenty-one years at the rate of a few cents a day, thus I have nothing." When a reporter asked if he had any advice for the youth of today, the tall, gaunt convict mused, "Stay away from the gun, get a job instead." In a scant three years, Ernest would be interred next to his brothers, a victim of chronic liver disease. That evening Wilbur's older sibling, Earl, newly released from a county jail in Kansas, joined his family at the wake.

On the morning of the 10th Underhill's coffin was moved to the Byers Avenue Methodist Church located at 18th and Byers in Joplin for the funeral. By the time the services began, the church's auditorium was filled over capacity with nearly 1600 people. Another curious 500 or more citizens stood outside on the lawn. The gathering would make history as the largest private funeral ever held in Joplin to date.

Reverend C. P. Mills of Topeka, Kansas (He was Wilbur's Sunday school teacher when he was a youth) conducted the service. His sermon focused on the theme "Man cannot tamper with the law." Following the service the doors of the church were flung open and the crowd was allowed to walk past Wilbur's open coffin. The body was described as being clad in a blue suit, white shirt, and blue tie. When an hour had expired, the coffin was closed to the frustration of several hundred persons still standing in line and loaded into the hearse for the trip to the Ozark Memorial Cemetery. Two of Wilbur's brothers-in-law and four nephews, including Frank Vance Underhill, acted as pallbearers. To the relief of most folks living in America's heartland, the man who had come to be known as the persona of evil was lowered into the grave next to his brother George

Byers Street Methodist Church today. Photo by Naomi Morgan

after a short graveyard service attended by the family and approximately 350 persons.

Wilbur Underhill would have the distinction of being the first major underworld figure of the so-called "Midwest Crime Wave" of the early 1930s to be slain by federal agents. In the months following the badman's death J. Edger Hoover, the director of the Department of Justice's Bureau of Investigation (the forerunner of the FBI) would be ordered by Attorney General Homer Cummings to eliminate by whatever means possible a long list of "Public Enemies." Apparently, Cummings and his boss, President Franklin Roosevelt, were deeply troubled by the fact the public was beginning to look at these big name criminals, especially the rural bank robbers, as heroic figures. Roosevelt was aghast that America's youth might come to think of these outlaws as perverse role models.

Hoover took the President and Attorney General at their word, coming up with a bold plan. Recognizing the

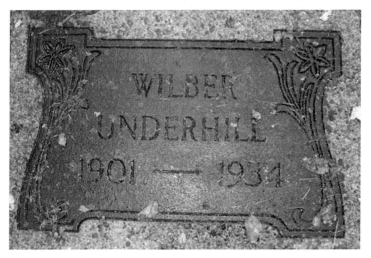

Wilbur Underhill's grave, Joplin, Missouri. Photo by Naomi Morgan

fact the majority of his bureau's "Bookworm" agents were mainly deskbound clerks who didn't stand a chance against these heavily armed desperadoes, he decided to fight "Fire with Fire." The director determined to recruit a hand picked squad of hired gunmen or professional "Shootists" to go after the big name criminals, especially those he considered culpable in the "Kansas City Massacre" incident (Which included just about every well-known hood currently at large in the Midwest). Hoover began his recruitment of these new agents from the ranks of police and sheriff's departments in Oklahoma and Texas. Two of those personally selected by the director were Oklahoma City Detectives Clarence Hurt and Jelly Bryce, who had previously proved their worth by participating in Underhill's slaying. This group of hard-bitten lawmen was formed into a so-called "Flying Squad" under the command of Agents Melvin Purvis and Sam Cowley. Although it was never made public, the "Flying Squad's" orders were apparently to pursue and kill on sight any of the "Public Enemies" on Hoover's list of most wanted. Over the next two years the squad proved to be as efficient and deadly as Hoover could ever have imagined, slaying such degenerate luminaries as Charles "Pretty Boy" Floyd, "Baby Face" Nelson, and "Ma" Barker and her deadly brood, as well as the legendary John Dillinger.

Chapter Eighteen
Epilogue

Back in Oklahoma, state and federal officers were still hard at work attempting to kill or capture Underhill's former crime partners. On January 18, 1934, a letter postmarked Lakin, Kansas arrived at the offices of the *Daily Oklahoman*, the state's largest newspaper. The correspondence originated from Bob Terrill, who police suspected of being the individual that successfully escaped from the automobile carrying Elmer Inman and Grace Cunningham, which officers had shot to pieces upon the conclusion of a high-speed chase just north of Seminole on the night of January 6. Terrill wrote, "I'm no friend of either Underhill or Inman, nor did I rob the Coalgate bank. I'm an escaped con trying to go straight by working for a living." The fugitive's correspondence led directly to his arrest by a squad of fast moving federal agents and his prompt return to life behind the stark gray walls of "Big Mac," thus proving the old adage it is sometimes best to keep silent.

On January 19, Bob Brady, Jim Clark, Frank Delmar, and four other inmates escaped over the walls of the Kansas State Penitentiary. While Delmar and Clark were able to hijack a car and make it back to Oklahoma, Brady and the others were forced to continue their journey toward freedom on foot. On the morning of the 22nd a farmer living eleven miles southeast of the community of Paola spotted the fugitives attempting to cross an open cornfield still dressed in their prison issues. He immediately contacted the authorities. A short time later, a posse made up of heavily armed officers and national guardsmen arrived on the scene.

When challenged, Brady, armed with an old sawed-off pump shotgun he had stolen from a farmhouse the previous night, showed fight attempting to fire on the officers but unfortunately for him the shell in his gun misfired. He then began to flee but a well-aimed blast from a shotgun loaded with buckshot raked the desperadoes backside sending him sprawling headfirst into the muddy field. His companions, seeing the results of the short lived gun-duel promptly surrendered and were sent back to Lansing while what was left of "Big Bob" was transported to the local funeral home where for the next two days a steady stream of several hundred morbidly curious citizens filed past his body as it lay in state.

Interviewed the following morning at her parent's small tarpaper shack in Oklahoma City, the outlaw's widow, Leona Brady, sitting at a battered kitchen table covered by a cheap checkered oilcloth and surrounded by her parents and three brothers, was asked how long she had been married to Bob? She replied, "Three years," then burst into tears saying, "We were so happy. I tried visiting him in Lansing just before Christmas but they wouldn't let me see him nor leave him anything but some fruit. He was trying to go straight, but they wouldn't leave us alone, " adding, "The cops, they pick me up every time I go out to get a newspaper."

Leona Brady. Courtesy Daily Oklahoman

She then drew herself erect, wiped away her tears, lit a cigarette and took a couple of deep drags before commenting, "I knew something had happened, I felt it in my bones all day yesterday." Suddenly her face brightened when she asked the reporters if Bob had taken any cops with him on his way to eternity. When they replied in the negative, she looked downcast then calmly responded, "Well, he ought to have killed fifty."

Robert G. Brady Jr. was interred at the Rosedale Cemetery near Ada, Oklahoma under the watchful eye of a score of local peace officers and federal agents. Ironically, Brady's

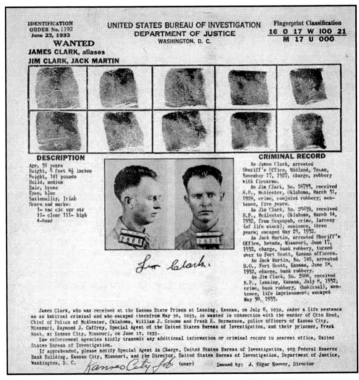

U442-Wanted poster for Jim Clark. Courtesy Mike Webb

father had also died at the end of a smoking gun barrel when Bob was only a year old.

Meanwhile, while Brady's corpse was being lowered into the frozen earth, Elmer Inman and Ralph Roe were standing tall in front of the man in the court of the honorable Judge George Eacock, answering the charge of aiding and abetting Wilbur Underhill. Testifying for the prosecution, Joe Smally, the real-estate agent who had subleased the Dewey Street cottage to the pair, identified Roe as the man who had presented himself as J. H. Reynolds and Inman as the individual who signed the rental agreement as Joe Sullivan. Both men entered pleas of not guilty and bond

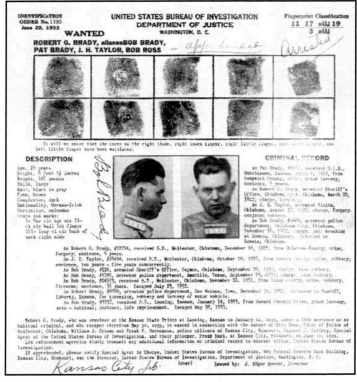

Wanted poster Big Bob Brady. Courtesy Mike Webb

was set at $10,000 for Inman and $5000 for Roe. Inman made bond and immediately slid back into a life of crime. Roe couldn't come up with the dough and was held in jail until he eventually pled guilty to the charge and was sentenced to six months in the federal pen.

At exactly noon on January 25, four unmasked men entered the First National Bank of Wellington, Kansas. One of the individuals, identified as Ford Bradshaw, was holding a machine gun while the other three were armed with fully automatic Lugar pistols equipped with shoulder stocks. After looting the institution of $4126.00, the gang fled in a new Pontiac Sedan with banker Hubert Richards forcibly attached to the running board for use as a human shield.

Five days later, on the afternoon of January 30, a posse made up of seven Tulsa city detectives and Wilbur's old nemesis Joe Anderson, along with several other Kansas officers raided a small residence located at 3331 East 7th Street in Tulsa capturing Clarence and Otis Eno. Also apprehended was a small-time thug named James White along with Mary Eno, Gypsy Bradshaw Eno, and the ever-present Hazel Winn. Seized in the raid were a dozen rifles, pistols, and sawed off automatic shotguns, along with a Thompson machine gun and a Browning automatic rifle. Absent from the apartment was Ford Bradshaw who had been spotted there just hours before the raid. Parked in the street in front of the house was the late-model Pontiac Sedan used in the recent robbery of the Wellington bank. The trunk of the car was loaded down with several hundred rounds of 30-06 ammunition much of it Dum-dum (Hollow point) bullets.

Reporters interviewed that evening, a dry-eyed Mary Eno Staley, the boy's ma, at the matron's quarters at central police headquarters. She informed the assembled newsmen, "I have had so much trouble with the boys I'm hard-

---

ened to it. I did everything I could to keep 'em out of trouble. I sent them to school, but they never attended choosing instead to play hooky. They would not go to church nor Sunday school. They soon became involved in petty troubles then it got worse," adding, " The law says they are bad boys and I guess they are." She further stated, " Several times after Tony (Otis) and Clarence got out of prison they found jobs but were dismissed when the employer discovered they had records. Two of my boys, Virgil and Louis, are missing and I don't even know if they are alive or dead. Lord how I tried to keep 'em straight." Incidentally, some $800 in cash was found on the old lady's person during the raid.

Moment's later Tulsa City Detective Earl Gardner stood up and told the reporters, "I can paint you a less sympathetic picture of her boys. All five brothers are habitual criminals who travel in a social class whose activities are written on police blotters across this country. Their rap sheets don't tell the whole story, they are guilty of a

News report of Eno brother's capture. Courtesy Okmulgee Daily Times

multitude of crimes they were never convicted." Truer words were never spoken. Mother Eno's sons were indeed hard-core career criminals. While Clarence and Otis had served half their lives behind bars, brother Earl had done time in prisons in Colorado and Oklahoma as well as Leavenworth while Virgil was a convicted forger several times over, and Louis had done jolts in the Nebraska and Missouri State pens. At one a point in the mid-1920s, all five lads were simultaneously held in various prisons across the nation. (Probably some sort of record)

The day after their arrest, the two Eno brothers were whisked to Kansas for safekeeping where Clarence, who had escaped from the Okmulgee County jail in December, was wanted for his suspected involvement in the robberies of the banks in Galena, Wellington, and Baxter Springs. He was also sought for questioning as to the hijackings of financial institutions in Chelsea and Okmulgee, Oklahoma as well as Nebraska City, Kearney, and Syracuse, Nebraska.

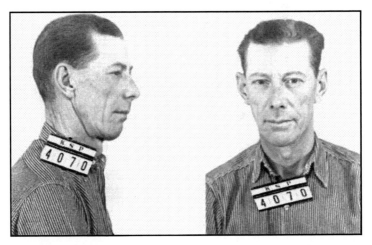

An older but not wiser Clarence Eno. Courtesy Kansas Department of Corrections

He and his brother eventually plead guilty to knocking off the First National Bank of Wellington, Kansas and were sentenced under the habitual felons act to 20 to 100 years apiece hard labor at the Kansas State Penitentiary in Lansing. Their cohort, Jim White, was convicted of the same heist and received a sentence of 10 to 50 years.

In the weeks following the brother's extradition to the "Sunflower" state, news reports appeared suggesting their transfer from Oklahoma to Kansas was accomplished by improper methods. According to a statement made by Major Wint Smith, head of the Kansas Highway Patrol, "The pair was extradited in an informal manner. The Tulsa officers somehow got lost while transporting them to the Tulsa County Jail. The first thing my men knew the two

Clarence Eno's 1953 pardon from the Governor of Kansas.
Courtesy Kansas Department of Correction

cars carrying the prisoners suddenly appeared in Caney, Kansas just over the border. Of course my men immediately arrested them in the name of Kansas."

Records show that over the years Clarence Eno evolved into a troublesome inmate constantly facing disciplinary charges for such rules violations as gambling, using dope, and possession of alcohol. In 1938, he and his brother Otis were both suspected of involvement in an abortive breakout attempt. The pair was promptly sentenced to Cellhouse #2 (the hole) indefinitely by order of Deputy Warden Bert Kesselring for "The safety of the institution." Clarence finally gained his freedom from the walls of Lansing in December 30, 1953 when Kansas Governor Edward Arn commuted his sentence to thirty years and granted him a full pardon. After working a few months at a downtown Kansas City barbershop Clarence got itchy feet and relocated to Philadelphia, Pennsylvania where in March of 1954 he was charged with the attempted robbery of a convenience store. He was sentenced to a year in the Eastern State Penitentiary. Beginning in early 1955 Clarence along with brother Otis, who had been paroled in mid-1954, and an ex-con named Charles Pearson participated in a series of armed holdups of Safeway grocery stores in Kansas and Missouri. The trio was captured in June near Topeka, Kansas, and transported to Carthage, Missouri, to stand trial for the January 7, 1956 hijacking of a store in Joplin. Otis was convicted of the robbery in early July and sentenced to twenty years confinement at Jeff City. While being transported from the Jasper County Jail to nearby Joplin for arraignment, Clarence and Pearson assaulted their escort, Deputy Earl Denny, severely beating him about the face and shoulders with their handcuffs. Upon releasing themselves from their shackles, the pair fled from the patrol car on foot. The following day the duo was tracked down by bloodhounds and captured in a wooded area near the Kansas border. Clarence was sentenced to a twenty-year term at the Missouri State Penitentiary for his crimes. The fifty-four-year-old outlaw died of a heart attack in his prison cell on July 20, 1959. Although Clarence Eno achieved little notoriety outside the Midwest, he will go down in history as one of the most active bank robbers of the public enemies era.

****

On the afternoon of February 1, 1934, Coal County Sheriff Walter Clark received a tip indicating Eugene Glenn Clark, alias Glenn Davis, who had been named by George Nash as being one of a pair of men who had visited his farm in the company of Wilbur Underhill the morning after the Harrah robbery, had been spotted driving through Coalgate on Highway 75 heading toward Calvin. Sheriff Clark quickly formed a posse and began pursuit. Meanwhile, he alerted officers in Calvin to be on the lookout. An hour later, a Constable Shaddock seized Clark in the company of his wife while the pair was motoring through the town's business district. According to the constable, the pair were unarmed and offered no resistance.

Moments after the arrest took place, Sheriff Clark arrived and took custody of the suspect, transporting him back to Coalgate where he was brought before the witnesses from the bank robbery who refused to identify him as one of the bandits. On questioning the young man denied any involvement with Underhill. Unconvinced of his innocence, Clark had the youth lodged in the Coal County Jail for the evening. The next morning Deputy U S Marshal Allen Stanfield, Detective A. B. Cooper, and Oklahoma County Deputy Bill Eads transported the prisoner to

Ada where he was brought before George Nash in an effort to identify him. The moment Nash recognized the lad; Clark dropped like a rock to the floor in a dead faint. Upon being revived, the suspect was asked if he cared to revise his statement.

Convinced the law had him over the barrel, Clark proceeded to sing like a night at the opera, admitting he, Underhill, Houston Nash, and a man who claimed to be Ed Davis, were responsible for the failed Harrah bank raid. He elaborated, saying after they had botched the job, Underhill lost his temper informing his partners, "The hell with this business, I'll show you mugs how to make some real money." The trio, minus Davis, then fled back to the Nash farm where they parted ways. Clark emphatically denied any involvement in the Coalgate robbery claiming he was at his home in Crowder with his wife when the job was pulled, saying, "Underhill was sure sore when he read in the papers where that deputy said the Harrah deal was the work of amateurs. He told me, 'If I ever see that red-headed cop (Deputy Bill Eads) I'll show him an amateur!'" Asked how he had become involved with Underhill, he stated, "Through the Bradshaws," adding, "I first met Wilbur in late September of last year. At first, I just ran errands for him and the boys, it was kind of a thrill." It appears Clark was one of a dozen or more hangers-on who drifted in and out of the Bradshaw Gang over the years, probably involved in one of their many ongoing criminal enterprises, which included bootlegging as well as livestock rustling and armed robbery.

Houston Nash was immediately transferred from the Federal Jail in Muskogee where he was being held for harboring, to the Oklahoma County Jail in Oklahoma City where he and Gene Clark were officially charged with the Harrah bank raid.

In mid-May Eugene Clark turned state's evidence testifying against Houston Nash as to the Harrah bank robbery case. Jackson Smith, the Harrah night watchman who had previously identified Underhill and Elmer Inman through photos as two of the hijackers proved a major disappointment to prosecutors when he refused to positively identify either of the suspects in a lineup. In his defense, it must be stated the poor man had not only been severely terrorized by the gang of hijackers but also blindfolded in the early stages of the heist.

On taking the stand, Nash, with a straight face, attempted to pass off his tired old story to the Judge and jury of how he had merely accompanied the gang on the raid in order to gather background for a book he was writing on the life of Wilbur Underhill. He further claimed Eugene Clark was a "Chicken livered liar!" On finding the outlaw guilty as charged, the prosecutor got in the last word by recommending a stiff sentence, saying, "That he might have plenty of time to further pursue his literary talents." Nash was hammered with a fifty-year sentence and entered McAlester on Independence Day 1934. He was transferred to Granite Reformatory in 1937 and paroled in 1940 when Warden Fred Hunt recommended he be given his freedom due to his being a model prisoner over the past six years. In 1942, Nash was remanded back to McAlester due to a parole violation (Stealing tires from a Rogers County filling station). He would not again taste freedom until December 1954. A year after his release from prison, Nash was killed in a Texas oilfield explosion. As a reward for his active cooperation with authorities in the case against Houston Nash, Eugene Clark was released from custody and walked away a free man.

****

In the early morning hours of February 4, 1934, Ed "Newt" Clanton was slain in a shootout with a pair of officers in downtown Chelsea, Oklahoma. Also killed in the gun duel was Rogers County Deputy Sheriff A. P. Powell. Clanton's partner at the time of the shootout was suspected to have been Ford Bradshaw who once again narrowly escaped capture.

In the meantime, a gang made up of Jim Clark, Frank Delmar, Ennis Smiddy, and a youth named Aubrey 'Red' Unsell began a prolific robbery spree knocking over the banks of Goodland, Kansas on February 9, as well as those in Wetumka, Kingfisher, and Crescent, Oklahoma in May and June. On July 24, the gang was also suspected of looting a bank in Henderson, Kentucky.

On the afternoon of February 28, 1934, two-dozen Los Angeles, city and county officers raided a swanky apartment located in the fashionable Wilshire district of Los Angeles. The motivation for the massive raid stemmed from a hot tip lawman had received having to do with a "High powered gang" operating out of the residence. The informant also mentioned the name of the long missing "Pretty Boy" Floyd. Captured in the raid were three men who gave their names as Clifton F. Joe, William Morris, and John Richards. All three individuals were armed with pistols when arrested. When officers attempted to frisk the subject who had identified himself as Clifton Joe, the suspect jerked away from the officer who reacted by shooting him in the arm. A check of Joe's fingerprints matched those on a wanted poster issued by the Department of Justice for Ed Davis, one of the eleven Kansas Memorial Day escapees and a one-time partner of Wilbur Underhill's. Davis was soon implicated in four recent armed robberies in the Los Angeles area. Agents of the FBI rushed to LA to question the fugitive as to any role he may have played in the Kansas City Massacre. Within months, Davis would be convicted of kidnapping/robbery and sentenced to life imprisonment in the California penal system. In 1937, he was involved in a botched escape at Folsom prison in which a guard and the Warden were slain in the melee. Davis was later executed in San Quinton's gas chamber.

Less than a week after Davis's capture, Ford Bradshaw and his girlfriend entered a juke joint named the Plantation Club located square on the Arkansas-Oklahoma border in the little community of Arkoma. Reacting to the loss of approximately $100 to an illegal gaming device, he commenced to tear the place to the ground. After terrorizing the bar for several hours, a posse of officers armed with shotguns subdued the heavily intoxicated outlaw. On being led out the back door in handcuffs, Bradshaw suddenly jerked away from the officers fleeing toward his parked car, which was loaded down with shotguns and rifles. A part-time Laflore County Deputy Sheriff named Bill Harper responded by emptying his .45 automatic into the desperadoes exposed backside. With Bradshaw's death, officers throughout the Midwest sighed a breath of relief. Over the past several years, he had made a reputation for himself as one

Ed Davis on his capture in LA.
Courtesy Los Angeles Times

of the most prolific and vicious criminals to ever come out of Oklahoma.

A couple of weeks after Bradshaw's death, twenty-eight state and Federal officers accompanied by four newspaper reporters staged a dawn raid on a small farm owned by an Ira Brackett located seven miles southwest of Mannford, Oklahoma capturing Charlie Cotner, Glen Roy Wright, and several other wanted fugitives without incident. News reports suggested the suspects were all deep in their slumbers, hung over from a night of revelry when lawmen stormed the residence. Apparently, the fugitives were not in the habit of being awakened before the rooster crows.

Discovered at the scene was a stolen truck equipped with a winch, four stolen cars, a large quantity of nitroglycerin, acetylene cutting torches, and several abandoned safes along with an assortment of automatic pistols and rifles. Cotner, who was suspected of involvement in numerous bank robberies and burglaries in four states includ-

Modern day view of the location of the Plantation Club (long torn down) where Bradshaw was slain. Photo by Naomi Morgan

ing those in Baxter Springs and Galena, Kansas as well as Stuttgart, Arkansas while in the company of Wilbur Underhill and Ford Bradshaw, was immediately transferred to McAlester for safekeeping. The outlaw was later extradited to Kansas where he was convicted of participating in the October 30, 1933 robbery of the Galena National Bank. On May 18, Cherokee County Judge John Hamilton sentenced him to twenty to one hundred years in the Kansas State pen at hard labor. Authorities in Stuttgart, Arkansas immediately placed a legal hold on Cotner thus preserving their right to try him for the 1933 robbery of the Peoples National Bank on the event of his release from the Kansas Penitentiary

In 1936, while still serving as an inmate at Lansing, Cotner was charged along with Glenn Leroy Wright, John McAtee, and Nick Peterson with the 1934 slaying of Night Marshal Robert J. Hammers in Clearwater, Kansas (*Note: Half brother of Judge Fred Hammers who presided over Wilbur Underhill's 1931 judicial hearing regarding the slaying of Officer Merle Colver). It appears while making his rounds on the night of March 14, Hammers discovered a group of individuals attempting to break into the Clearwater bank. A gun battle broke out which resulted in the marshal's death. Sedgwick County Sheriff Charles Hoover, aided by Kansas State Investigator Joe Anderson, spent the better part of two years making the case against the trio. Although it was never proven exactly who was the triggerman in the Hammers

Charley Cotner. Courtesy Wichita Eagle

murder, Cotner and Peterson were both convicted of First Degree Murder on February 23, 1937 and sentenced to "Natural Life."

Ironically, according to Kansas prison records; Cotner was paroled into the custody of the president of a Vian, Oklahoma bank in 1952 after serving some eighteen years behind bars. The noted outlaw was given a complete pardon and restoration of his civil rights on March 12, 1959.

****

The morning after Cotner's arrest, Robert Trollinger and a companion named Frank Layton were captured by a contingent of Howell County and Missouri Highway Patrol officers while sleeping in a stolen car parked next to an isolated tourist camp near Willow Springs, Missouri. Although both men were packing pistols, neither offered resistance. Lawmen discovered a "small arsenal" of weapons in the car's trunk, which included a machine-gun, several pistols, and three high-powered rifles. Hidden beneath a wool blanket in the backseat officers found a steel vest, a quantity of ammunition, and a sack of roofing nails along with seven stolen license plates from Oklahoma, Texas, and Missouri. Like Charley Cotner, Trollinger, whose hair had been dyed dark red in an effort to change his appearance, was wanted for questioning in connection to a half-dozen armed robberies in four states. The fugitive was quickly extradited to Nebraska to face the music over his suspected involvement in the September 20, 1933 $9000 robbery of the First National Bank of York. Frank Layton was transported to Texas where he was wanted for a filling station heist. A week after Trollinger's arrival in Nebraska he pled guilty to bank robbery and was sentenced to ten years at the State Penitentiary in Lincoln. He was paroled in 1941.

At noon, on May 24, 1934 three men entered the

Kissee Jewelry Store in Claremore Oklahoma robbing its owners, Mr. and Mrs. W. E. Kissee at gunpoint of approximately $238 in cash and over $1500 in jewelry and guns. After securely binding the pair with rope and taping their mouths, the trio made good their escape. Witnesses identified the leader of the hijackers as Elmer Inman. A few weeks later, Inman, along with a young gunsel named W. A. "Shine" Rush, were suspected of stealing a spanking new Plymouth automobile at gunpoint off the busy streets of Seminole, Oklahoma.

Around this time, a forty-seven-year-old ex-con from McClain, Oklahoma named Walter Philpot was arrested and put on trial for his suspected participation in the July 3, 1933 Clinton, Oklahoma bank heist. Upon hearing of the trial through the prison grapevine, Ed Davis came forward confessing his part in the robbery naming his companions as Harvey Bailey, Jim Clark, Bob Brady, and Underhill. Custer County (Clinton is located in Custer County) Sheriff G.G. Simpson reacted to Davis's statement saying; "We have a very weak case and with the confession of Ed Davis I seriously doubt the guilt of Walter Philpot." Representatives from the Oklahoma Attorney Generals office promptly refuted Davis's claim stating, "Davis has a minus rating in truthfulness as far as we are concerned." Detective A. B. Cooper who had arrested Philpot and claimed the reward offered by the Bankers Association chimed in, saying, "He did time in McAlester with Philpot and is just trying to cover–up for his pal." Despite the fact the two females taken hostage in the raid were unable to identify Philpot as one of the hijackers and the prosecution was only able present a vague circumstantial case, Philpot was convicted of the crime and sentenced to 25 years in McAlester. On receipt of the prisoner, Prison Warden Jess Dunn duly informed the press, "If he is innocent I think something should be done about it by the Governors office if the court offers no remedy."

****

Several weeks after Philpot's conviction, Federal Judge Edger S. Vaught dismissed charges of harboring a fugitive against Hazel Underhill while Lon and Seedel Johnson were given six month suspended sentences on the same charge.

****

On the afternoon of August 1, Jim Clark, who was suspected of pulling off a half-dozen recent bank robberies was captured by a posse made up of a bevy Kansas operatives including Joe Anderson, along with a score of Tulsa officers in the parking lot of an apartment house located at 1335 South Peoria Avenue in Tulsa. Also captured in the raid was Clark's current moll, nineteen-year-old Golda Johnson, and her sister along with Bob Brady's widow, Leona, and a small-time thug known to his underworld associates as "Charles White" who in reality was an undercover agent of the Kansas State Highway Patrol named Earl Silverthorne. Apparently, Silverthorne had infiltrated the gang by befriending Leona Brady who had unwittingly led the shamus directly to Jim Clark's doorstep. Moments after his arrest, a handcuffed and heavily manacled Jim Clark was placed in the backseat of a waiting unmarked patrol car and spirited back to Lansing.

When informed of Officer Silverthorne's true identity by a reporter from the *Tulsa World* later that evening in her cell in the Tulsa County Jail, Leona Brady responded by saying, "That dirty rat!" Adding, "I guess I'm not as smart as I thought I was. He sure fooled me." When the correspondent asked how she had met her notorious lover, Golda Johnson responded, "At a dance in Muskogee when I was fifteen," adding, "They don't have anything on me pal." Incidentally, Golda was the daughter of the notorious Charles Johnson, a one-time member of the old Henry Starr Gang. Johnson was currently serving a lengthy term in Leavenworth Federal Penitentiary.

According to Major Ellis Christensen, on the trip back to Kansas, Clark profusely thanked him and his fellow officers for not shooting him during the raid, saying, "You could of shot us all and been heroes." Christensen also allowed how upon nearing the gates of the prison the bandit inquired if the officers had a shot of whiskey on them. Christensen responded by handing the outlaw a half full pint of Old Crow, saying, "Go ahead." Clark retorted, "I'm sure going to need it when I see those walls again." After taking a healthy swig, the desperado smiled at his captors saying, "I should of known you guys would get me."

In January 1935, Clark was convicted on federal bank robbery charges (May 31, 1934 Kingfisher heist) and given a 99-year sentence. The outlaw would serve the next thirty-odd years behind bars at both Leavenworth and Alcatraz before being paroled back into society in 1965. Upon his release, he traveled to Warner, Oklahoma where he went to work on the ranch of a boyhood friend. In 1967, he was married and the newlyweds bought a trailer-home located near Lake Fort Gibson. The couple later relocated to a residence in Wagoner, Oklahoma where Jim took a job managing a parking lot owned by of all things the Commercial Bank and Trust of Muskogee. According to family members, soon after gaining his freedom Clark traveled to Arkansas attempting to find the large sack of silver coins he and his comrades had hidden in a hollow tree in the aftermath of the 1933 Black Rock bank job. Apparently, he was unsuccessful in the endeavor owing to his inability to locate the tree in question due to the many changes in the landscape occurring over the past three and a half decades. Another interesting antidote told by one of Jim's nephews concerns the time a pair of FBI agents stopped by Clark's trailer seeking his advice on how to go about capturing the perpetrators of the recent Hulbert bank robbery. Evidently, the old bandit got a big kick out of this turn of events.

Although he was constantly badgered to tell his life story, he firmly resisted the temptation until author L.L. Edge contacted him in the early 1970s. When Edge, who was writing a book concerning the 1933 Memorial Day breakout, informed Clark his old pal Harvey Bailey was cooperating in the venture he finally consented to be interviewed. Over the next few years, Clark met several times with the author. Interestingly, Clark's version of events often times varied from that of his old crime-partner. In a letter dated November 14, 1973, He wrote Edge: "I have been reading several articles from Harvey Bailey lately. The accuracy is off in these articles. Could be that his age is playing tricks on his memory." In contrast to Bailey who chose to live in the limelight re-telling his exciting exploits to all who would listen, Clark preferred to spend his twilight years in a quite fashion, spending his leisure time fishing, gardening, and bird watching. For the remainder of his life, even while actively assisting L. L. Edge in the writing of his book, Clark steadfastly refused to have contact with Bailey and other characters from his sordid past claiming any association would taint his present life. On the other hand, one wonders if his motivation for not communicating with his ex-crime partners was truly a simple desire to live a life of solitude or perhaps a very real fear of retribution. According to a 1957 Leavenworth prison report, Clark was suspected of being the "Kingpin of Gambling" at the institution having in his employee a small army of henchmen, otherwise known as "Leg breakers" in prison jargon, doing his strong-arm collections over a period of years. One can assume he made more than his share of enemies while doing time at Leavenworth and had little desire to clue them in to his present whereabouts. In the final years of his life, Jim and his wife visited kin in San Francisco, California. According to one of his step-sons, while crossing the Bay Bridge from Oakland his wife blurted out, "Look Jim, there's Alcatraz." The retired outlaw reacted by quickly covering his eyes with his hands refusing to even glance at the rocky bastille. James Nolan Clark died of a heart attack in 1974 and is buried at Elmwood Cemetery in Wagoner, Oklahoma.

Just days after Clark's capture in Tulsa a posse made up of thirty officers unsuccessfully raided an isolated farmhouse located six miles south of Pawhuska, Oklahoma in an attempt to capture the outlaw's running buddy, Frank Delmar, The following day, Delmar was apprehended near Claremore by a squad of machinegun totting federal agents. Delmar would spend the rest of his life behind bars dying of natural causes in 1959 at Leavenworth Federal Penitentiary. According to prison officials, the fifty-eight-year-old

Leavenworth Federal Penitentiary. Photo by Naomi Morgan

Delmar never sent nor received a single letter nor heard from any visitors during his twenty-four years of incarceration. As for Clark's other recent crime-partners, Aubrey Unsell was captured near Duncan, Oklahoma, on September 10, while Ennis Smiddy was apprehended on Christmas morning 1934 by a posse of federal agents at his father's farmhouse near Waurika, Oklahoma, while he was in the process of opening his presents. He and Unsell plead guilty to robbing the Kingfisher bank and both were sentenced to fifty-year terms. Smiddy died at Alcatraz in 1941 of a liver ailment at the age of 38.

****

Above: Jim Clark after his release from prison. Courtesy Lester Clark
Right: Clark's girlfriend, Golda Johnson, photo sent to him while he was serving time at Alcatraz-marked on rear "Passed by censor-USP Alcatraz 1940." Courtesy Lester Clark

Meanwhile, back in Oklahoma Ralph Roe and Jack Lloyd were picked up at a residence in Mannsville in a police raid occurring on the evening of July 26, 1934. Parked outside the home was a pair of automobiles, one registered to Hazel Underhill and the other stolen out of Bonham, Texas. Both men were held several days for questioning on auto-theft charges until Hazel showed up with her ever-faithful cigar-chomping attorney, James Mathers, and arranged for her new lover's release on a writ of habeas corpus. Lloyd was not so lucky. Officers kept him in lockup undergoing several weeks of intense grilling regarding not just the hot car rap but also his suspected involvement in the Coalgate robbery.

Shortly after noon on September 10 Roe and the recently freed Lloyd, armed with handguns, walked into the Farmers National Bank of Sulphur, Oklahoma forcing teller Kathryn Patton and Assistant Cashier David Collins along with a trio of customers to lie on the floor. While Roe gathered up the cash (approximately $3000) placing it in a sugar sack, Lloyd watched over the hostages. According to Collins, he once looked up hoping to catch a view of Lloyd's face but the bandit warned him to "Get your face to the floor or I'll put a pill right between your eyes, Bub." Collins did as instructed. The bandits then left the bank taking

Federal Judge Robert Williams.
Courtesy Kenneth Butler

Collins as a hostage shoving him off the running board of the moving car several miles outside of town.

On the evening of October 1, a Pushmataha County officer arrested the pair of fugitives at a tourist court near Clayton, Oklahoma. Both men were transported to the Carter County Jail in Ardmore where witnesses positively identified them as the stick-up men involved in the Sulpher bank job. Lloyd was also officially charged with assisting Wilbur Underhill in the robbery of the Coalgate bank.

In January, the pair was moved to the Federal Jail in Muskogee where they were among the first persons ever charged in US history with violating the newly created "Dillinger Law" which allowed for the use of the death penalty in certain robbery with kidnapping cases (Hostage taking).

On January 17, 1935, Jack Lloyd's trial began with fireworks when Muskogee Chief of Detectives John Wolsey presented Federal Judge Robert L. Williams with a crudely carved wooden gun found

Wooden gun found in Jack Lloyd's cell He was obviously emulating the methods of John Dillinger who had recently used a hand craved wooden pistol in a sensational escape from a jail in Crown Point, Indiana. Courtesy Muskogee Phoenix

that morning in Lloyd's cell. Lloyd admitted it was his and then surprised the Judge by pleading guilty to the Sulphur bank heist, saying, "Sure I robbed the Sulphur bank. An ex-con can't get a job from decent folks. Every time a robbery occurs within two hundred miles of my home the cops pick me up." US Attorney Cleon Summers recommended the death penalty, stating, "It is the only way to stop these punks!" Ignoring the government council, his honor sentenced the outlaw to 144 years in Federal prison.

The following day Ralph Roe was led into court in irons due to his being declared a severe escape risk. Sitting in the back of the courtroom was Roe's perky sweetheart, Hazel Underhill. Wilbur's bereaved widow was reportedly smothered in a rich fur coat and bathed in expensive jewelry. Incidentally, Roe's attorney was again Hazel's legal representative, James Mathers.

Following a short trial, in which he pled not guilty and half-dozen witnesses responded by testifying under oath he was a patent liar, the defendant was found guilty and sentenced to 99 years. Immediately after the conclusion of Roe's trial, Federal Marshal Joe Wilson and a contingent of G-men transported him and Lloyd to Leavenworth Federal Penitentiary. The pair was transferred by rail

Theodore Cole. Courtesy Muskogee Phoenix

to Alcatraz, the nation's legendary maximum-security prison, on October 3, 1935. They were booked into the notorious prison as inmates #260 (Roe) and # 264 (Lloyd).

At noon on December 16, 1937, with a heavy fog shrouding the rocky island bastille, Ralph Roe and a fellow Okie named Theodore Cole who was serving fifty years on a kidnapping rap sawed through the bars of the prison's mat shop and slipped into the icy cold San Francisco Bay on a makeshift raft constructed of discarded oil drums and rubber tires. The prisoners were discovered missing after the 1 pm headcount and moments later the island's alarm, which could be heard across the bay in San Francisco, was sounded. Coast guard cutters were immediately dispatched to search the waters off the island. The FBI and highway patrol along with area police departments responded by setting up dozens of roadblocks in the bay area. A massive manhunt was conducted but no sign was found of the escapees. Not then, not ever.

According to the final report issued by the US Bureau of Prisons, the pair drowned in the bay's heavy cur-

Alcatraz, main cellblock. Courtesy US Bureau of Prisons

rents, their bodies washing out to sea. Since 1937, the two have been reportedly sighted at various locations including a Tulsa Hotel and lounging on the beaches in Mexico and Florida. None of these sightings were substantiated. According to other sources, they made it to South America and were living in luxury off the vast resources Roe had illegally obtained from his earlier bank robberies. An odd statement considering Roe's cut from his robberies for the five years prior to his capture amounted to a measly few thousand dollars, most of which went to attorney fees or paid to those who harbored him. Although no credible evidence has ever been presented which would indicate Roe and his partner made it out alive from the depths of San Francisco Bay, it must be pointed out that every year for several decades on the anniversary of Eva Mae Nichols death a fresh batch of roses mysteriously appeared at her grave. After observing the

Pamphlet distributed by US Bureau of Prisons showing Alcatraz Island circa 1961. Author's private collection

appearance of the flowers for several years, Eva's family approached the caretakers who informed them they had never noticed who had left them; they simply materialize out of the blue.

****

On the afternoon of February 17, 1935 Eugene Clark, the informant from the Harrah bank caper, was arrested at his home in Crowder, Oklahoma on a tip originating from a underworld stool pigeon. Apparently, the snitch had relayed information to State Crime Bureau agents implying Clark had been involved in the 1933 Tryon bank job. In a stroke of appalling bad luck, one of the witnesses to the robbery, William Vassar, who was an attorney at the time of the heist, had since been elected Lincoln County District Attorney (Tryon is located in Lincoln County).

On the morning of March 2, Clark was brought before County Judge Walter Hill to answer a charge of Rob-

Guard tower, Alcatraz Island. Author's private collection

bery With Firearms. The defendant, eyes downcast, pled not guilty. At the same hearing, the three witnesses to the robbery including the County Prosecutor officially identified him as one of the perpetrators of the crime. The defendant's trial was set for March 27. When interviewed shortly after the hearing by the local press, Vassar was asked what he thought about prosecuting a man that once held a gun to his head. He calmly responded, "We swapped horses. Now its my turn!"

On the opening day of trial Owen and Bernice Gallamore, (Now married) the couple who had been taken hostage by the bandits the night before the bank robbery, showed up in court positively identifying Clark as one of their kidnappers. Reacting to the couple's testimony, the defendant frantically joined his attorney in a heated conference. Moments later he changed his plea to guilty as charged and threw himself on the mercy off the court. District Judge Leroy G. Cooper subsequently sentenced him to 25 years at hard labor. Clark was released on parole in March 1942. Incidentally, over the years, Clark's name has often been mentioned as a good candidate for the stool pigeon involved in Underhill's capture and subsequent death.

George "Dewey" Shipley, captured with James Camp in Kansas. Courtesy Tulsa World

On March 11, 1937 an unemployed welder from El Reno, Oklahoma named James Arthur Camp (alias James McVey) along with Lillie Mae Womack (alias Bobby Owens) and Wilbur Underhill's old running buddy, George Dewey Shipley, were arrested as a result of a police raid on a ranch near Emporia, Kansas. Both Camp and Womack were charged with aiding Eugene Clark in the 1933 Tryon bank robbery while Shipley was whisked to Texas to face a charge of looting the Coleman National Bank on February 2, 1934 to the tune of $24,000. On his arrival at the Lincoln County Jail, Camp was positively identified by the Gallamore's as being Clark's accomplice in their October 8th kidnapping near Purcell. On April 8, Camp pled not guilty at his preliminary hearing and was bound over to the October session of the district court. The following day Womack pled the same and was also bound over for trial. Although Camp vigorously asserted he was in Shawnee making illegal booze at the time of the robbery, he was convicted on October 10 by a jury of his peers and sentenced to 25 years at the Oklahoma State Penitentiary. He was paroled back to the free world on December 13, 1941 and drifted back into obscurity. Miss Womack was somehow able to escape serious consequences for her part in the affair.

****

On the day marking the one-year anniversary of the Claremore jewelry store heist, an eighteen-year-old amateur sleuth named Joe Morgan, the son of state criminal identification expert W. H. Morgan, was sitting in a beer parlor in downtown Tulsa when he noticed a familiar face, but just could not place it. Suddenly, it dawned on him, it was a face he had observed many times while studying his father's vast collection of wanted posters. He stood up casually strolling out the bar into a neighboring drug store where he called the police department informing the dispatcher he knew the whereabouts of the elusive Elmer Inman. Moments later, a squad of plainclothes Tulsa cops streamed into the drinking establishment putting the pinch on the noted outlaw.

Shortly after his arrest, Inman was transported to Rogers County where he was quickly arraigned in front of Justice of the Peace E. J. Humphrey who ordered him held pending preliminary hearing for the crime of robbing the Kissee Jewelry Store. Elmer was then incarcerated in the antiquated Rogers County Jail located on the third floor of the courthouse.

On the evening of August 8, 1935 Inman jimmied open the door to his cell with a key fashioned out of a metal jail issue spoon he had pilfered earlier in the week. Rushing past the female section of the jail, he kicked open a locked wooden door then fled down a flight of stairs to the second story courtroom where he leaped out an open window on to the hard ground. Unfortunately for him, he fractured his foot on impact and was forced to hobble across the street where he collapsed on a porch holding his leg moaning in pain. Moments after the escape jailor Giz Hardin sounded the alarm. A posse soon spotted the outlaw. When deputy Oce Denbo approached the fugitive he aimed a big horse pistol his way saying, "Get your hands up!" to which a frustrated Inman replied, "Go ahead and shoot, I don't give a damn!"

The badman was tried and convicted of the Kissee Jewelry heist on September 18, 1935. District Judge N. B. Johnson sentenced him to a term of two years at the Oklahoma pen. Inman's lawyer immediately appealed the sentence. On March 16, 1936, a partially blind and crippled Inman limped out the front gates of "Big Mac" free on appeal bond.

In October, Ottawa County Sheriff Dee Watters arrested him and thirty-two-year-old Claire Adams at a residence on Route 66 near Chelsea, Oklahoma for suspicion of stealing a travel-trailer from a tourist court near Ardmore. According to police reports, an automatic pistol was found on Inman at the time of his arrest. The pair was quickly transported to the Carter County Jail in Ardmore to await disposition of the case. How the mighty had fallen. From his involvement in headline grabbing $20,000 high risk burglary jobs only a half decade before, the noted safe cracker had lowered himself to hijacking vacationers campers from isolated parks.

The forty-six-year-old thief was convicted of theft and was held in Carter County until the state appeals court affirmed his two-year sentence from Rogers County and Inman was returned to the big house.

Elmer was finally released from the Oklahoma Penitentiary April 8, 1939. He and his latest long-suffering spouse (he was married several times) immediately packed up and moved to Venice, California, where they spent the war years. As far as can be ascertained, he never again stepped foot in Oklahoma even to attend the funerals of his parents. In 1950, he relocated to 229 East Main Street in Medford, Oregon where he established the Inman Jewelry Company, which one might assume from Inman's past behavior may have been a front for a fencing operation. On the evening of November 18, 1955 Inman lost control of his new Packard Sedan at the intersection of State Highway 99 and Shasta Dam Boulevard near Project City, California and was broad sided by an oncoming semi-truck. He and a passenger were killed outright. His wife was severally injured but survived. The legendary cat burglar was buried at the Redding, California Cemetery.

****

At the dawn of the 21st century, very few persons who were involved in the Wilbur Underhill saga remain alive. The last of Underhill's criminal associates, Frank Sawyer, passed away in 1987 while Charlie Cotner and Chester Purdy died within months of one another in 1983. The trio of octogenarians were reportedly all long reformed but filled with spirited memories of those distant adventures from their outlaw pasts, which they willingly imparted to those who would lend an ear.

In Purdy's case, his road to self-betterment was a rocky one. It appears the badman was paroled in 1933 due to his contracting TB. A few months after his release, Purdy and a crime-partner were involved in a botched kidnapping of a wealthy Lincoln County oilman. Apparently, the victim in this case reacted to his imminent abduction by shooting Purdy in the arm with a load of birdshot. The failed kidnapper was arrested at the Nowata Hospital only hours after the event by officers who reported the outlaw's left arm had been amputated. Once again, he was shipped back to "Big Mac." He was again paroled in 1947 but returned to prison the following year upon being charged with a Dodge City, Kansas burglary. Purdy was paroled for the final time in 1959 and pardoned by the Governor in 1965 as the result of his attorney's claim the desperado was on deaths door and wished to meet his maker with a clean record. Seems the sixty-six-year-old Purdy had more life in him then he let on. Three years after his pardon he was arrested by the FBI and charged with burglarizing a Texas bank. He lived quietly in Tulsa under virtual house arrest for the next dozen years until he drove his car into the back of a rental truck one Sunday morning and died of his injuries within hours of the crash.

As for Sawyer, upon his return to McAlester in 1933 he spent the next two decades causing his keepers as much

---

grief as a single man is capable. In 1940, he and Glenn Roy Wright along with a pair of other cons attempted to scale the walls at "Big Mac" using an improvised ladder. A pair of tower guards responded by broadsiding the quartet with a series of shotgun blasts, which severely wounded Wright and forced the surrender of Sawyer and the others who were promptly tossed into the "hole." Eight years later, Sawyer savagely murdered a fellow inmate named Raymond Wright using a nine-inch homemade dirk. Prison officials were unable to discover a motivation for the killing and Sawyer was sentenced to a second life term. In June 1956, the fifty-seven-year-old con and a partner escaped the institution by hiding in the back of a soft drink truck. He was recaptured a week later near Wilburton, Oklahoma. Several years later, he was transferred to the Kansas State Penitentiary to serve out his sentence concerning the Fort Scott robbery. In 1969 Sawyer was paroled to the care of a relative in Texas where he took up house painting as a profession living to the ripe old age of eighty-seven.

Underhill associate Jesse Littrell, who began his career in banditry on horseback, passed on in 1952 and is buried in Marlow, Oklahoma. Although Harvey Bailey would name him as one of the participants in the 1933 Black Rock, Arkansas bank robbery, Littrell was never officially charged with the crime. In 1939 the fifty-three-year-old outlaw was convicted of bootlegging and sentenced to a third term at "Big Mac."

Wilbur's pal Bruce Brady died in California in 1975 while Memorial Day escapee Lewis Bechtel spent the twilight of his years on the west coast as well, dying in Calaveras County, California in 1971. Marion Pike, who harbored the Kansas escapees in the immediate aftermath of the breakout, passed on in the late-1970s. Harvey Bailey died in Joplin, Missouri on March 1, 1979. His burial site is located just a few blocks from that of the Underhills.

As for Underhill's adversaries, Ralph Colvin retired from the FBI in 1940 after twenty-two years of service. He immediately accepted an appointment as the Chief of Police of Tulsa, Oklahoma. He passed away in 1951 at the age of 73 and is buried at Tulsa's Rose Hill Cemetery.

Clarence Hurt retired from the bureau in 1955 after a sterling career. During his time as an agent, he was involved in the capture of such underworld notables as Harvey Bailey and Alvin Karpis. Hurt, along with Agent Charles Winstead shot and killed John Dillinger in front of the Biograph Theatre in Chicago on July 22, 1934. In 1958, Hurt successfully ran for the position of Sheriff of Pittsburg County Oklahoma. The legendary G-man died in 1975 and is buried at McAlester, Oklahoma.

Stanley Rogers, who commanded the raiding party that captured Underhill at the Owens Furniture Store, went on to serve five terms as Oklahoma County Sheriff. His lengthy administration was noted for numerous advancements made in modernizing the department. Just months after Underhill's death, Rogers, acting as president of the

Grave of Clarence Hurt. Photo by Naomi Morgan

Oklahoma Peace Officers Association, led a massive 1000 man posse into Eastern Oklahoma's notorious Cookson hills in a Herculean effort to track down the likes of Charles "Pretty Boy" Floyd, Ford Bradshaw, and the Barrow Gang who were suspected of hiding out in the heavily forested district. During the war years, he served as head of security at the US Army Ammunition Depot at McAlester. Rogers died in 1974 at the age of 85. His son, who accompanied his father on the Underhill raid, became a prominent Oklahoma City physician.

William L. 'Bill' Eads retired from the Oklahoma County Sheriff's Department in the early 1950s. He then served ten years as the Chief of Police of Nichols Hills, Oklahoma prior to his death in 1964.

After leaving the Okmulgee County Sheriff's Department "Big John" Russell served as a county tag agent before being appointed assistant deputy warden of the Oklahoma State Penitentiary in McAlester in the mid-1930s. He passed on in 1977 and is buried at the Okmulgee Park Cemetery near his old partner, Mark Lairmore, who died in 1939 of a heart attack while working as a Tulsa city detective.

Upon his retirement from the Burns Detective Agency in 1938, where he had served as an operative for twenty-two years, A. B. (Archibald) Cooper established his own private detective firm in Oklahoma City. He ran unsuccessfully for Oklahoma County Sheriff in both 1938 and 1950. In 1951, he accepted the position of lead investigator for the Oklahoma County prosecuting attorney. Cooper passed on at the age of seventy in 1954.

Jake Sims, who came within a hairs-breath of capturing Underhill at the Nash farm in 1933, retired as Chief of Police of Seminole, Oklahoma in order to accept the position of Director of the Oklahoma Bureau of Investigation in the late 1940s. He died in 1966 and was buried at Maple Grove Cemetery in Seminole.

Wilbur's mother, Nancy Almira Underhill, died at age 81 in 1951 while the outlaw's sister, Dorothy, who never married, passed on in 1971 and Earl in 1974. All three are buried near Wilbur and brothers Ernest and George at Joplin's Ozark Memorial Park Cemetery. The outlaw's nephew, Frank Vance, died in 1982 and is buried in the Kansas City area. Hazel Underhill moved to California and departed this world in 1979.Her ashes were interred next to her notorious brothers and first husband in a small cemetery located in Nowata County Oklahoma.

****

Seventy years have passed since Wilbur Underhill's violent demise, but wont as we are to forget this man who was surely the essence of wickedness, he has his place in history. His capture and subsequent death marked the beginning of the end of the great Midwest crime wave and greatly assisted in the establishment of the modern day FBI. As the old philosopher once said, "For a man to truly know good he must first know evil."

Sources

Books

Edge, L. L.-*Run The Cat Roads*-Dembner Books-NY-1981

Hall, Jesse A. -Hand, Leroy- *History of Leavenworth County,* Kansas-Historical Publications- Topeka, Kansas- 1921

Past and Present of Montgomery County, Illinois-S. J. Clark

Publishing Company, Chicago, Illinois-1904

Johnson, Lester D. -*The Devils Front Porch*-University Press of Kansas- 1970

Winters, Robert-*Mean Men: The Sons of Ma Barker*-Rutledge Books, Danbury, Conn.-2000

Bailey, Harvey with Haley, J. Evetts-*Robbing Banks Was My Business*-Palo Duro Press-Canyon, Texas-1973

Hounschell, Jim-*Lawmen and Outlaws, 116 Years In Joplin's History*-Fraternal Order of Police #27-Walsworth Publishing-1989

Helmer, William-Mattix, Rick-*Public Enemies: America's Criminal Past*-Checkmark Books-NY-1998

Horan, James- *The Desperate Years*-NY- Bonanza Books-1957

Hamilton, Carl- *In No Time At All*-University of Iowa Press-1957

Lamb- Arthur- *Tragedies of the Osage Hills*-Red Corn-Pawhuska, Ok. 1964

Svobida, Lawrence-*Farming the Dust Bowl*- Caxton Printers and the University Press of Kansas-1940-1986

Wallis, Michael-Pretty Boy: *The Life and Times of Charles Arthur Floyd*-St. Martins Press-NY-1992

Shannon, David A. -*The Great Depression*-Prentice-Hall-Englewood Cliffs, NJ. –1960

Burrough, Bryan-*Public Enemies*-Penguin Books-NY-2004

Morgan, R. D. -*The Bad Boys of the Cookson Hills*-New Forums Press-Stillwater, Oklahoma-2002

Morgan, R.D.-*Desperadoes: The Rise and Fall of the Poe-Hart Gang*-New Forums Press-Stillwater, Oklahoma-2003

Morgan, R. D. -*The Bandit Kings of the Cookson Hills*-New Forums Press-Stillwater, Oklahoma-2003

Spears, Sarah Singleton-*Yesterday Revisited: An Illustrated History of LeFlore County Oklahoma*-LaFlore County Newspapers Limited-Poteau, OK. –1991

Okmulgee County History-Okmulgee County Historical Society-1985

A History of Sequoyah County 1828-1975- Sequoyah County Historical Society- 1976

Welsh, Louise, Townes, Willa Mae, and John A. Morris-
A History of the Greater Seminole Oilfield-Western
Heritage Books Inc.-1981

Houts, Marshal-*From Gun To Gavel: The Courtroom
Recollections of James Mathers of Oklahoma*-
Morrow-1954

McCullough, David-*Truman*-Simon and Shuster-NY-
1992

McReynolds, Edwin, Marriott, Alice, and Faulconer,
Estelle- *Oklahoma: The Story of It's Past and
Present*-University of Oklahoma Press-1961

Esslinger, Michael- *Alcatraz: A Definitive History of the
Penitentiary Years*- Ocean View Press-Carmel, Cal.
2003

Reynolds, John-*The Twin Hells*: *A Thrilling Narrative of
Life in the Kansas and Missouri Penitentiaries*-Bee
Publishing Company-Chicago-1890

Stanley, Jerry-*Children of the Dust Bowl*-Crown Publish-
ers-NY-1992

Livesey, Robert and Karpis, Alvin-*On The Rock*-Paper
Jacks Ltd. Ontario, Canada-1981

Morris, John W. -Editor-*Drill Bits, Picks and Shovels: A
History of Mineral Resources in Oklahoma*-Okla-
homa Historical Society-1982

Articles and Periodicals

Hunting the Human Cougar of the Southwest-Manley Wade Wellman and Capt. Thomas H. Jaycox-Master Detective-McFadden Publications-NYC-November 1934

Seminole City Street Directory-Oklahoma 1933

The Crimson Trail of the Tri-State Terror-Startling Detective-May 1934

Bob Brady: Forgotten Depression Outlaw-Rick Mattix-Oklahombres- Winter 1992

The Tri-State Terror: The Saga of Wilbur Underhill in Oklahoma-Mike Koch-Oklahombres-Four Part Series-1994

Kansas State Penitentiary Biennial Reports-1928-30-32-34-Courtesey Kansas Department of Corrections-Bill Miskell

Dixon's 1926-Oklahoma-Kansas Mining Directory-Courtesy Dobson Memorial Museum-Miami, Oklahoma

The End of the Tri-State Terror-Agent Paul Hanson-U.S. Department of Justice document

The Tri-State Terror Dies After Bloody Gun Battle on Shawnee Streets-Jim Bradshaw-Shawnee News Star-October 1999

The Day They Went Over The Wall- David Dary- *Kansas City Star*-Star Sunday Magazine-May 20, 1973

Correspondence

*Unpublished collection of letters from author L. L. Edge to Jim and Hazel Clark circa 1972-74 as well as a mass of unpublished handwritten notes from Jim Clark concerning his version of the 1933 Memorial Day escape and the Underhill-Bailey Gang's 1933-34 bank robberies-. Also, three-page letter written to L.L. Edge from Jim Clark dated 1973. — Courtesy Lester Clark Collection

*Unpublished collection of 27 letters written to Dorothy and Almira Underhill from Wilbur Underhill circa 1924-1933- Michael Webb collection.

*Handwritten recollections of Major Ellis Christensen concerning the 1934 capture of Jim Clark-circa 1973-Courtesy Lester Clark collection.

Newspapers on microfilm

Oklahoma

Claremore Progress

Muskogee Times-Democrat

Muskogee Phoenix

Okmulgee Daily Times

Okmulgee Democrat

Tahlequah Arrow-Democrat

Haskell News

McAlester News Capitol

Shawnee Morning News

Daily Oklahoman

Seminole Producer

Sallisaw Democrat-American

Sequoyah County Times

Henryetta Free Lance

Miami News Record

Coalgate Record-Register

Coalgate Courier

The Oklahoma News

Kingfisher News

Lincoln County Republican

Chandler Daily News

Harrah Herald

Heavener Ledger

Bristow News

Tulsa World

Sapulpa Herald

Watonga Republican

Vian News-Press

Vinita Leader

Tulsa Tribune

Clinton Daily News

Kansas

Chetopa Advance Clipper

Oswego Independent Observer

Wichita Eagle

Wichita Beacon

Galena Times

Canton Pilot

Baxter Springs Citizen Herald

Coffeyville Daily Journal

Garnett Evening Review and Journal

Leavenworth Times

Missouri

Neosho Daily Democrat

Neosho Times

Joplin Globe

Joplin Herald

Kansas City Star

Other

New York Times

State Journal –Frankfort Kentucky

York Daily News Times-Nebraska

Fort Smith Elevator-Arkansas

Research Facilities

Arkansas

Main Library-Central Arkansas Library System-Little Rock

Fayetteville Public Library

Fort Smith Public Library

Oklahoma

Buckley Public Library-Nancy Hamlin

Northeastern State University Library

Muskogee Public Library–Grant Foreman Research Room

Okmulgee Public Library

Tulsa Central Library

Claremore Public Library

Nowata Public Library

Stillwater Public Library

Bristow Public Library

Vinita Public Library

Miami Public Library

McAlester Public Library

Shawnee Public Library

Ada Public Library

Seminole Public Library

Clinton Public Library

Henryetta Public Library

Harrah Public Library-Metropolitan Library System

Coalgate Public Library

Coal County Genealogy Society

Oklahoma State Penitentiary Musuem-John East

Three Rivers Museum-Muskogee-Linda Moore

Dobson Memorial Museum-Miami

Kingfisher Public Library

Watonga Public Library-Carol Wray

Kansas

Canton Public Library

McPherson Public Library

Wichita Public Library

Galena Public Library

Coffeyville Public Library

Garnett Public Library

Leavenworth Public Library

Missouri

Mid-Continent Library-Independence

Missouri Southern University Library-Joplin

Joplin Public Library

Neosho Library

Kansas City Public Library

Springfield Public Library

Other

Shasta County Public Library-Redding, California

Kentucky Department of Libraries and Archives

Assistance and Documents

Kansas

Wichita Police Department

Wichita Chamber of Commerce

Sedgwick County Sheriff's Department

Kansas Department of Corrections-Bill Miskell-Brett Peterson

Labette County Sheriff's Department-Sheriff William C. Blundell

Kansas State Historical Society

Baxter Springs Heritage Center and Musuem

Oklahoma

Oklahoma Department of Corrections-Rich Green

Muskogee County Sheriff's Department-Charles Pearson

Oklahoma State Historical Society

Coal County Clerk of Court

Rogers County Clerk of Court

Muskogee County Clerk of Court

Okmulgee County Clerk of Court

Sequoyah County Clerk of Court

Lincoln County Clerk of Court

Ottawa County Historical Society

Okmulgee County Commissioners Office

Okmulgee Park Cemetery

Green Hill Cemetery–Muskogee

Lincoln County Historical Society-Pioneer Museum

Shurdan-Kelley Funeral Home-records

Missouri

Missouri Department of Corrections

Office of the Secretary of State

Missouri State Historical Society

Barton County Commissioners Office

Joplin Chamber of Commerce

Jasper County Clerk's Office

Ozark Memorial Cemetery-Joplin

Dillon's Funeral Home-records-Joplin

Others

U.S. Department of Justice-Bureau of Prisons

Nebraska State Historical Society

Colorado Historical Society

Federal Bureau of Investigation–Official case files
pertaining to Wilbur Underhill

U.S. Census-1860-1930

Special Titles from New Forums Press

call 1-800-606-3766 or go to www.newforums.com to order!

Oklahoma Cowboy Cartoons
–by Daryl Talbot

Award-winning cartoonist Daryl Talbot returns with this collection of cartoons depicting the funny side of modern cowboyin'. If you've ever owned a horse or worked on a ranch (or wished you did), you'll get a kick out of this lighthearted look at ranchin' and ropin'.

1999 (ISBN: 1-58107-014-4; 64 pages, 5 1/2 x 8 1/2, soft cover)   *$ 7.95*

Between Me & You & the Gatepost— Rural Expressions of Oklahoma
(2nd, enlarged edition)
–by Jim Etter, illustrated by Daryl Talbot

A new and bigger edition of this popular collection of homegrown expressions and euphemisms that have distinguished the speech of Oklahoma folks for a coon's age and may do so 'til the cows come home. Take the bull by the horns and buy this book, and you'll be grinnin' like a possum eatin' persimmons!

1999 (ISBN: 1-58107-015-2; 44 pages, 5 1/2 x 8 1/2, soft cover)   *$ 7.95*

Hilarious History: The Funniest True Stories and Legends of Stillwater and Payne County
-by D. Earl Newsom

A collection of many true stories of the early days of Stillwater and Payne County that in retrospect are hilarious, although they often involved bitter controversies at the time: adultery, fist-fighting attorneys, bootlegging preachers, and preachers' bitter debates (and fist fights). Taken from contemporary newspaper accounts.

1999 (ISBN: 1-58107-016-0; 60 pages, 5 1/2 x 8 1/2, soft cover)   *$ 7.95*

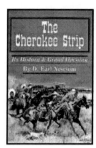

The Cherokee Strip—Its History & Grand Opening
–by D. Earl Newsom

The opening of the Cherokee Outlet, popularly known as the Cherokee Strip, on September 16, 1893, was one of the great spectacles of American history. Relive the excitement in this outstanding volume. Includes a history of the Cherokee Nation; the towns of Alma, Blackwell, Enid, Newkirk, Perry, Ponca City, and Woodward, along with the 101 Ranch. Illustrated with 160 historical photographs.
1992 (ISBN: 0-913507-27-X; 209 pages, 6 x 9 inch, soft cover) **$13.95**

Ragged Edges: Unusual Rag-Time Compositions
–by John Wilson

Here is a true delight for those interested in early Oklahoma history. Ragtime was the music of the period of the land-run and early statehood , the music that inspired, entertained, and delighted the pioneer forefathers of Oklahoma! You will be tapping your feet to Professor Wilson's skillful rendering of Eli Green's Cake Walk, Mandy's Ragtime Waltz, The Watermelon Trust Slow Drag, and others. And, those who play the piano will certainly enjoy trying their fingers at these invigorating tunes. **Includes audio cassette.**
1998 (ISBN: 0-913507-98-0; 122 pages, 8 1/2 x 11, soft cover, lay-flat binding) **$25.00**

A Distant Flame: The Inspiring Story of Jack VanBebber's Quest for a World Olympic Title
–by Jack VanBebber as told to Julia VanBebber

The autobiography of a sickly and partially handicapped Oklahoma boy who developed his abilities to become an NCAA champion wrestler at Oklahoma A&M, win a 1932 Olympic Gold Medal, and eventually be known as one of the ten greatest amateur wrestlers of all times. A must for young readers and sports fans.
1992 (ISBN: 0-913507-26-1; 192 pages , 5 1/2 x 8 1/2, soft cover) **$13.95**

The Story of Exciting Payne County
– by D. Earl Newsom

A virtual encyclopedia of Payne County, its towns and villages, and its people since the 1889 land run. Included are detailed histories of the major towns (Stillwater, Cushing, Perkins, Yale, Glencoe, and Ripley), histories of the once thriving oil towns, brief histories of more than 20 villages that have virtually disappeared, maps, photos, lists of county officials, and dates of major events in every community.
1997 (ISBN: 0-913507-91-1; 272 pages, 8 1/2 x 11 inch, hard cover) $29.95

Stillwater History - The Missing Links
-by D. Earl Newsom

Fascinating events, Stories and Pictures not included in Previous Books. D. Earl Newsom's final book dealing with Stillwater history and at his request a limited edition was published. The Madeline Webb Murder Trial, the Mathews Murder Case, the Ku Klux Klan, Stillwater's Movie Histories, "Doc" Whittenberg, the Ramsey Oilfield,Stories behind Street Names and Hotels, Taxis and Buses.
2000 (ISBN: 1-58107-027-6; 72 pages, 8 1/2 x 11 inch, soft cover) $15.95

Claiming the Unassigned Lands
-by Clyde Shroyer

Mr. Shroyer has researched and gathered family information, backing it up with historical research to accomplish the task of telling his family story and their role in Oklahoma History. Recommended by the 1889er Society
2000 (ISBN: 1-58107-025-X, 390 pages, 5 1/2 x 8 1/2, soft cover) $19.95

Remembrances of Sapulpa (Vol 1.)
–by Virginia Wolfe

Compiled from the author's weekly column for the *Sapulpa Daily Herald* celebrating Sapulpa's centennial, this first volume of a projected ten-volume series tells the story of Sapulpa's growth and development as seen through the eyes of many of its founding families and leading citizens. Liberally illustrated. A real nostalgia trip!

1998 (ISBN: 1-58107-010-1; 138 pages, 8 1/2 x 11 inch, soft cover) $25.00

The First Generation—A Half Century of Pioneering in Perry, Oklahoma
-by Fred G. Beers

A glimpse at the earliest days of Perry, Oklahoma, and the Charles Machine Works, Inc., the manufacturer of Ditch Witch® equipment, through five decades from a bald, treeless prairie at the middle of the great land rush of 1893 to today's bustling, verdant community populated by picturesque descendants of hardy pioneer stock.

1991 (ISBN: 0-913507-22-9; 384 pages, 6 x 9, hard cover) $19.95

Hiram and the Rattales
–written and illustrated by Joan Bartlett Brozek

A unique look at Oklahoma and American history as seen through the eyes of a special family of rats living in southern Oklahoma. Papa Rattale tells his children the stories of the great events of American history as handed down to him by his ancestors. A book that makes American and Oklahoma history come alive for the young and the young at heart.

1988 (ISBN: 1-913507-39-3; 90 pages, 5 1/2 x 8 1/2, soft cover) $ 7.95

Y-O-U and The I-O-A Way
-by Lea Ann Donnelley Walker
and Richard Green

A chronicle of the Oklahoma Lions Boy's Ranch, its philosophy, and the Main and Donnelley families who founded it, told by the daughter of cofounder H.F. Donnelley. Liberally illustrated, including many facsimile documents. Proceeds from the sale go to support of future programs of the Ranch.

1998 (ISBN: 0-913507-90-3; 170 pages, 8 1/2 x 11, soft cover)   *$20.00*

Thunder in the Heartland –
Parables from Oklahoma
-by Jim Marion Etter

Just as truth is often stranger than fiction, sometimes it takes a touch of fable to give a true story the luster of immortality. At least, this seems so with Oklahoma, where, except for monumental events like the 1995 Oklahoma City bombing, many significant moments in history have been largely forgotten. They have been left to sleep in the memories of a few and on microfilmed pages of yesteryear's newspapers, in obscure library books or in dusty court records.

Except for the one based on the bombing itself, the following stories, all of which are fiction inspired by fact, are an attempt to awaken a few of these happenings, circumstances and traditions that in fact *are* the Sooner State. Any similarity between some fictitious name and that of a real person, of course, is a flat accident.

Author Jim Etter has completed an excellent collection of compelling stories with which all Oklahomans can identify. A must for your reading pleasure!

2000 (ISBN: 0-58107-034-9; 214 pages, 5 1/2 x 8 1/2, soft cover)   *$14.95*

Here's the perfect guide to take you down memory lane as you drive the most famous nostalgic route in history –

Route 66
in Oklahoma!

Featuring

- An in-depth essay on music from Oklahoma
- Notable music histories of Oklahoma cities, towns, and tribes on Route 66
- Notable musicians from Oklahoma Cities and towns on Route 66
- Where to hear live music, sing karaoke, and find a good jukebox
- Annual music events along Route 66 in Oklahoma
- Museums and other places with a musical focus
- Route 66 Maps for the U.S., Oklahoma, and tribal nations in Oklahoma
- Where to collect vinyl and other music memorabilia

2004 (ISBN: 1-58107-090; 200 pages, 5 1/4 x 8 1/4) $10.95

The Bandit Kings of the Cookson Hills

Author R. D. Morgan chronicles the true adventures of a loose-knit confederation of daring bank bandits originating from the infamous Cookson

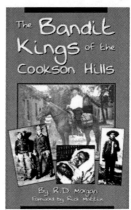

Hills of Eastern Oklahoma who terrorized the Arkansas-Oklahoma borderlands for more than a half decade following the close of the First World War.

The original leader of the group was Henry Starr, the Cherokee bandit, who claimed to have robbed more banks than any man. Upon his death, a middle-age storekeeper along with an audacious young war hero named Ed Lockhart took over the helm.

In a time when most Americans were captivated by the "Teapot Dome" scandal, the death of President Harding, and the gridiron adventures of Notre Dame's "Four Horsemen," folks living in the Ozark Mountains watched with fear and fascination as the outlaw band committed their bold depravations. Although the gang's take rarely amounted to over $2000, it must be remembered the average yearly income for a family of five in 1922 amounted to $2100. A gallon of gas cost eleven-cents and a loaf of bread fetched only nine pennies.

2003 [ISBN: 1-58107-082-9; 5 1/4 x 8 1/4 inch]   *13.95*

The Bad Boys of the Cookson Hills

Their reign of terror lasted 18 long months!

R. D. Morgan continues the stranger-than-fiction true tale of the Cookson Hills Bandits. Here is a detailed description of a vicious crime and the eighteen-month long manhunt to track down the criminals involved. It details the history and crimes of a loose-knit gang of bold outlaws originally known as the Cookson Hills Gang, then the Ford Bradshaw Gang and finally the Underhill-Bradshaw Gang whose members blazed a path of robbery and murder through Oklahoma, Kansas, Nebraska, and Arkansas in 1932-34. It also chronicles the efforts and sacrifices of a handful of brave lawmen that tracked them down.

2002 [ISBN: 1-58107-059-4; 5 1/4 by 8 1/4 inch]   *$13.95*